Dodd's Luck

Golden Coast Publishing Co.

Dodd's Luck

The Life and Legend
of a Hall of Fame
Quarterback and Coach

by Robert Lee
"Bobby" Dodd and
Jack Wilkinson

Published by Golden Coast Publishing Co., Savannah, Georgia.
Designed and produced by Lisa Lytton-Smith.
Hand-colored photograph by Kathy Riggs, Statesboro, Georgia.
Edited by Kathleen Durham and Van Jones Martin.
Proofread by Rusty Smith.
Typeset by J. Michael Matascik for Curry Copy Center, Savannah, Georgia.
Printed and bound by Interstate Book Manufacturers, Inc.

Library of Congress Card Catalog Number 87-081407
ISBN 0-932958-09-5
Printed in the United States of America.

The publisher would like to thank the following people for their gracious assistance in finding and selecting the photographs for *Dodd's Luck:* Anne Bartlow, Head, Archives Department, Price Gilbert Memorial Library, Georgia Tech; Emily Fine, Sports Information Department, Georgia Tech; Diane Hunter, Richard Holman, and Bud Skinner, *Atlanta Journal/Constitution;* Mark Whitworth, Publicity Assistant, University of Tennessee; Phil Davis; and John Dunn and Gary Goettling, Georgia Tech Alumni Association.

Photographic credits:

Van Jones Martin, page vi.

The George Griffin Collection, Institute Archives, Price Gilbert Memorial Library, Georgia Institute of Technology, page 270.

Georgia Tech Sports Information Department, pages 152, 180, 234, 271-274, 276.

Atlanta Journal/Constitution, pages 134, 244, 269, 270-272, 276.

University of Tennessee Sports Information Department, page 268.

Paul Duke Collection, page 269.

Author's Private Collection, pages xvi, 14, 32, 50, 66, 82, 96, 116, 164, 198, 212, 220, 266-271, 273-275, 277.

To Mimi, a wonderful wife and mother.

Contents

ACKNOWLEDGMENTS

They say I'm lucky—and I am. Sometimes I think I'm the luckiest guy in the world to have had the family and friends that I've had. In this book I've mentioned many of the people who have been so important to me, from my childhood in Galax to my wonderful years with Georgia Tech.

In addition, there is a group of friends I would like to acknowledge in a special way. Their encouragement, support, and friendship are dear to me and played a big part in my decision to do this book. They are: Paul Duke, Dave Center, Jack Johnson, Richard Beard, Foster Yancey, Billy Queen, Gene Gwaltney, Ashley Verlander, Allen Morris, Fuller Callaway, Kim King, George Mathews, Bud Lindsey, Sid Goldin, Bill Terrell, and Neill Faucett.

Thank you, men. I love and respect each one of you.

Bobby Dodd

FOREWORD

I was fortunate to have played and coached under Bobby Dodd—to have really understood the principle of the integrated mission of a coach with regard to both the playing and the player's life. He was so sincere and dedicated to this.

Some coaches speak well of the integrated mission, but Coach Dodd exemplified to his players that he truly cared about them. There was no doubt in anyone's mind that off the field Bobby Dodd was like a second father. And he treated every person as he would treat his own son, or want to be treated himself.

The direction that I received from Coach Dodd at Georgia Tech has consumed my thinking, my actions, and my planning my entire life.

I had good parents who taught me "It's not whether you win or lose, but how you play the game." When I came to Georgia Tech, Bobby Dodd was the perfect example of that. At Georgia Tech I learned how to play the game.

Later, when I was an assistant to Coach Dodd, I realized that I was in a profession where many people would do anything to win—to win at all costs. But at Georgia Tech we played by the rules. The thing that stands highest at Tech is the honesty and integrity of the program. Bobby Dodd is responsible for that.

He taught us to care, because he cared. He taught us to be concerned, because he was concerned. He taught us that honesty is sacred, is absolute, and is eternal.

Frank Broyles

Sunday evening, November 24, 1985. I was in the kitchen, doing the dishes, when the phone rang shortly after seven o'clock. Naturally. He'd waited until the second half of the NFL TV doubleheader had ended before calling.

"Hello, Jack? Coach Dodd. My wife made me call you up and tell you how much I liked that story."

In the *Atlanta Journal-Constitution* that morning, in the Dixie Living section, there appeared under my byline an article entitled, "Tech's Living Legend Alive and Well." After spending much of a week with him—in his office at the Georgia Tech Alumni House, at home, in his box at a Tech-Tennessee game, and, of course, at the Bitsy Grant Tennis Center—I'd written my perception of Bobby Dodd at 77, the sunset strip of life. I was pleased with the piece. Apparently so was he.

"Jack," he continued over the phone, "people have been after me for a long time to do a book about my life. If I ever get around to doing it, I think I'd like you to write it."

I was flattered, extremely so, and told him so. Later, I told my wife, Lucy, about our conversation. The prospect of doing a book about Bobby Dodd was intriguing, no, exhilarating. I'd never written a book and now one of the most prominent figures in 20th-century Georgia had raised that possibility. I had a hard time falling asleep that night.

Growing up in Lynbrook, New York, in the 1950s and 1960s, I'd heard about Bobby Dodd and Georgia Tech. The Yellow Jackets. The Ramblin' Wreck. Grant Field. Gold helmets. White jerseys at home, long before the Dallas Cowboys ever existed, much less made that football fashion statement. Unorthodox training methods that bordered on blasphemy. Great teams, even greater bowl successes, and Dodd's greatest accomplishment of all: his care, concern, and compassion for his players.

By the time I finally saw Grant Field in person, though, Bobby Dodd was neither the athletic director nor the head football coach. In 1979, while working with the *New York Daily News*, I flew to Atlanta to do a story about Norm Van Brocklin, the fiery NFL Hall of Fame quarterback and former Minnesota Viking and Atlanta Falcon coach. That year, having recently undergone surgery, Van Brocklin was back in football as an assistant to Pepper Rodgers, then the head coach of his alma mater, Georgia Tech.

I was curious how those two would coexist. Van Brocklin: ferocious, acerbic, the definitive old school football man. And Pepper: bell-bottoms and boots, perms, everything that was antithetical to the old guard in the west stands at Tech.

As practice began that day, I noticed a female sportswriter leaning against the fence that surrounds the Astroturf inside Grant Field. As a head coach, Van Brocklin never would have tolerated a woman at his practices. But then, a female sportswriter was absolutely acceptable compared with what was going on in the south end zone. There, the Tech players were stretching, loosening up for practice. Two enormous loudspeakers stood in front of them. And between the speakers lay Miss Burma Irby, an aerobics instructor clad in a skimpy leotard and contorting herself in the late afternoon sun in front of one hundred cases of pent-up adolescent testosterone.

While the speakers blared some infernal disco beat, Burma Irby led the Yellow Jackets in stretching. "Now stretch . . . stretch . . . stretch-stretch-stretch-stretch," she cooed. "Now push . . . push . . . push-push-push-push." I though I was on location at a Mel Brooks film. *Blazing Libidos.*

And I wondered what Van Brocklin thought, standing stiffly—motionless at midfield, sucking on a cigarette and trying to comprehend Miss Burma Irby. At least the Dutchman was a newcomer to this trashing of Tech tradition. I tried to imagine what all this was like for Bobby Dodd. Surely, this was not the Georgia Tech I had heard, and read, so much about so long ago.

Neither was the team that opened the season that Saturday in Grant Field. Alabama—blessed 'Bama and the Bear—trampled Tech 30-6. It was the start of a 4-6-1 season for the Jackets, and the beginning of the end for Rodgers, who was let go at the end of the season.

Not until the late fall of 1985, when I began to work on the Dodd newspaper article, did I really begin to know, to understand what the Bobby Dodd era at Georgia Tech was all about. When I started researching this book, I developed a keen appreciation for the man and the times. An appreciation Van Martin, our publisher, has had nearly all his life.

Growing up in south Georgia, Van had been a devout Tech fan, born to the breed. His father was a Tech man, class of 1931, and instilled that in his son. In 1959, Van Martin, then 12, took his set of plastic cowboys and Indians and began cutting and painting and sculpting the figures. Some were painted Baylor green and gold, others Tech gold and white. One was bent to resemble a placekicker. With that, Van Martin recreated one of the most memorable scenes in Georgia Tech football history: Pepper Rodgers's last-second field goal that beat Baylor 17-14 in the 1952 Orange Bowl. One Indian had to have his headdress cut off so he wouldn't block that kick.

Such was the spell that Bobby Dodd and Tech cast over thousands of little boys—and not so little boys—in Georgia and throughout the South.

Now, 35 years after that bowl game, Van Martin is publishing this book.

Before this project began, Coach Dodd was a bit wary. He remembered how much time I'd spent with him to write that story and wondered how much of his time I'd occupy now. That concerned him. Bobby Dodd is a man of habit, one who likes his life exactly as it has been for some time now: routine. Unlike Bear Bryant, this is a coach who got out early, got lucky medically, and continues to get the most out of life. It's been two full decades since Dodd last coached, more than a decade since he retired as athletic director. Since then, his schedule has seldom varied.

By mid-morning, he's at his office in the Tech Alumni House, where he works as a consultant to the Tech Alumni Association. After lunch, every weekday afternoon is spent on his beloved green Georgia clay at Bitsy Grant Tennis Center in Buckhead.

When we first met there in November 1985, the temperature, like the old coach himself, was in the high 70s, unseasonably warm. Many men, some young enough to be his grandsons, sat in the shaded sanctuary of the clubhouse veranda overlooking courts one, two, and three. But the bow-legged bowl legend was out there on number three, sweating and hustling yet another younger man out of a buck or five, ten if he wasn't careful.

In between matches, or in case of inclement weather, Dodd can be found in the clubhouse, playing cards, playing checkers, playing something, anything. Then he's home by the dinner hour, home at Sherwood Forest, to the Tech yellow brick ranch house with black shutters on Robin Hood Drive. Follow the road to the yellow brick ranch and that's where you'll find Alice, Bobby Dodd's wife of 53 years, whom he always calls Mimi.

"I lead a pretty routine life, and I like that," Dodd had told me in 1985. "I like to do the same things every day."

Doing interviews was not on the daily agenda. So I planned to stagger our taping sessions, do them periodically, judiciously. Fortunately, much of Bobby Dodd's life has been recorded, and many lives have been touched by him, so there was ample outside research to do.

Shortly after we started working together, I began getting phone calls from him. "Jack? Hello, podner. When are you and Ol' Coach gonna get together again and talk?" Dodd embraced this project with the same fervor he's brought to everything he's done in his life. A fervor that was so apparent the day we formalized plans for the book.

Wednesday, June 26, 1986. Georgia was beginning a month-long, record-breaking stretch of 95°+ temperature. We were in the cool of the Capital City Club downtown—where Dodd is a long-time member—meeting for lunch in a private dining room on the second floor. Van Martin was there, along with Bobby Dodd, Jr. Coach Dodd was resplendent in a seersucker summer suit, blue button-down Oxford shirt,

Georgia Tech yellow power tie, no socks, and a new pair of white Puma artifical turf football shoes.

Only Bobby Dodd would ask an ex-New Yorker to write his biography, the story of one of the legendary figures in southern football. And only Bobby Dodd would walk into the Capital City Club sans socks and wearing football shoes. And get away with it.

He'd been working that morning at Grant Field, at the Bobby Dodd-Bill Curry Football Camp for high school and junior high players. After that practice session, after showering and dressing, sneakers and sockless seemed more sensible than wing tips. So Dodd drove over to lunch, and no one cared a bit about his footwear. Or if they did, they said nothing.

When I think of Bobby Dodd now, I don't see football shoes and bare ankles. I don't see the suit and fedora he always wore on game days while seated in a chair at midfield, orchestrating the action on the field before him. Instead, I think of the side door, the kitchen door, at his house. The blinds don't quite cover the entire window, leaving a small clear crack at the bottom. When I ring the doorbell, I usually see the feet first: two big old feet, size 13, in sweat socks. Then the door opens.

"Come in, boy," he always says. Coach Dodd usually wears an old pair of gray sweatpants, with a hole torn in the right knee; a long-sleeved thermal undershirt; and his favorite camel's hair blazer. We'll walk into the den, where a game of some sort is on TV, and sit on the couch. And then we'll start to talk, and a whole new world, many worlds, open up.

He'd talk for hours, about so many people and places and things. Occasionally, he'd jump up and demonstrate proper punting or casting technique, or the trick play at Tennessee where the center wound up with the ball and nearly scored, or the Kingsport Play, as successful at Tech as it was in high school. And he'd talk about the people who played for him, and worked for him, and cared for him so very much. They still do.

Some 15 years ago, I was a small-college quarterback at Hofstra University on Long Island. I was slow afoot, weak-armed, and hardly played a down after my sophomore season. And I was totally embarrassed on the first day of classes my senior year, when a geography professor read the roll and asked if I'd ever played football.

"A long time ago," I replied.

"There was a quarterback here a couple of years ago named Wilkinson," the professor recalled. "Weak arm. Very weak arm."

I dropped geography the next day.

Reflecting on my football career, and reflecting on the research and writing of this book, I've reached a three-part conclusion about Bobby Dodd:

I would have loved to have played for him.

I would not have been good enough.

It wouldn't have mattered. He would have treated a scrub like me just like he treated his 21 all-Americans. With dignity.

There have been so many people whose time, patience, influence, and understanding have helped make this book a reality. Coach Dodd and I offer our most sincere appreciation.

To Lucy, Katharine, and Alison, for their love and support, and most of all, their patience. And for letting me lock the attic door when I had to.

The *Atlanta Journal-Constitution* allowed me the time and freedom to write this book. For that, and much more, I am indebted to Guy Curtright, Bill Kovach, Dudley Clendinen, Mary Lee, Keith Thomas, Debra Johnson, Allen Hauck, and Thomas M. Stinson, and I am forever indebted to Betty Parham and Glenn McCutchen.

Paul Shea and Chuck Perry are rare and treasured founts of friendship, literary advice, and common sense.

Live from New York, it's Ira Berkow, Larry Klein, and Phil Berger, without whom this book would have had less life.

My brother, Tom, and sister, Kathleen, helped keep me going up close and long distance. Tom also threw in a quiet, alternative place to work and an endless supply of stale chips.

For unmatched hospitality and history, I will always be thankful to Glenn and Kay Pless of Galax, Virginia, Witt and Helen Langstaff of Kingsport, Tennessee, and Tom and Nancy Siler of Knoxville, Tennessee.

Rick Sabetta and Tom Merritt have never let me down. Never have, never will.

The sports information offices of several schools were crucial to the completion of this book: Mike Finn and Georgia Tech, Claude Felton and Georgia, Bud Ford and Tennessee, and Bob Bradley and Clemson.

To Don Smith and the people at Harris Lanier, especially Gary Powers and Regina Moodie, for their expertise and the use of a Lanier Typemaster, on which the book was written.

I can never fully thank John Crittenden, for getting me started in the business, and Ray Sons, for saving me from the kitchen at the Pot Belly Pub and keeping me in the business when no one else would give me a chance.

The young lefthander, Kim King, was, at times the quarterback of this endeavor and absolutely essential to its success.

Kathleen Durham helped me write legibly and read coherently. Lisa Lytton Smith gave us the framework in which we worked, and designed the book, as always, so well. Rusty Smith was meticulous—a trait not usually found in Bulldogs.

And Van Martin was the guiding force and spirit behind it all—shaping, reshaping, cajoling, putting up with far too much and putting out this book. Many, many thanks.

And to the Dodds—Coach, Mimi, Bobby, and Linda—for allowing me into their lives, and for their time, concern, candor, station wagon, sustenance, and best of all, friendship.

For the regal Lucy Keeble, and for Mom and Dad.

Jack Wilkinson

The Dodd family in 1913. Top row,
Edwin and Susan; middle row, Edwin Jr.
(Pat) and Ruth; in front, John and Bob.

Chapter 1
The First Star of Galax

THEY ASSEMBLED IN FRONT of their home, in the proper photographic pose of the day. It was a spring day in 1913, and the Dodds stood still long enough for a family portrait to be snapped. On the second step of the stairs leading to the front porch stood Edwin Dodd and his wife, Susan. There was Edwin: three-piece suit, gold watch chain shimmering, a round-collar white dress shirt, hair slicked down, and a serious, almost stern countenance. And Susan: radiant in a long-sleeved white dress that kissed her white shoetops, arms clasped behind her back, yet her face as dour as her spouse's.

One step below stood the oldest of the four children, Edwin by name but known to all as Pat: cabby's hat, white shirt and tie, hands thrust into the pockets of his knickers. Beside him the only daughter, Ruth, also in white, like her mother, hands at her side, hair pulled back severely, unsmiling.

And down on the sidewalk stood the little ones, John and Bob. That's what Bobby Dodd was known as while growing up. Bob. Bobby came years later. John and Bob sported bow ties with their white shirts and dark shorts. Just one thing was missing. Two, actually: their shoes and socks.

The barefoot boys, standing at attention. Little Bob, just four years old, looking straight at the camera. He does not look down at his feet, which are covered in mud. Which is not exactly what Edwin and Susan Dodd had in mind when they thought to take a family portrait.

But even then, as now, Bobby Dodd liked to enjoy himself and life. And if that meant running around in a muddy yard before a family photo session, so be it. He knew how to enjoy himself without getting into real trouble, knew how to keep his nose clean. His feet, though, were another matter.

He was born a Blue Ridge boy, born at the base of the Blue Ridge Mountains, in a tiny frontier town in southwestern Virginia called Galax (pronounced GAY-lax). He has not returned to his birthplace in more than four decades, but, to this day, Bobby Dodd thinks of that place as home.

"I'm a Virginian," says Dodd. "I claim Galax as my home. The Blue Ridge Mountains and Galax. That's my heritage."

Ralph McGill, the late, great editor of the *Atlanta Constitution* wrote often and lovingly of Dodd, usually referring to him as "the tall Tennessean." McGill, a Nashville native, had seen Dodd play football at the University of Tennessee in Knoxville. Most others, though, have always associated Bobby Dodd with Georgia Tech. Indeed, the two have become so intertwined as to become inseparable. But Robert Lee Dodd is a Virginian, in his mind, in his heart, and in his bloodlines.

Edwin Dodd appropriately named the youngest of his four children for his hero, General Robert E. Lee, a Virginian, a southern gentleman, and one of the most respected military strategists in American history. Yet Robert Leé Dodd's Virginia roots grow deeper than his birthplace and namesake.

In 1607, a group of English colonists, adventurers, and entrepreneurs sailed the Atlantic and settled on the Virginia coast. They established Jamestown, the first permanent English colony in America. Among that company of colonists were three brothers from York, England: John, James, and William Nuckolls.

One of their descendants, Charles Nuckolls, left the coast in 1780 and moved to the rugged southwestern part of Virginia, where he bought one thousand acres of land on the New River and Cripple Creek. Other members of the Nuckolls family soon followed him westward.

One hundred twenty-eight years later, three centuries after the first Nuckolls arrived in Virginia, Susan Viola Nuckolls Dodd gave birth to Robert Lee Dodd, an heir worthy in name and demeanor of his cavalier heritage.

Like the Nuckolls, the Dodds also trace their ancestry to England. George Dodd arrived in Boston in 1650. Later relatives settled farther south in North Carolina and Virginia. One became an ambassador to Germany; another, William Dodd, was a captain in the American Revolution. William's great-grandson, Lorenzo R. Dodd, fought for the Confederacy in the Civil War and was wounded at Dry Creek at the Battle of White Sulphur, Virginia. A century later, John Dodd, Bobby's only surviving sibling, actually interviewed a Confederate veteran while researching the family history. The old man recalled that "Lieutenant Dodd was retreating hastily across the creek, when he was shot in the lower dorsal region."

After the war, Lorenzo—or Ren, as he was known—and Berkeley, his father, left Buchanan and headed farther west into southwestern Virginia, first to Bland and finally settling in Tazewell. On September 5, 1869, a son was born to Lorenzo and Harriet Dodd and was christened Edwin Witten Dodd. Bobby Dodd's father.

For years, Ren Dodd owned and operated a livery business in Tazewell, as well as a hotel. As did many hotels of that era and area, the Dodd Hotel featured a regular poker game of some renown. The drummers, or traveling salesmen, who stayed at the hotel often spent much of their nights playing poker or shooting pool. Edwin Dodd grew up watching and learning pool and poker, game skills he later passed on to his sons just as Ren Dodd had done.

At the turn of the twentieth century, Edwin Dodd, then 30, married a woman eight years younger. On March 5, 1900, Dodd wed Susan Viola Nuckolls in her hometown of Oldtown, eight miles west of what would become Galax. Their first two children were born in Glade Spring, Virginia: Pat in 1901 and Ruth in 1903. By the time John arrived in 1906 and Bobby in 1908, the Dodds had moved to Galax.

Galax is a mountain town (the Appalachian Trail runs down Main Street) located in a high valley, which runs south from the Potomac River into North Carolina. The countryside is rolling, gentle, grassy hills. Farms abound still. The Blue Ridge Parkway sits seven miles to the south.

When the town was officially founded in 1903 in an area known as Anderson's Bottoms, it was known as Bonaparte. No one knows why. The name was changed to Galax—for the heart-shaped leaves abundant there—shortly after the Norfolk and Western Railway Company extended its rail line 2.72 miles and linked the town to Fries, Virginia, on December 3, 1903.

The railroad brought new people and new prosperity and also helped remove the mud. Galax easily could have been called Little Muddy. Mud was everywhere, not just on young Bobby Dodd's feet. There were deep, dangerous mudholes, some right on Main Street, in the heart of town.

One mudhole was so deep, a fence rail could be pushed down into it and disappear. Local legend has it that a young boy was plowing near that mudhole when his mule was frightened, bolted, and ran right into the bog. Both plow and mule sank from view. A taller tale tells of a man walking down Main Street when he spotted a hat in the mudhole. He walked over, picked it up, and discovered a man's head underneath. When the pedestrian asked the stranger if he was all right, the man in the mud replied, "I am, mister, but I'm a little concerned about the horse I'm riding." A canal was constructed in conjunction with the railroad and the problems with mudholes were eased.

After the railroad was extended to the area, a horse and mule trader named J. P. Carico and several other men formed a land company, bought most of the land that is now present-day Galax, and hired an engineer to lay out the new town. On December 17, 1905, the first lot sales drew a large but unenthusiastic crowd.

Many prospective buyers couldn't fathom the wide streets and sidewalks. Surely, they thought, this place wouldn't prosper to the point where street cars would be necessary. Why squander all that good ground, particularly at such steep prices? In the main part of town, prices ranged from $100 to $250 for a corner lot; a few blocks away, lots went for $50. Most people left, disgruntled.

Edwin Dodd, though, stayed and paid.

By the time Bobby Dodd was born, the population of Galax was pushing six hundred. Of those six hundred, Edwin Dodd had one of the best jobs in town. He helped develop the financing to open the Galax Furniture Company, which thrived in an area abundant with virgin timber. Edwin Dodd became the first manager of the furniture company, the biggest industry in town.

"I had an extremely happy life," Bobby Dodd said, "with a wonderful mother and a wonderful daddy. I was spoiled a little bit, but I had a great life.

"My daddy was a great guy. He was always in good humor and kept the family pretty much in good humor. He had a good job and a good salary. I believe he was paid five hundred dollars a month. I remember he showed me his checks. That must have been a fabulous salary for that day.

"My daddy loved people. He loved his family. He loved music. More than anything, he taught me and my brothers and sister to enjoy life. My daddy played with us, and we had a great time. He was a fun daddy. He created a lot of pleasure for us, and we all enjoyed it."

The house in which Bobby Dodd was born—in front of which he posed barefoot—sits on the corner of Grayson and Lafayette, at 312 Grayson Street, on the west side of town. The porch has since been enclosed. "A pretty modest bungalow," John Dodd called it. Two bedrooms upstairs, with the master bedroom on the main floor. For a while, John and Bobby slept on a trundle bed that slid out from beneath their parents' bed. Yet life was cozy, not cramped, in the Dodd household, and also comfortable and fun.

"We had a little shed, or barn," John Dodd said, "with a little pony and later a mare. We didn't get the pool table till we moved into the second house."

The second house, the big house, was right up Lafayette Street, built up on a hill on a triangular corner lot at Lafayette and Stuart Drive. Then, it sat on the outskirts of town, four or five blocks walking distance to the Galax Furniture Company. The Dodd boys used to ride their sleds down the hill out back, using a brush pile for a jump.

Today the old Dodd house at 310 Lafayette is a boarding house where an older couple rents out rooms on the first and second floors. Despite its white aluminum siding and storm windows, it has the forlorn look of a house that has seen far better days. And it has.

Bobby Dodd was five when the family moved into the new frame house built in 1913. The house on Lafayette had two floors, a spacious basement, and a wraparound porch. The three boys shared an upstairs bedroom, while Ruth had her own room. Mrs. Dodd maintained a flower room in the cupola and kept milk in her spring room. Irene Alderman, Bobby Dodd's first cousin, still lives in Galax. She remembers that house and how immaculately Mrs. Susan Dodd kept it. She called Mrs. Dodd Aunt Viola.

"The living room had light pink velvet chairs and a settee," Mrs. Alderman said. "The dining room was in the middle of the house. It had a fireplace with green ceramic tiles all around it." There was also a fireplace in the kitchen, where Mrs. Dodd, a wonderful cook, concocted delicious dishes. The house had all the amenities, too.

"We had running water and a bathroom," John Dodd recalled proudly, "which an awful lot of people didn't have at that time." They even had electricity, that marvel of the age which had finally come to Galax in 1908, the same year Bobby Dodd was born.

Most importantly, the house had a large side yard which, to a child, seemed enormous. "Boy, it was big," Bobby Dodd remembered. "It looked like a football field, one hundred yards to a little boy like me. That's where I learned to pass and punt and play football, really, in that yard. My older brother Pat was on the high school team. Big stuff to us was to get out there in that yard and tackle that other fellow. Punt, pass, and tackle.

"We'd play two, three, four on a side. Go to school early to play before school, then play after, too. Our clothes were always torn."

They'd play back behind the Methodist church, too, with kids like Sam Hampton and Jack Schooley, who lived across the street from the Dodds. Football wasn't the only game played in the Dodd household, though. "My daddy taught me to play cards—all the games of the time, and later bridge and gin rummy," Dodd said.

Edwin Dodd also taught his children gymnastics. "My daddy put mattresses up in the attic to practice gymnastics. He taught me how to stand on my head, walk on my hands, do flips, cartwheels, things a lot of boys don't have the opportunity to learn.

"After supper, we'd usually end up in the attic doing cartwheels and everything." Bobby Dodd would later perfect these stunts in high school, then put them to good use as a young assistant at Georgia Tech, where he would bet players milkshakes that he could walk ten yards on his hands faster than they could. And he usually could.

"We'd either do gymnastics after supper," Dodd said, "or shoot pool."

Ah, pool. After moving into the bigger house, Edwin Dodd bought a pool table at a bankruptcy sale after a local pool hall had gone out of business. He put the pool table down in the basement of the big house, and he and his offspring played often. Others watched enviously.

"They had the only pool table in town," Irene Alderman said.

In pool, as in other activities, Bobby Dodd took his cue from his father. "My daddy taught me to be a good pool player," said Dodd, who later made his mark—and some enemies—with his pool cue. Even today, he has a pool table in his basement. Even today, Dodd uses his original, peculiar style when shooting a game of eight ball.

"He was a great pool player," John Dodd said. "But he was so short when he started playing that he just had it laying on his hand, in his palm, with his other hand under the cue stick." Instead of holding the cue dangling down by his waist and stroking it, little Bobby Dodd had to raise his right arm, as if he were giving a clenched fist salute, put the cue in his palm, and stroke it. It looked funny; still does. But the older men he hustled in later years saw nothing funny in it at all.

Edwin and Susan Dodd encouraged their children to play something else besides football and games of chance. "All of us chose an instrument to play," Bobby Dodd said. "Pat played the saxophone, mother the guitar, John the piano. I played the violin."

Jack Benny had nothing to worry about. Each August, Galax still holds an Old Fiddler's Convention, where pickers come from miles around to play the bluegrass music Bobby Dodd loves so well. Loving it and performing it, however, are two different things.

"After I played violin for a year, my parents decided to have a recital," Dodd said. "That ended my violin career, because I was not gonna take part in any recital. I didn't like going to violin lessons, anyway. My buddies used to tease me about that. So I switched to the ukulele."

Arthur Godfrey had nothing to worry about either. "The ukulele was a lot of fun," Dodd said. "I could copy my mother on her chords. But only Pat got good at playing instruments. None of us ever got to be worth a tutti-frutti at it except Pat. He did play some and had his own orchestra later on. But we had music in our family, and we had fun in our family."

In 1916, one of the first Model-T Fords puttered into Galax. A Model-T cost about $750 then. The contrasts between the combustible engine car and the country town of Dodd's youth were striking. A local man named Bob Caldwell drove that first Model-T down the dirt path that was Main Street and pulled up next to two oxen pulling a covered wagon.

Oxen and other livestock were common sights on Main Street in those days. Farmers would drive cattle, sheep, and even turkeys down Grayson Street and into the pens at Chestnut Yard, at the railroad station, before loading them onto the train.

Susan Viola Dodd's influence on her family extended far beyond the encouragement of music appreciation. Her children adored her, and Bobby Dodd recalls her lovingly. "My mother was the finest mother, the finest wife, the greatest cook you ever saw," he said. He can still give a loving, longing litany of his mother's best dishes. "Whipped cream pie," Dodd said, his eyes almost glazing over. "Potato soup. And bread, fresh bread at all three meals—rolls or hot bread or salt-rising bread. It was different then, you ate all three meals at home. No one went out to restaurants. And my daddy came home from work for lunch. He'd walk home for lunch, and Mama would have fresh bread for every meal."

Mama's menu continued. "Buckwheat cakes," Dodd said, closing his eyes and smacking his lips. "I'd give $25 for buckwheat cakes now. When my sister was living here up the street in those apartments, where WSB-TV is, she'd make buckwheat cakes for me. My sister didn't fool with 'em much, though, 'cause they smelled with that yeast. But I loved buckwheat cakes. And I miss 'em.

"Mama could cook anything, and she'd put up preserves and jellies. And Mama's scalloped potatoes. I loved scalloped potatoes. Pies. Desserts.

"Now, we didn't know what it was to have meat like they do today, like a filet. We didn't know what a filet mignon was, or a T-bone. Only thing my mama bought was...I don't know what it was called but we called it a country steak. I can remember when she served it to us. It had gravy over it. I can see her now, she beat it, kinda like with a hammer thing, to make it soft and tender, and I can see her beating it now in the kitchen. When she served it, she always served it with creamed gravy. I loved the creamed gravy, but I didn't like the meat much, 'cause it was too tough and my teeth were too bad. But I loved that creamed gravy. I never ate steak when I was in college, and I hardly eat steak today."

"She was a Nuckolls," said Glenn Pless, a distant relative of Bobby Dodd's "and all the Nuckolls were great cooks."

"But Mama," Dodd said, "was supposed to be the best of all."

Mrs. Dodd was loved for more than her cooking, though. And so was her husband. "I remember what kind people they were," Irene Alderman said. "Very kind and civic-minded. They spent a lot of money on other people, probably too much money.

"Each Christmas, Uncle Edwin and Aunt Viola brought us a real nice toy. We wouldn't have had much of a Christmas without them."

Christmas in Edwin Dodd's house began on Christmas Eve. The tree was always standing in the cupola, beautifully decorated. Dodd would let each of his children open a present or two on Christmas Eve and the rest on Christmas morning. Bobby Dodd followed this custom with his children. "Kids love it," Dodd said. "They get two Christmases.

"We always had a nice Christmas. My daddy was generous and bought things for a lot of people."

One year, Bobby got a tricycle for Christmas. "A *bigggg* tricycle," he remembered. An old-fashioned tricycle, with an enormous front wheel. Bobby rode it everywhere through the house, and his mother was terrified he would ram the furniture. Eventually, he would pedal it outside on the dirt streets.

Later, he graduated to a Christmas bicycle. "An Iver Johnson," Dodd said proudly. "We'd put a big plank on the fence, ride it up, the plank goes down, then you go down the other side. But you had to do it fast or you fell off the other side. Woooooo!"

One Christmas, Edwin Dodd bought his two youngest sons greyhound puppies. "I don't know what in the world possessed him," Bobby Dodd said, "but can you imagine in Galax, Virginia, what in the devil you're gonna do with greyhounds? Everybody in Galax had a shepherd dog, or collie, or beagle, or mixed breed. Hell, everybody had a dog. But a greyhound? John had his about three months when it got sick and died. I kept mine, full grown. I'd run with him, but a greyhound was out of place in the Blue Ridge Mountains."

Mr. Dodd's generosity extended beyond the Christmas season. During World War I, rationing put many goods in short supply. Irene Alderman recalls how she and her sister Kit would cry because they had no sugar to put on their oatmeal. One morning, their Uncle Edwin left a pail of sugar outside their kitchen, so his nieces would have sugar with their morning oatmeal.

By then, Edwin Dodd was doing very well financially. "He was just a good businessman," John Dodd said. "he owned a grocery store—the Cash Racket—and a small movie theater, too. He brought a lot of Hawaiian groups into the theater and always entertained them after the show at our house. He also owned a drug store and soda fountain."

Dodd's good business sense certainly helped when the Galax Furniture Company burned to the ground in 1917.

"Furniture factories were fire traps in those days—all wood," John Dodd said. "I remember seeing the fire from the cupola in our second house about three o'clock in the morning. All our family was up watching the fire four or five blocks away. When a furniture factory caught on fire back in those days, there was nothing you could do for it. You just had to let it burn."

The ashes had barely stopped smoldering when Dodd found another job, managing another furniture factory in Bluefield, West Virginia, about 60 miles north of Galax on the state line. The Dodds lived in Bluefield for nearly a year, the longest year in Bobby Dodd's life.

"That just broke my heart," Dodd said. "I didn't want to leave Galax where all my relatives were and all the young kids my age, first cousins most of 'em. We got to Bluefield, it was a new world to me. They sent me to school.

"They took me to school each morning, and when recess came, I ran for home. I went home every recess. I never stayed longer than recess. ...Mama wouldn't punish me, she would just take me back the next day. But I never went back after recess. Mama felt sorry for me. I was unhappy. I guess I was crying, and I wanted to be with my mama. And I didn't know anybody there. They were all strangers to me, and I didn't like 'em. I don't know how long that lasted. She may have finally let me drop out of school, because I never remember going to school a full day there.

"And a strange thing happened. We're in a picture show one night, my daddy took us to the picture show, and somebody came in and tapped him on the shoulder and said, 'Mr. Dodd, the furniture factory's on fire.' The furniture factory catches on fire, it couldn't be a greater fire, it's all timber, all wood, and it just burned to the ground. And we moved back to Galax."

Edwin Dodd helped raise the funds to build another furniture factory in Galax, managed the factory, and returned his family to its home on Lafayette Street (which Dodd had been renting out). "I was happy then," Bobby Dodd said. "The only real sad part of my young life that I remember was in Bluefield. I hate to say it, but I was glad that furniture factory burned down."

Back in Galax winters were harsh. When it snowed, which it did often, the Dodd boys and their friends would block off their streets and sled down those hilly dirt paths. They also built fires to warm themselves between rides. At Christmastime, many local boys would tramp into the woods, cut down cedars, carry them back into town, and sell them as Christmas trees. Many families would often go "galacking," collecting galax leaves in bags and selling them for holiday floral decorations.

Come spring, though, and especially come summertime, it was baseball time. "Baseball was big stuff in Galax," Bobby Dodd said. "Football was very popular but, strange thing, we never saw a basketball game in Galax. We didn't know what basketball looked like. But baseball was big stuff.

"The big social event of the week was the baseball team playing the neighboring town. Everybody had a baseball team: Pulaski, Whitfield, Roanoke. On Saturday afternoon, you had a baseball game and everybody in town went out and watched the baseball team play."

They played in Felts Park, or the Fairgrounds, as it was also known because of the occasional horse races there. It's a 16-acre park smack in the middle of town, behind the old YMCA.

"Back then, Felts Park had soft, spongy turf," Glenn Pless said, "so you couldn't get hurt."

Bobby Dodd managed to get hurt there once, though, in a baseball game composed of kids teams from the north and south sides of town (Center Street divides Galax in half). "Bob was the captain," recalled childhood friend Sam Hampton. "He liked to make teams, tell us things, from when he was a little fella on up."

This day, Sam was pitching. Bobby Dodd was catching. But he missed a foul tip, and it hit him squarely in the throat. In those days, kids had no such equipment as a catcher's mask or chest protector.

"It scared me to death," Hampton said. "Bob couldn't talk and was coughing like crazy. But that rascal, he kept playing. He switched to pitcher, and I caught. I don't care what the score was, that Bob Dodd was still in there scrapping. There wasn't no quit in that Bob."

There was another catcher in town with far more renown than Bobby Dodd, though. "The catcher on the town baseball team was ol' Jim Anderson," said Dodd, "who was our town policeman and he was my second cousin. And, of course, I was very proud of ol' Jim...but because he was a baseball player, not because he was a policeman.

"Now ol' Jim pulled a play that I have never seen before," Dodd continued. "I've never seen it or heard of it before. I'd go down to the police station every Saturday morning, and ol' Jim would sit there with a big Irish potato and a knife, and he'd peel that Irish potato white until he'd get it just the size of a baseball.

"Come Saturday afternoon, ol' Jim would have that Irish potato in his hip pocket. As soon as the visitors got a runner on third base, that's when ol' Jim would pull his play. He'd reach back in his hip pocket and he'd get that Irish potato and he'd cup it in his hand where no one could see it. And he'd signal for a pitchout. And when that baseball hit his mitt, he took that Irish potato and threw it ten feet over our third baseman's head. And here comes that runner, diggin' for home. And here's ol' Jim with the baseball.

"And ol' Jim would tag him and the damnedest fight you ever saw would start. 'What's this?!' And our umpire would say, 'You're out!' And then the other team would really holler, 'You can't call us out! Your baseball's out there in left field!' "

Which is where Glenn Pless was playing when ol' Jim Anderson first used the hidden potato trick. "Nat Hester's on third base, leading, and Jim throws the ball wild, beyond third base into left field. I went running after it. I thought, 'My Lord, here we've lost that ballgame.' When I picked it up, I saw what it was but I still threw it in."

"That's when they had the big argument," Sam Hampton said.

"I can still hear big Jim: 'You show me in the rule book where it says anything about an Irish potato!' " Pless said. "After about thirty or forty minutes, they decided maybe it wasn't quite right and played it over."

Ol' Jim was convinced it was right. "He did that every week, you know," Dodd said. "You didn't scout anybody back then. Until finally, ol' Jim got a little arrogant and he tried it over at Low Oak. And I remember they carried him back in an ambulance. That's the last time the play was ever used. They just beat the hell outta him.

"I was ten years old at the time, and getting old enough to enjoy sports. I was interested in sports all my life. . . . I guess in many ways, I was kind of a Tom Sawyer or Huckleberry Finn. I just hated school. I didn't get in a lot of trouble, but I had to be active. I was kinda hyper. I had to be playing football, I had to be doing something.

"I couldn't sit around and read. I hated to read. You know, I didn't want anybody reading to me. If I'd a had a fishing hole, I'd a been out fishing, but I didn't have a fishing hole. So the next thing we could do, really, was play football and shoot pool a lot."

So Bobby Dodd did both. Better to live like Tom Sawyer and Huckleberry Finn than to have to read about them. "He was always playing ball," Irene Alderman said. "Played on an empty field. Whether it was baseball or football, he was always playing ball."

"I was planning on playing high school football in Galax," Dodd said. "My dream was to play in the VMI-VPI football game in Roanoke, Virginia, on Thanksgiving Day. That was the biggest event in Virginia. They were big rivals. The only school I would have thought about going to would have been VPI, which was in Blacksburg.

"Blacksburg wasn't too far away from us [about 45 miles northeast of Galax]. VMI was in Lexington, and I wouldn't have gone to VMI anyway 'cause it was a military school and I would've hated that. But I would've gone to VPI."

And he well might have, had the Galax Furniture Company not been sold in 1921 to the Vaughan-Bassett Furniture Company of Bassett, Virginia. "I think my daddy may have made some money on the sale, and I think he may have saved some money also out of his salary," Dodd said. "I know he had some money. I don't know how much, have no idea. But back then, ten thousand dollars was like two hundred thousand dollars today."

"Our father was apparently doing pretty well," John Dodd said. "Besides those other business interests he had, he'd been involved with some timber business. They called 'em cross ties, mining ties, all kinds of things, timber products.

"Once the furniture company was sold, he decided he'd just close everything out then and move to Kingsport. He was trying to buy some business

11

over there in Kingsport that would develop good for the kids."

So Edwin Dodd moved his family 75 miles southwest to Kingsport, in the east Tennessee hill country. "I don't know why he chose Kingsport," Bobby Dodd said. "But that changed my life."

The 1921 Kingsport High football
team. Bobby Dodd is in the front
row, third from left. Jitney Blankenbecler is second from the right in
the middle row.

Chapter 2
The Dodds and Football Come To Kingsport

THE DODD FAMILY ARRIVED in Kingsport, Tennessee, in early September 1921, just in time for the start of the school year. More importantly, they arrived just in time for the start of the first football season at Kingsport High School.

Kingsport was in its infancy then but already burgeoning. Like Galax, it owed its lifeblood to the railroad—in this case, the Clinchfield Line, or the CC & O.

By the Dodds' arrival in 1921, Kingsport was growing quickly. "It was a booming little industrial town," Bobby Dodd remembered.

"A fantastic new little town," John Dodd called it. "Our father wanted to go there because he'd heard it was such a good place to start a business."

A great little city, known as the Model City, whose residential streets resembled spokes sprouting from the hub of a wheel. In 1921, the population of Kingsport was about five thousand. "Everybody knew everybody," said Jitney Blankenbecler, a lifelong resident of Kingsport, the mayor from 1950 to 1951, and a high school football teammate of Bobby Dodd's.

Quite quickly, everybody came to know the Dodds. "When we got to Kingsport," Dodd said, "my daddy bought a grocery store, along with his brother-in-law, Aunt Annie's husband, Kemper Hampton." Edwin Dodd also bought an interest in a timber tract near Kingsport and, as Bobby Dodd remembered, "a beautiful home in Kingsport," one very reminiscent of the house they'd left behind in Galax. The house—the address is now 821 Broad Street—was white clapboard, with a large porch and a vacant field next door, where the Dodd boys and their friends played football. Bobby Dodd had a bedroom on the second floor.

The house, on the corner of Broad and West Ravine streets, stands three blocks from the heart of downtown Kingsport. It still looks similar to when the Dodds lived there, save for the foreign cars in the driveway and the Astroturf carpeting on the porch.

That house appealed to Bobby Dodd more than the grocery store. "The greatest thing about the grocery store," he said, "and the only thing I liked about it—I never worked there in my life, I hated it—but when they bought that grocery store, they inherited a little motorsickle that they used to deliver some groceries.

"It was a Cleveland, I remember it just as well. It was about like the small Hondas of today. Real small, about one or two cylinders. Light. Real small. And when I saw that motorsickle, boy, that was what I needed. I wanted that motorsickle worse than anything."

But Mr. Dodd would let his 12-year-old son have it only on Sundays. "I had the best time riding that motorsickle. The streets were *paved*, and I could ride that motorsickle all around. I'd see my buddies and I'd wave to 'em, and I'd get the biggest kick out of that motorsickle that I ever had almost out of anything. It was just about five times as good as that first tricycle you got when you were a kid."

As exhilarating as motorcycle riding was, two other activities held even more fascination for Bobby Dodd: playing football and shooting pool. Unlike in Galax, though, Dodd took his cue stick out in public in Kingsport.

The pool hall was called Bill Richardson's Pool Room. It stood in the middle of downtown, in a row of brick storefronts just across Main Street from the railroad station. "By the age of 14, I could shoot pool as well as anyone in town," Bobby Dodd said proudly. "I loved to play nine-ball. That was a gamblin' game. You played for 25 and 50 cents. Back in those days, that was pretty big money.

"I managed to win a dollar or two each day in the pool room. My daddy had to give special permission for me to play, of course, 'cause I was underage. And I kept my dollar bills in my drawer in a Brownie camera. But my older brother Pat saw me counting my money one day, and I had to give him about half of it to bribe him not to tell Mama and Papa all about what I'd been doing."

Mama and Papa probably knew anyway. Most everyone else in Kingsport knew how well Bobby Dodd could shoot pool. "The town pool shark," said Jitney Blankenbecler, who heard Dodd was winning so much money shooting pool that he hid it in the grandfather clock at home, so his parents wouldn't ask where all the money'd come from.

Not everyone admired this little guy with the peculiar cue stroke, though. "They eventually had to take him out of there because he was making such a killing money-wise playing pool," John Dodd said. "I don't know who was making the complaints, but he was taking some of the old-time gamblers real bad.

"One of Bob's friends, a linotype operator at the Kingsport Press, backed him. Squeak Watkins was his name. He took a liking to Bob and put him in the pool room and financed all of his betting. Both of them were splitting the money. It got to be such a well-known fact in town, the police had to just go in and take him out. They just couldn't let him stay there.

"He was about 12 years old, and he was taking these 30, 35, 40 year olds, old-time gamblers in a pool hall, and they didn't think any kid in short pants could possibly take 'em. Bob was unusually good at pool. He was also unusually good in badminton, tennis, golf, and any damn thing you could name."

Especially football. Even that first fall in Kingsport, when Bobby Dodd—just a seventh grader—played on his first organized football team. Which, coincidentally, was the first football team ever organized in Kingsport.

At least the Dodds had played some football and seen some high school games back in Galax. Said Jitney Blankenbecler, "Everybody else here *played* in the first football game they ever *saw*. We had a group of guys who didn't know one end of the ball from the other." Actually, the football was more rounded then. "Daggone near a basketball," Jitney said.

The team was organized by a volunteer coach, Don Williamson, who claimed he had played collegiate football at the University of Rochester in upstate New York before coming to Kingsport. "He didn't know any football," Dodd said. Williamson owned a printing shop and in his spare time helped found the enduring Kingsport tradition of football.

The boys didn't embrace the new-fangled game immediately, however. "There was a lot of apprehension about all this diving and falling and catching fellas," Blankenbecler recalled. "But after a few times, you forgot all about that. It was the kind of game that just sucks you in and never lets you go."

In the 1921 team photo of the inaugural Kingsport High School football squad, Bobby Dodd sits in the middle of the front row. "I look like the waterboy," admitted Dodd. He wears something on his head, something that resembles a casserole dish more than a football helmet. And he is having the time of his young life.

"I'm in the seventh grade, and I made the team—I'm twelve years old and weigh a hundred pounds, and it was the biggest thrill probably of my life," Dodd said. "It didn't matter to me that we got beat the first game, 59-0, that we didn't win a game. I was on that team at 12 years old and a hundred pounds."

And it mattered not that Bobby Dodd was so tiny they didn't even have a football uniform that fit him. "I wore unionalls that first year," Dodd said. "A unionall is like an overall, except it just covers you all over. It doesn't have straps on the shoulders, it just covers you all over, kinda like a flight suit for a pilot. Arms and legs. It was khaki colored."

His mother sewed padding into the unionalls for protection. Many of Dodd's teammates didn't wear headgear that first year. "Too damn expensive," said Dodd.

Kingsport High School then included grades 7 through 12. Although he was a skinny, slow, weak seventh-grader, Bobby Dodd made the varsity. "Because I knew football, I'd played football," he said. "These other kids had never seen a football before. And I could tackle. And I could catch the ball and throw the ball. And John, my brother, made the team, too. I believe he was a quarterback the first year."

Bobby was a second-string end. "I was a wide receiver most of the time," Dodd said. "and the reason I was a wide receiver was, you know, they didn't have bleachers, they didn't have seats. People stood on the sidelines, just like where the players stand today. They stood right up against the sidelines.

"So I'd go out on the kickoff—our team was receiving—I'd go out and stand on the sideline, where our spectators were. I was a layout man, see. Which is illegal today, but back then it wasn't. And they snapped the ball and I went down the sideline and I'd catch the pass.

"And they'd scream, 'He's not in the game! He hasn't got on a uniform!' But it didn't make any difference, we had our own officials—you know, we played at home. When we played at the other places, I almost got killed sometimes. The other places were rough."

There were only 18 players on the Kingsport roster that first season. "A lot of times, we could only scrimmage half the line," Blankenbecler said. "We couldn't go 11 on 11."

"Most of the time," John Dodd said, "we had to use the faculty to have a scrimmage."

Practices were held at the original Kingsport High School, which later became the junior high and is now George Washington Elementary School. The old high school was on East Sevier Street, just three blocks from the Dodd home. Games were held on Saturday afternoons. Kingsport players had to put on their uniforms at the school, then jog about three-fourths of a mile through open fields to the gridiron downtown. Bobby Dodd started his football career, ironically, on Legion Field, a name he would come to know, and loathe, years later in Birmingham, Alabama.

There were no stands that first football season in Kingsport. Bleachers were erected in 1922, but in 1921, spectators stood along the sidelines, crowding the field and providing camouflage for the little layout man. Just how small was Bobby Dodd?

"A couple of fellas tell the tale that a couple of fellas picked him up one game and threw him over the line for a touchdown," Jitney Blankenbecler said. "That's false."

Even when the bleachers were built, though, many Kingsport fans continued to ring the sidelines. Years later, Bobby Dodd would dread taking his Georgia Tech team into Baton Rouge to face LSU on Saturday nights.

But Tiger Stadium had nothing on Legion Field in Kingsport, or on the hostile arenas in several other Tennessee towns.

"Tough towns," Dodd said. "In Kingsport, they'd pull a knife on you on the sidelines—the visiting team, of course. At Erwin, Tennessee (Erwin High in Unicoi), they threw rocks at me one time while I was playing safety. And we had a free-for-all at Johnson City."

Unlike contemporary football players, whose helmets are hard plastic shells with extravagant cage facemasks, those Kingsport pigskin pioneers couldn't really rely on their headgear for protection if a fight broke out. "We had helmets," John Dodd said, "but they were just about so thin and poor, you just about got your head beat off anyway. They were just soft padding, about like a horse blanket, with their leather on the outside. They were not stiff like today. They were soft."

But then, at least they were designed specifically for football. Many of the original Kingsport players wore makeshift football cleats. "The players had to provide their own helmets and shoes," Blankenbecler said. "Most of us just took a regular pair of shoes and put on some cleats."

Duly dressed, if not duly impressive, the Kingsport Panthers (their original nickname; it later became, and remains today, the Indians) brought the game of football to their town. "Some crazy things happened back in those days," John Dodd chuckled.

The Panthers opened their first season against powerful Virginia High and promptly lost 59-0. They lost their home opener, too, 14-0 to Johnson City. In fact, Kingsport was shut out in its first five games, losing all five by an aggregate score or 134-0.

Some rules were quite different then. Only two or three officials refereed games. One ref always leaned into the huddle to listen when a substitute reported in. "You couldn't talk for one play back then," Blankenbecler said. When a ballcarrier went out of bounds, the ball was spotted right there on the sideline for the next play. There were no hash marks then; if the center lined up just inside the right sideline, his teammates were all lined up to his left.

The Panthers didn't score until their sixth game, kicking a field goal but still falling to Tennessee High 64-3. The following week, they finally scored a touchdown and actually won a game, 7-0 over Abingdon, Virginia. Just who scored the touchdown, though, is still hazy.

Kingsport football records indicate that a boy named Josh Denham ran 12 yards for the first touchdown in Kingsport High history. Both Dodd brothers and Jitney Blankenbecler insist it happened differently.

John Dodd: "We were driving down near the goal line. Bob was on the sideline with the coach; I was at quarterback and the coach put Bob in the game at end. We had practiced a pass to him—not the trick play, this was legitimate. But they didn't even see him, didn't realize that he was separated from the crowd. So he ran down the sideline and caught a pass from me, and that was the only score of the whole damn game.

"When the officials called it a touchdown, the Abingdon team started the damnedest fight you ever saw. Our coach, Don Williamson, a rather fat, heavy fella, ran out on the field. About this time our captain, Shorty Poston—he was a fullback who used to dive over the line at the goal—drew back to hit one of the Abingdon men and hit our own coach flush in the nose. I think Coach Williamson was the only casualty of the game."

Other than Abingdon, which became the first Kingsport football victim, and the only victim that first season. The Panthers finished with a 1-7-1 record, losing a second time to Johnson City before holding that school to a scoreless tie in their third meeting, the season finale. Regardless of the record, though, football had come to Kingsport.

A few months later, something even more important came to Kingsport: LeRoy Sprankle.

"I've always said," said Bobby Dodd, "that of all the people in Kingsport—ministers, the leading people, J. Fred Johnson was the leading citizen—Sprankle had more influence on the whole town than any other one individual. As our teams got good, then they started getting good cheerleaders, everything went along with athletics. Like at Valdosta. Hell, they got a great band down in Valdosta 'cause of their football team.

"So, Sprankle had a great influence on the little town of Kingsport, Tennessee. And after we all got out, we all realized how much influence he had on our lives. We didn't think about it that much when he was coaching us, you know. But when you get out and get older, you realize, 'That guy had a great influence on my life.' I was very fond of him. Later in life, I told him so."

Sprankle came to Kingsport from Canton, Ohio, in the winter of 1922. Having served in World War I, he worked as a draftsman in Canton for the Timken Roller Bearing Laboratories. He also played semi-professional baseball and basketball. He was a catcher for the Noaker's Ice Cream team. Sprankle had longed for a career in baseball until he was injured in a construction accident, struck in the eye by a flying object. The minor injury dashed his dreams of a baseball career.

Sprankle arrived in Kingsport to coach the first high school basketball team. He had played basketball—as well as football and baseball—at Mt. Union College in Alliance, Ohio.

"Round, chubby, friendly," is how Jitney Blankenbecler remembers

Sprankle. "Absolutely honest. Loved his boys. Would do anything for his boys."

And literally did. For 13 years, Sprankle coached every athletic team at Kingsport High: football, basketball, baseball, and track. He even had a gymnastics squad called "The Royal Tumblers." One of his most royal and loyal tumblers was Bobby Dodd, who had learned his gymnastic basics back in Galax, after dinner, on those mattresses in the attic.

Naturally, Dodd also played football, basketball, baseball, and track for LeRoy Sprankle. "He was a very competent young man," Dodd said. "He took me under his wing and had me play all sports so I didn't have time to get into trouble. He begged me to stay in school, which I did enough to be eligible for athletics."

Sprankle lived in the fire department when he first arrived in Kingsport. For awhile, he ate many of his meals at Jitney Blankenbecler's home, a practice followed by many bachelors new to town who boarded (and in some cases roomed) at other Kingsport households. Sprankle spent most of his waking hours, though, in the building next door to the fire department. The high school.

He immediately improved the school football team. Kingsport opened the 1922 season with five consecutive victories. Three were shutouts. Kingsport twice defeated Greeneville, which had shut out the Panthers the previous season 19-0. This time, the Sprankmen, as they became known, clobbered Greeneville by a combined score of 153-19.

Kingsport finally lost its sixth game, 40-12, to Erwin. The score indicated no improvement from the previous year, when Erwin prevailed 26-0. But this time, Kingsport trailed by just 14-12 when Erwin scored 26 points in the final five minutes.

In that Erwin game, though, Bobby Dodd *officially* scored his first Kingsport touchdown, at least according to Kingsport football records. Dodd, then playing some quarterback but still primarily a receiver, caught a 40-yard pass from Jitney Blankenbecler.

Kingsport would lose only one other game that season, 7-6, to Virginia High. The Panthers finished with an 8-2 record. The next year, as the Indians, they would fare even better.

Again, Kingsport opened the season with five straight victories. This time, though, they were all shutouts. Only the opener was close. Luke Lowe drop-kicked a 30-yard field goal for the only score of the game. There followed a 94-0 rout of Marion, Virginia, in which halfback Matt Lunn scored 41 points.

The third victory for Kingsport, 25-0, came over a collection of local, non-high school players called the Cotillion Club All-Stars. Two games later, Lunn again scored 41 points in a 95-0 mauling of Newport. The Indians finally lost, 14-0, to Virginia High. After tying powerful Knoxville

Central High 7-7 in the next-to-last game of the season, Kingsport finished 8-1-1 and won the 1923 mythical Tennessee state high school championship.

During winters, Bobby Dodd played basketball but not on Sprankle's varsity team, at least not initially. "I wasn't a good basketball player," Dodd said, "because we had never seen a basketball back in Galax. But I went out because Sprankle got me interested in basketball. He was a good basketball coach, by the way, real good. And when he started basketball, he made me go out.

"I was small then, and I wasn't particularly suited to basketball—but then, I wasn't particularly suited to football, either. I could tackle and handle the ball, though. At first, I didn't make the basketball team. It took me two, three years before I was a regular on the basketball team. Tickled me to death when I finally made the regulars. But I didn't know basketball well enough, and I didn't have any real talent. See, I was small, and I wasn't particularly fast, and I didn't know the game. So I didn't make the basketball team right away.

"But Sprankle had me out every year. I played on what he called his midget team the first year. He had a midget team, and I was on the small team but did not play varsity. Then I moved up. Ended up about the third year, I was playing varsity football, basketball, baseball, track, and gymnastics. I was making five letters a year."

Even after moving up to the varsity basketball team, though, Bobby Dodd still epitomized the midgets.

"We were playing Rogersville, a little town about 30 miles away, in basketball," Dodd said. "I'm on the basketball team, but I'm real small. And after the game, a man came to me—I never saw him before—and he said, 'Young man, would you be interested in becoming a jockey?' I was that small. I said, 'I don't even know anything about jockeys.' I didn't even know what a jockey hardly was. ...I remember well that later that night, the lights went out in the Rogersville gym, and we had to sit there for about an hour while they got the lights back on. Ol' Rogersville. The first sweetheart I ever had was from Rogersville. A girl named Virginia Margraves.

"But anyway, I ended up as a good basketball player. That was my favorite sport. I had more talent in basketball than I did in football. I was what they call the point guard. They didn't call it that then, but I brought the ball down, I fed the ball to the other people. I was the quarterback of the basketball team, just like I was in football."

Come spring, Dodd played baseball for Sprankle. He played both second and third base. He occasionally batted in the cleanup spot. "I was a pretty good baseball player. In track I tried the pole vault, because it took a little bit of gymnastic skill. So I high jumped and pole-vaulted, and I made the track team.

"Sprankle always had me doing something. He had me doing two sports many, many times. We were practicing football and basketball overlapping. And we'd overlap basketball and baseball. And we'd overlap baseball and track, they were on at the same time. So I was doing one or two sports all during the year, and then he had us playing baseball during the summer on some team, some mill team, or he'd coach us. So we were doing something with him all the time, and I didn't have time to get in trouble.

"The only thing was," Bobby Dodd sighed, "I just hated school worse than any Indian."

Indeed, the quintessential Georgia Tech man, the coach who would stress academics, who would pride himself on the number of players he would graduate, who would go to great lengths to help those players graduate—often keeping players on scholarship five and six years, sometimes even seven—hated school.

"Despised it, just despised it," Dodd corrected. "My whole family disliked school, 'cept for John. We thought, 'There's something wrong with John.' But Pat never finished high school. Ruth never finished high school. And the only reason I went to school was so I could play football and basketball.

"See, I never thought about going to college. All I was ever going to do was stay eligible enough in high school to where I could play. They didn't have any eligibility rules, I don't think. So long as you just went to school, you could play.

"I hated school, just hated it. I was looking out the window all the time, wanting to be out there playing on that practice field, wondering what's going on out there. There wasn't anything in school that pleased me except physical ed and gymnastics."

It wasn't that Bobby Dodd was dumb. On the contrary. "He could have been one of the smartest boys ever in Kingsport if he wanted to," Blankenbecler said. "He had the capability." He merely lacked the academic inclination.

"I had a pretty good memory," Dodd said. "If you gave me something to memorize, I could remember it. I could remember right now, hell, I can remember Edgar Allan Poe, and Burns, and Shakespeare, and things I learned. I can tell you a lotta things like that 'cause my memory's good. But I don't want to sit down and have to memorize something."

Not unless there's some green, not grades, riding on it. In high school, Bobby Dodd memorized the capitals of the then-48 states. Then he'd bet people he could name the capital for every state they could name. "Things like that, they interested me," he said. "See, that's competition. But I hated math. I hated science. I never took physics in college. I never took anything past zoology, and I had to take it. Psychology wasn't too bad for me, I didn't mind it too much. I didn't mind history much; that was mostly memory."

Dodd may have been disinterested in schoolwork, but he was neither defiant nor disruptive in the classroom. Basically, he was just *there*, killing time before lunch, before practice, before the next ballgame.

"My teachers loved me," Dodd recalled. "My homeroom teacher one year, she said, 'Now Robert, *please* study, please do better, I want you to pass my course.' "

That teacher was Nancy Wylie, Dodd's math teacher at Kingsport High and his senior year homeroom teacher. In an article in the September 23, 1962, edition of the *Atlanta Journal-Constitution Sunday Magazine*, Miss Wylie remembered Dodd. "I can't recall that he ever disobeyed rules," she wrote. "He just sort of ignored them."

She also described him as the most relaxed student in school, a composure that was one of Dodd's greatest assets on the athletic field. "He was usually found leaning against a wall," Miss Wylie wrote, "hands in his pockets, feet crossed."

Miss Wylie recalled that once, during a checkers game, an opponent urged Dodd to make a move. Dodd replied, "I haven't rested up from the last move yet."

Nancy Wylie may have been partial to Bobby Dodd because she, too, enjoyed sports. During Kingsport football games, she charted the team's plays, the way assistant coaches now do at all high school, collegiate, and professional games. Being nearsighted, she had to stand on the sideline with the players to see the action. From that vantage point, Miss Wylie once saw Bobby Dodd wipe his muddy hands on a referee's clean, striped shirt. Then, he threw a perfect pass.

Miss Wylie wasn't the only teacher who liked Dodd. "The teachers, they'd give me every break they could," Dodd said. "I wasn't mean in school, you know, I didn't smart aleck, or smart off. I was docile and friendly, and they liked me."

A strikingly appropriate saying accompanied Dodd's yearbook photograph in the tenth grade. It read: "Happy am I, from care I'm free; why aren't they all content like me?"

Outside the classroom, Dodd did wonderfully well, even off the playing field. "On that playground apparatus, he was one of those guys who would damn near go over the top on the swings," Jitney Blankenbecler said.

"And the girls would all go, 'Wooooo!' The girls didn't look at me, but they all loved him.

"Dodd was even a good marble shooter. Dadburned, he was good at everything. I've always thought of Bob as the all-American boy. He was mischievous, but he was never in any dirty trouble."

"There was nothing I saw Bob do that he didn't excel in," said Frank "Gabby" Merideth, another Kingsport classmate and teammate. "He had a high IQ. He shot pool well. He played poker well. He swam well. He was great on the football field, played basketball and baseball. He could even dance well. There was nothing he couldn't do."

Bobby Dodd's life was altered dramatically, and permanently, in 1921 when his family left Galax for Kingsport. In 1924, his life changed again, this time tragically.

Edwin Dodd did not prosper financially in Kingsport. While the rest of the city boomed about him and his family blossomed, Edwin Dodd struggled. In addition to his share of the grocery store and his timber interest, he later bought a downtown drug store. It was located on Main Street, across from the railroad station and just a couple of storefronts down from the pool hall.

"After Daddy bought it, he changed the name to the Bon Ton," Bobby Dodd said. "I don't know where in the world he got that name. But the Bon Ton was a big mistake."

Like most old-time pharmacies, the drug store also featured a soda fountain, which was exceedingly popular with Dodd's children and their friends.

"All four of us children worked there," Bobby Dodd said, "and we brought our friends in and gave 'em free milk shakes and free sodas and free everything. My sister brought all of her friends in. By the time we got through giving away everything—and it was probably mismanaged, anyway—it lost money. I wasn't interested in the finances. I wasn't interested in the Bon Ton, really, except to go in there and get milk shakes and take my friends in there.

"But the Bon Ton was a disaster. And the grocery store turned out to be a loser, too."

More than adolescent generosity caused the decline of the drug store. Even in the 1920s, downtown commercial decay was a problem. "The Bon Ton lost a lot of its patronage," John Dodd said, "because of the change in the town. The town moved away from Main Street, about halfway between

25

Main Street and Sullivan Street. It's like certain parts of town get too old, and they just outgrow 'em."

Edwin Dodd's failing timber holdings compounded his financial woes. "I don't know if somebody cheated him out of any money or not," John Dodd said, "but he seemed to think things weren't done right. It later went bad and had something to do with his mental attitude later on."

For the Dodds, life was no longer as financially secure as it had been in Galax. That troubled Edwin Dodd greatly. He worried constantly. And he started drinking more heavily.

At 14, Bobby Dodd drove his papa around in the family's old Ford. "I loved to drive him," Dodd said. "He would kinda choose me, I guess because maybe he was drinking, and he didn't want the others to know it. But I was driving him. I was very close to him."

Close enough to know that Edwin Dodd's fears weren't just financial. "I think my daddy thought he had cancer of the prostate," Bobby Dodd said. "Which, by the way, I've had. Runs in the male members of our family. All of 'em had it. John. Pat. Me. My daddy thought he had a malignancy. He may have thought he was gonna die.

"And he must have started drinking. But I never knew he drank, never smelled whiskey on him in my life. But they say he drank a lot in later life, from about the time I was 12, when we moved to Kingsport, till he died when I was 16. During those four years somewhere, he started drinking."

"Prostate problems were common then, as they are now," John Dodd said. "In those days, though, there wasn't much you could do for the damn thing. Surgery. The number of deaths was pretty bad. You didn't have the drugs you have now to keep infections out while you were doing an operation.

"He thought he had cancer of the prostate, but I talked to his family physician later, and he didn't seem to think that they ever pinned it down, that they ever got a sure biopsy on his prostate. But I felt this worry caused Papa to do what he did."

Early one March morning in 1924, about three o'clock, Edwin Dodd left his comfortable home on Broad Street. He walked about a half a block, took out a loaded Smith & Wesson .32, put the pistol in his mouth, and pulled the trigger. A neighbor heard the shot and ran to the Dodd home. John and Pat hurried outside, looking for their father.

They found him in a driveway, lying in a pool of blood. An ambulance arrived momentarily and rushed Edwin to the hospital. Back at the house, the other children were all awake and crying now. Mrs. Dodd tried to comfort them.

"Mama knew Papa was out gonna take his life," Bobby Dodd said. "He'd written a note to her, and she'd found it when she heard him leave the house, but it was too late."

Miraculously, Edwin Dodd survived his suicide attempt. The .32 caliber bullet passed through the rear of his head, missing both his spinal column and the stem leading to his brain.

Edwin Dodd remained in the hospital for a couple of months. His family all came to visit him. "He was conscious, but I don't remember much about seeing him," Bobby Dodd said. "I probably cried. It was tragic. You know how you'd feel. I felt like I was closer to him than any of the other children."

"I can't recall him ever coming back home," John Dodd said. "And I can't recall really talking to him, you know, as a son to a father after that."

The nightmare didn't end with the first suicide attempt, however. The phone rang at the Dodd house one day. It was the hospital calling. Edwin Dodd had gotten some drugs and taken a fatal overdose. He was 54 years old.

"It was very depressing," John Dodd said. "It was hard to believe that happened. But you finally learn to accept it. You think of it as being something you're ashamed of, that you can't talk about. It was a stigma."

After his father's first suicide attempt, John Dodd quit high school for a year to run the Bon Ton. Although he worked there 16 hours a day, "it really wasn't much of a profit-making deal at all. It was really more of a lark. We weren't old enough to appreciate how serious the financial end of it was."

Susan Dodd was. She was a widow now, with four children. She had to manage a household as well as her dwindling finances, and had to come to terms with her own grief as well as her children's. "Mama was a stout woman," Bobby Dodd said. "She took it like a trooper. She got over it, and she never showed it."

"This was all such a shock that we don't remember quite all that we should," John Dodd said. "But I do remember that Mama took it pretty good, much better than most women would. She was pretty strong. I'm sure it hurt her terribly, but she carried on real well."

The Dodds moved into a comfortable bungalow around the corner, at what is now 126 East Sevier Street, a halfblock up from the old high school. A smaller house than their last two homes, it resembled John and Bobby's birthplace in Galax. Shortly thereafter, Pat Dodd moved out. Then Ruth got married and moved out, too. With Bobby and John still living at home and not much money coming in, Mrs. Dodd rented out one bedroom to a schoolteacher and cooked meals for four young men.

"All of 'em high-type boys," Bobby Dodd said. "They all enjoyed each other."

And the Charleston. "That was the big thing at lunch, everybody would practice the Charleston. They'd hold onto the mantel in the living room—they didn't have any women as partners—and everybody learned to

Charleston. Had great times with 'em, we all enjoyed 'em, and I guess Mama made enough money where she could take care of me and John and feed us all. I never heard her complain about money."

Although his life had been shattered domestically, Bobby Dodd was resilient. He continued to thrive athletically. He had firmly established himself as LeRoy Sprankle's quarterback in the single-wing offense—a starter and a star. The 1924 season, Dodd's sophomore year, began a spectacular three-year period for Kingsport football.

The Indians opened the 1924 schedule against Big Stone Gap, Virginia. Leading 59-0 at halftime, they cruised to a 97-13 victory. In a 46-0 rout of Abingdon, Dodd rushed for two touchdowns, caught another, and threw for two more. Virginia High tied them 6-6, but the Indians were still undefeated after eight games, when Dodd, with his team trailing Blacksburg (Virginia) High 6-0, threw a touchdown pass, sneaked a yard for another touchdown, and drop-kicked the extra, and deciding, point in that 13-12 triumph.

Undefeated entering the ninth and final game, and seeking its second straight state title, Kingsport anticipated playing Knoxville Central High, the popular and logical choice. But Central backed out of the ballgame. Instead, Kingsport played Knoxville High, which posted a 20-6 upset, preventing Kingsport from repeating as state champions.

After winning its first two games of the 1925 season, Kingsport lost 7-6 to hated Knoxville High when Bobby Dodd—who had just thrown a 35-yard touchdown pass to Harry Cox—missed the extra point. In the next four games, Dodd threw 11 touchdown passes. The first of those came against his old hometown of Galax.

Dodd passed for four touchdowns against Galax. He also passed the word among his Kingsport teammates: "Now that one is my cousin, so don't hurt him. And he's my cousin, too, so don't hurt him, either." Kingsport easily prevailed, and no kin was injured.

Sprankle continued to coach and counsel Bobby Dodd, now more a second father to the boy. On Friday nights before Saturday football games, Sprankle had Dodd meet him at the fire department to discuss strategy and the game plan for the following day. Dodd was then expected to go straight home and go to sleep.

The night before the Tennessee High game, however, the coach found young Dodd and two of his teammates out after curfew. The next day, Sprankle made them sit out the first half of the game. By the time Dodd came in, Kingsport was up 38-0. The Indians proceeded to score 62 second-half points for a 100-0 win. That season Kingsport outscored its opponents 433-22 and won 10 of 11 games.

By Bobby Dodd's senior year, the football program at Kingsport High School—actually its entire athletic program—was firmly established as one of the best in east Tennessee. From its meager beginnings in 1921, when the principal and teachers joined that small squad of 18 for practice, Kingsport now had anywhere from seven to nine full teams dressed out, from the seventh grade to the varsity.

"We had a lot of emphasis on football because there wasn't anything else to do around here," said Dr. Shelton Reed, now a retired surgeon who still lives in Kingsport. One hundred twenty-five boys tried out for football at Kingsport High when Reed was a seventh grader, and Bobby Dodd a celebrated senior.

"Everybody worshipped Bobby because he was a showy guy," Reed said. "He didn't know a stranger. He had no inhibitions. And he was always a leader. It immediately comes across that he's a leader."

In his senior year, Dodd was the leader of an extraordinarily talented backfield nicknamed the Pony Express. Equally extraordinary was the fact that anyone would consider Bobby Dodd, with his speed, a pony.

"It's just a miracle I could play with my speed, or lack of speed," Dodd admitted. "There was hardly a single person on any of the football teams I played on in high school and college who couldn't outrun me in the 50 and 100-yard dash.

"It was really embarrassing. I wouldn't run with 'em 'cause I knew they'd beat me. They were always challenging me, those fat tackles would challenge me to a race. I wouldn't accept because I was extremely slow. I was fairly quick with my hands and could throw the ball pretty good and kick pretty good, but when it came to running, I just wasn't there. I just didn't have it.

"And believe me, in a game where speed is so important as it is in football, it was nothing short of a miracle that I was able to play. I guess I played more than anything because I really loved the game and really wanted to play."

"Bob was slow and tripped on his own feet a lot of time," John Dodd said. "But he really outguessed the other team. I think that really came down through our father. I think our father and all our uncles were athletically minded, and would have been good players if they'd tried to do that.

"But Bob, he could just outthink anybody. If they had a weakness in what they were doing, playing tennis or whatever it was, he generally found out what it was and just put the heat on them.

"But the more pressure there was on *him*, the better Bob came out. He seemed to do whatever it was—a pass or a kick or whatever—better when the heat was on than in practice."

And, as the saying that accompanied Bobby Dodd's yearbook photo in the 11th grade read: "What he lacks in brawn, he makes up in brain, for his rapid thinking has often turned defeat into victory."

So even in high school, Dodd displayed all the attributes that served him so well as a collegian and later a coach. He was innately intelligent, inspiring, imaginative, highly competitive, well liked, and lucky.

But Bobby Dodd's greatest asset, both as the bowlmaster at Georgia Tech and back at Kingsport High, was this: Long before anyone had coined the phrase "Dodd's Luck" people believed in him.

"We had complete confidence in him," Jitney Blankenbecler said. "That's my strongest memory of him. If he said do it, we knew that was the right thing to do."

Dodd and his teammates did most everything right in the 1926 season. They opened with an astonishing 198-0 annihilation of Norton, Virginia. Norton never crossed midfield and Kingsport set what was then the record for most points scored in a high school football game. Sprankle played his first team the entire first and third quarters, when the Indians scored 128 points, 73 in the third quarter alone.

The Wonder Teams, they called Kingsport in those years. The Pony Express backfield consisted of Dodd at quarterback and running backs Paul Hug, James Duncan, and Frank Merideth, who was primarily a blocking back. The Pony Express galloped on after Norton, winning their next three games by a composite score of 193-0. Wisely, Abingdon and Rhea County, the next two opponents, canceled out.

Three more games, three more victories, by a 173-0 total. Against the Milligan College junior varsity, Dodd drop-kicked two 20-yard field goals and a 30-yarder, kicked four extra points, averaged 50 yards on punts and, surprisingly, even scored a touchdown.

After seven games, Kingsport had not allowed a point while scoring 546. But the Indians then lost on a late field goal to dreaded Knoxville High, 3-0. It was the end of their 15-game winning streak, and the first time they'd gone scoreless in 29 games.

They dropped the finale, too, losing 15-6 to Middlesboro, Kentucky in the mud. Still, Kingsport finished the season with a 7-2 record, averaged 60.7 points per game, and outscored the opposition 550-18. Shelton Reed recalls Bobby Dodd's final high school game: "I can remember Bob going off the field for the last time and everybody cheering." (Indeed, Bobby Dodd was voted most popular, as well as most athletic, in his senior class.)

In his five years as a quarterback, Bobby Dodd scored 30 touchdowns, passed for 37 more, kicked 51 extra points and seven field goals, and scored 252 points.

"And then a strange thing happened that changed my entire life," Dodd said. "The high school principal—Charles Kaufman was his name—came to me and he said, 'Robert, you can't play anymore football. You've played six years.' Well, this hurt me, this hurt me bad. See, I'd planned to make high school football my career! I loved high school football.

"And Mr. Kaufman said, 'As you know, you're failing all your work.' I knew that. He said, 'I'll make a deal with you.' Can you believe a high school principal did this? He said, 'If you pass all your courses, you'll have 14 credits. It takes 16 to graduate. You've been in high school six years and only have 14 credits. But if you study and pass your courses, I'll give you two credits you didn't even take, and I'll give you a diploma, because I want you to go to college.'

"Well, I'd never had any idea of going to college. But I realized, 'If I'm gonna play any more football, I've gotta go to college.' So I told him I'd do it. And for the first time in my life, I studied. I had to get some books—I didn't have any books!"

So Bobby Dodd studied. As his senior saying in the yearbook noted: "Bobby doesn't like to study, but when he does, his brilliant mind is revealed." Not quite brilliant, perhaps, but bright enough.

"I passed all of my courses," Dodd said, "and then the principal gave me a diploma. Shocked everyone in Kingsport. Nobody thought I was gonna graduate from high school.

"And now, I'm going to college."

And that is a story all to itself.

Punting with style, 1928.

Chapter 3
The Reluctant Volunteer—
Bobby Dodd Goes To College

CALL IT "Bobby Dodd Goes to College." It is an autobiographical, buoyant, joyous journey across the early landscape of his life. Bobby Dodd has told his story hundreds, perhaps thousands of times. He still tells it every time he's called to speak at a function, public or private. Some of it is even fact.

"Now I'm going to college," Dodd begins. "And I got this buddy with me, Paul Hug, and he is the finest athlete in the South. He's a straight-A student, 185 pounds, could outrun anybody in the state. Great athlete, best wrestler in the school, best boxer in the school. He and I are going to college together, and I say where we're going, 'cause I'm the quarterback.

"There were two schools offered us scholarships: Vanderbilt University and the University of Tennessee. I said, 'Paul, we're going to Vanderbilt, we're going to play for those Commodores and Coach Dan McGugin.' So come September 1, early practice, we head to Nashville. Hitchhiked. They didn't treat us like they treat players now. Got down to Nashville, we practiced for ten days. I wasn't having to go to school. I loved that. I was having the time of my life.

"And then one day, they came out on the practice field and said, 'Robert, your grades just came in. We've never seen grades like yours before. There's no way you can go to Vanderbilt.' Well, this hurt me. This is the middle of September, I've already turned down the University of Tennessee, which was the only school that offered me a scholarship beside Vanderbilt. So we didn't have any place to go. I said, 'C'mon, Paul'—remember now, I was the brains of the two of us—'we'll hitchhike to Atlanta, we'll go out to Georgia Tech.'

"So we thumb our way to Atlanta and go out to Georgia Tech. And that brother of mine, John, the smart one, he's at Georgia Tech. We come out here and see John. And he said, 'Bob, I hate to hurt your feelings, but you're too durn dumb to go to Georgia Tech.' And he was right.

"So I said, 'I know what we'll do. We'll go to the University of Georgia, anybody can get in there.' And we could have, but we couldn't get a scholarship. Well, we were about to go to Mercer, in Macon, and my brother called

Neyland, the coach at the University of Tennessee, and told him that we were down here about to go to Mercer. He said, 'Would you still take 'em at the University of Tennessee?'

"Neyland was mad as could be, but he wanted my buddy Paul. He said, 'I'll take 'em if you have 'em up here in the morning by ten o'clock.' My brother put us on a train out of Atlanta that night, we got to Knoxville the next morning at eight, we registered at the University of Tennessee at ten o'clock, and we played in a freshman football game that afternoon at one."

Hug and Dodd did indeed play a freshman football game, and once they played in a game for Tennessee, they were not only obligated to the Volunteers for that season but also were ineligible to play for another school. So Bobby Dodd just continued to do what he had always loved best—he played.

He played freshman football, basketball, and baseball, and he joined a fraternity, pledging Sigma Nu, mainly because his high school coach, Le-Roy Sprankle, was a Sigma Nu. Naturally, Paul Hug pledged Sigma Nu, too.

Bobby Dodd also played around a lot academically. "My freshman year was just delightful," he said, "nothing but a lot of fun. I didn't have to study much. In fact, I didn't study."

He followed that philosophy religiously for four years at Tennessee, the same philosophy he'd had in high school. His college class schedule seldom varied, either. "I took the easiest courses I could get," Dodd said. "I went to school three or four hours, three days a week, Monday, Wednesday, and Friday. I didn't like those labs.

"One year, I had to take a zoology, or biology lab and I didn't like that a bit. That made me come back after lunch and I didn't like those afternoon classes. Well, as I remember, I dropped that course."

Dodd took every physical education course he could, though, and history, too. He particularly remembers a husband and wife who taught history, Dr. and Mrs. Hamer.

"Mrs. Hamer'd give me a C, didn't make any difference what I did. She'd leave me in there—I'd cut exams—and she'd say, 'Now Bobby, you come back and take this exam.' And she'd leave me in the office with that damn history book right there. I wouldn't look at it, though. I wouldn't cheat if she wasn't in there. If she'd been in there, trying to catch me, I might've tried to cheat. I had a sense of honor. I knew she was gonna give me a C anyway.

"So I wrote what I knew, signed my name, and I got a C. So Mrs. Hamer and Dr. Hamer would pass me. They liked football. And I acted pretty decent in their classes; I didn't give 'em any trouble.

"And then I had a little ol' psychology teacher and she liked all the football players. Her name was Miss Stevens. Miss Stevens liked every football player and we all got in her class.

"Buddy Hackman got caught cheating one time in her class. Now Hackman was the dumbest guy that ever was. It wasn't uncommon for us to get the exam questions before the exams, maybe 30 percent of the time. We'd usually get 'em two hours before the exam. They came through the secretaries. The exams were mimeographed, and one of the secretaries would get copies of the mimeographed exam and give it to one of the football players she liked.

"I was smart enough to where I'd take the exam and get a girl and she was smart, so I'd say, 'Just tell me enough so I could pass.' I wasn't gonna make a B on it or an A, 'cause they knew damn well I didn't know that much, and I'm not that stupid. I, being a smart quarterback, knew to get only a D. Buddy, being a dumb ass, got an A. One hundred.

"That durn Hackman, he wrote every question perfect. They had a Watergate investigation and fired him from school. I told him, 'You oughta be fired. Any person that makes a hundred on an exam, as dumb as you are, deserves to be fired.' They never knew I was involved, but they fired Hackman outta school and he had to stay out about three months."

Although he played on three freshman teams, Bobby Dodd says the athletic highlight of his freshman year came in the spring, in the interfraternity track meet. He had already helped Sigma Nu win the interfraternity basketball tournament, but in that event, at least he had the assistance of four fraternity brothers.

"When it came time for the interfraternity track meet," Dodd said, "we didn't have anybody in the fraternity who was much good except my roommate, Hug, and he was on the freshman track team and was not allowed to compete. I was on the freshman baseball team, so I could compete.

"So I took another boy there in the fraternity who said he could high jump a little bit, and we went over to the track meet without the rest of the fraternity even knowing.

"Well, he entered the high jump and he ended up in third place and won a point or two. And I entered every field event: the shot, discus, the javelin, high jump, and pole vault. And I either won first or second in every one of those events. And when it came down to the last event, the javelin, I was throwing against the captain of the varsity football team, named Elvin Butcher. He was an ATO. Whoever won that javelin throw won the interfraternity track meet for his fraternity.

"I was throwing like mad. I was a competitor and I always wanted to win, always did my best in every game, nearly, that I ever played. And I threw my arm away, but I did win that javelin throw, and won that interfraternity track meet. And when I went back to the fraternity house that night with that trophy, which was about three feet high, you never saw such shouting and jubilation and screaming, and all the fraternity men ended up by getting pretty tipsy celebrating my victory in the interfraternity track meet."

Come the fall and football season of 1928, Bobby Dodd was now a sophomore, at least eligibility-wise. He was playing for Bob Neyland. For three seasons, this was the gridiron equivalent of the Odd Couple. Robert Reese Neyland and Robert Lee Dodd.

There was Neyland: Felix Unger goes to West Point. A strict, stern, ultraconservative military man. A graduate of West Point who came to Knoxville in 1926 with the rank of major. And there was Dodd: Oscar Madison with a twang. As fun-loving and casual and daring as Neyland wasn't. Seldom have two such opposite personalities coexisted so successfully, if not always peacefully.

In many ways, Neyland was a walking contradiction. He was responsible for many innovations in southern football, and football in general. But when it came to basic football philosophy and coaching, and winning football games, Neyland was very conservative. He based his approach on ground-game effectiveness, unyielding defense, and a total, efficient kicking game.

Consider Neyland's innovations.

He was one of the first coaches—and then the only southern coach—to use the indirect pass from the center to the quarterback. Instead of always snapping the ball back to the tailback in the single wing, Neyland sometimes put his quarterback under the center, as is standard today (although his quarterback often held his hands in mid-air between the center's legs, not up against his rump, and took the snap there).

As the first southern coach to use telephones during games, he got reports from his assistants atop the press box who could scout and spot the action and report to him on the sideline. He introduced the cup pass protection blocking to the South, as well as the six-man defensive line. He taught his tailbacks to run forward toward the line and pump fake, as if they were going to throw, then dodge, and then throw or run—a skill Dodd executed well.

Long before the term *hang time* was concocted, Neyland used a stopwatch to time his punters and passers during pre-game warmups to see how quickly they released the ball. He was the first coach to use lightweight jerseys of fine knitted yarn, the first tearaway jersey (Duke ripped 17 Tennessee jerseys in one game).

Later, in an age of black high-top football cleats, Neyland dressed his teams in low-cuts, reasoning they would allow his players' ankles more freedom. His teams wore extremely light hip pads (27 ounces) and uniforms.

On road trips, each player carried his uniform in a duffel bag, and unlike other southern coaches Neyland sequestered his team in private the day before away games. He housed the Vols in a tourist court, or motel, on the edge of the city. He rented out the entire court, reasoning his players would rest better there, with less distractions, than in a downtown hotel.

Neyland had strict training rules, too, including a limit of one glass of milk at the training table. Dodd adored milk—still does—and each night after practice and dinner at the training table, he headed for a sandwich shop and gulped two or three more glasses of milk.

While Neyland demanded, and gave, his players the best equipment, including high-priced (for then) cleats costing $16.50 or even $22.50, Dodd was perfectly happy with an old pair of kangaroo hide, high-top shoes. In fact, he wore the same pair of football shoes all four years at Tennessee.

"I wanted an old pair of shoes 'cause they felt good," Dodd said. "When you go to punt, you have to straighten out your toes, and with new shoes, it's hard, they don't feel good. When you start to kick a ball with new shoes, you don't have the feel on your foot. I actually could have kicked as good with no shoes on, barefoot, like they do today. In fact, I've kicked that way many times. But I had this old pair of shoes that were flexible and just about to fall apart, and I kept using 'em. All I had to do was get new cleats on 'em when I wore 'em out."

As much as Dodd loved those old shoes, he despised wearing ankle wraps, another Neyland training rule. He had strong ankles and considered wrapping too much trouble. Besides, it bothered his kicking. "I had to trick Neyland," Dodd said. "I'd put a little ol' piece of tape and a little ol' piece of adhesive around it, so it looked like I wrapped my ankles. But there wasn't anything there.

"Neyland caught us one time, me and McEver. He had everybody come up and he said, 'I want to check on ankles. Take off your shoes.' Everybody took off their shoes, and me and McEver were caught with no ankle wraps on. He ran us till our tongues fell out.

"And I never laced my shoes tight. Loose. Better for kicking, and I don't think it tired you as much. I think you cut off your circulation some.

"I wore those old shoes and I wore the same pair of shoulder pads every year. Everybody else had these cantilevered pads, pretty big pads. I just wore a pair that was nothing but a piece of leather, because I wasn't gonna do much blocking anyway. I had to do a little bit. But it hampered my throwing to have that damn big ol' shoulder pad. So I had these little shoulder pads they held out for me. They were always saying I was gonna get my shoulder busted, but I never did."

Bobby Dodd always wore uniform number 17, in every sport he played. "I picked it up somewhere in high school and stuck with it in college," he said. "I've always felt number 17 was my lucky number."

In the fall of 1928, though, none of it—not the old shoes, the bare ankles, the light-as-air shoulder pads, the lucky number 17—helped Dodd, at least not immediately. Despite Dodd's considerable success in high school and as a Tennessee freshman, his prospects for playing on the varsity that season looked as slim as his bony reflection in a mirror.

"I was very depressed," Dodd recalled. "It looked like the captain of the football team was gonna play my position. He was a punter, Roy Witt. It looked like he was gonna push me out of that backfield."

This was back in the era of single-platoon football and limited substitution, when a coach picked his best 11 players and played them both ways, on offense and defense. Although Dodd's undefeated freshman football team was remarkably talented, Neyland still had some talent returning from his 1926 and 1927 teams, which finished 8-1 and 8-0-1.

Dodd considered transferring when he thought he wouldn't get to start. Only his phys ed and coaching instructor A. W. Hobt knew this, and Hobt advised him to stay on. As Dodd would later so often, so wisely, so successfully tell his younger players at Georgia Tech, Hobt said, "Now don't get discouraged, your time will come."

"I said, 'Yeah, but I don't like sitting on that bench.' I played six years of high school football without sitting on the bench, and I wasn't gonna sit on it in college."

Dodd didn't have any particular alternative in mind when he considered transferring from Tennessee. "Just anybody who wanted me," he said. "It didn't make any difference to me where I went to school. All I was gonna do was play football. I didn't care what school I went to."

It never came to that. Just as in high school, just as at Georgia Tech, just as in most every facet of his life, Bobby Dodd was lucky at Tennessee. "I'll be dad-gum if Roy Witt didn't get hurt," he said, "and Neyland had no choice but to put me in."

Neyland didn't relish the choice, either philosophically or physically. "I wasn't the slowest man on the football team," Dodd said, "but I was close, and in single-wing football, where in the hell you are gonna put someone who can't run a lick? But they had to put me in there, because back in those days, you couldn't substitute a punter. Your punter had to be already out there. And he had to play. You take a guy out of the game, he's out.

"So when Witt got hurt, I'm the kicker. And I'm a good kicker. Neyland likes me as a kicker, and he likes me as a passer. But he didn't like me a damn bit as a runner, and I wasn't much of a blocker."

But in 1928, Dodd became the seventh sophomore of that undefeated freshman team to start for Neyland. They were nicknamed the Flaming Sophomores, a name and reputation forged in what was even then one of the most scorching kilns in college football: Tuscaloosa, Alabama, the home of the Crimson Tide, the University of Alabama.

Tennessee had opened the season by easily dispatching Maryville 41-0 and Centre College 41-7. Dodd had drop-kicked one extra point after the first of two Buddy Hackman touchdowns to edge Ole Miss 13-12. But now this was Alabama, which had been to the Rose Bowl the two previous years, beating Washington in 1926 and tying Stanford in 1927. Then, as now, 'Bama was the biggest name in southern football.

"Alabama, in Tuscaloosa, that's big stuff," Dodd said. "That was our first big game. We went there and everybody tells us Alabama is going back to the Rose Bowl again. They had a great team. The betting odds said five hundred dollars even money Tennessee wouldn't even score, which wasn't uncommon then."

Wallace Wade coached the Crimson Tide. Neyland met Wade for the first time on game day, and, despite his team's 3-0 start, Neyland suggested to Wade that the third and fourth quarters be cut short to prevent an Alabama rout. Wade said he didn't expect to run up a big score, but if so, he'd shorten the second half.

In the locker room, Neyland told his players not to look at Alabama when the Tide came on the field. "I think that's the only coaching error he made," Hackman would say in 1981, at the 50th reunion of the class of 1931. "When you tell people don't do something, they'll do it.

"They were wearing white jerseys that made 'em look like elephants. Neyland had thought that would put the fear of the Lord in us, like you were in a prize fight and nobody told you how big the other guy was. But we weren't scared of anybody, even if we were about 20 pounds lighter a man."

At least one Alabama fan shared Neyland's skepticism. As Herc Alley, Tennessee's 165-pound captain, trotted back to the bench after winning the coin toss and electing to receive, he heard a 'Bama fan bellowing that he'd bet two thousand dollars that Alabama would make more touchdowns than Tennessee made first downs.

Gene McEver had other ideas. He was known as the Wild Bull, a bruising running back from Bristol, Virginia, who was clearly the best of all the Flaming Sophomores. The night before the Alabama game, McEver roomed with Bobby Dodd.

"He said, 'If they kick that ball off to ol' Gene, to ol' Ephrem'—I don't know where he got that name, but he called himself that—'he's gonna run it back for a touchdown,' " recalled Dodd.

In the locker room the next afternoon at Denny Field, McEver told the rest of his teammates, "If I get that ball on the kickoff, everybody try to cut down a man. If you can't cut down a man, just move over and let me through."

The Volunteers dropped back to receive the opening kickoff, resplendent in their new light silk pants. Dodd and McEver exchanged their special handshake. Then McEver received the kickoff, some Vols cut down their men, others just moved over, and the Wild Bull charged 98 yards for a touchdown. Dodd's kick gave Tennessee a 7-0 lead it never relinquished. Most fans, and players, were stunned.

"You really had never heard of Tennessee much then," said Frank Howard, then a tough, squatty Tide guard from Barlow Bend, Alabama, ("It's three wagon greases from Mobile") who later became somewhat of a legend himself as coach at Clemson. Like most people back in 1928, when Frank Howard watched this country bumpkin named Dodd run, he could not believe his eyes.

"He couldn't run much faster than me," Howard said, "and I was a hydrant."

Still, Dodd and Tennessee led 7-0, but Alabama responded instantly, scoring in three plays to make it 7-6. It remained 7-6 until Dodd punted out of bounds at the Alabama three. An errant snap from center gave the Vols a safety, a 9-6 lead and, ultimately, a victory. In the second quarter, Bobby Dodd increased that lead to 15-6, passing to McEver for his second touchdown. By halftime, Alabama had cut Tennessee's lead to two points and shortened Dodd's playing time to two quarters.

On the final play of the first half, Alabama punted. Neyland had given strict orders to fair catch all punts. "I shouldn't have done it," Dodd said. "I tried to run when I should've made a fair catch. But we didn't know how much time was left, and I was trying to make something happen before the half."

There was no clock on the scoreboard in that era. The referee kept the time on the field. Trying to beat the clock, Bobby Dodd was bulldozed by two 'Bama players, Fred Sington and Molton Smith, two 220-pounders.

"They hit me in the back as I twisted and hurt my kidney," Dodd said. "Had to take me out."

Dodd was carried off on a stretcher and into the locker room, where Neyland reprimanded him for fielding the punt. Dodd never returned that day. "The only time I was hurt in my whole career," he said. "Hurt me bad. I passed blood, and they were afraid to let me play. I didn't play for about the next four weeks."

For the next two quarters that day, he watched Tennessee somehow hold off Alabama in a seemingly endless second half. "They ran all over us," Dodd said, "but they couldn't score."

That 15-13 triumph is still perhaps the most significant in Tennessee football. Neyland would go on to record the most enviable of records and to establish arguably the premier dynasty in college football history. In 21 seasons, Neyland won 173 games, lost just 31, and tied 12. His teams once went 33 games without losing, lost just once in 61, and won 31 of 33 games from 1938 to 1940. And Neyland would come to be regarded by many as the finest defensive football coach—if not football coach, period—of his time.

But with that upset of mighty 'Bama in 1928, Tennessee football was taken seriously for the first time. Certainly, the Tennessee student body took it seriously, deliriously so. The Volunteers returned to Knoxville by rail, and the following day, when their train pulled into the station back home, an enormous crowd greeted them, cheering madly.

Standing on a fire engine, some students unfurled a banner that proclaimed for the first time, "In Dodd We Trust." Bobby Dodd had some difficulty reading it, however. Years later, Houston Herndon, an end on that team, recounted the homecoming for Tom Siler, now retired, but the long-time sports editor of the *Knoxville News-Sentinel*.

"The train was coming into Knoxville," Herndon told Siler. "Dodd, who had spent the night in a stateroom still in great pain, asked me to help him get to the bathroom. He put his arm around my shoulder, and I maneuvered him into the tiny toilet. He was relieving himself when he passed out, flat cold.

"So there I was, holding him up and he was wetting all over the trousers of my new cream-colored suit. I couldn't let go or he would have fallen over the john. So I held him. But the way I looked, I couldn't go out and enjoy the cheers of that wild crowd."

Dodd spent a week in bed at the university infirmary and did not return to action until the last game of the season. Without him though, Tennessee crushed Washington and Lee, Carson-Newman, and Sewanee, then survived rival Vanderbilt 6-0. The Kentucky game ended, alas, in a scoreless tie after an apparent touchdown pass to Hug was nullified by an official's ruling that he had stepped out of bounds.

That tie conceivably cost Tennessee a trip to the Rose Bowl. The

following weekend, Florida came to Knoxville. The Gators were undefeated, high scoring, and reputed to be the best team in the South. They
seemed destined for the Rose Bowl. Bobby Dodd, however, had other
ideas. Great ideas. Maybe the long layoff from the injury gave him more
time to prepare. Maybe the frustration of watching the futile efforts of his
team against Kentucky inspired him. Whatever the reason, Dodd worked
magic against the Gators.

What unfolded that Saturday in Knoxville, John Dodd insists, "was
my brother's most fantastic accomplishment as a player."

Hundreds of folks from Kingsport had come to Knoxville, as they
usually did every time Dodd and the Vols played at home. Neyland, an
absolute fanatic for preparation, practice, and execution, was in the
hospital with the flu and missed practice the entire week. So Tennessee
was ill-prepared for Florida.

"They didn't have any preparation for the game," John Dodd said.
"Bobby ran three or four plays and saw that Florida was ready to kill
everything they were gonna run. So he told Hug they were gonna run the
old Kingsport play."

A play that Dodd would later use with great success at Georgia Tech,
a play in which Dodd and Hug would collaborate on a bootleg pass, un-
beknownst to their teammates. While everyone else would be enthusi-
astically running and blocking the play called in the huddle—a sweep to
the left side—Dodd would fake a handoff to the tailback, wrap his large
hand around the ball, hide it on his hip, and then roll around right end and
look upfield, where Hug invariably would be wide open.

Early on, Dodd completed seven of eight passes against Florida and
gave Tennessee a 13-0 lead. Some of those were the Kingsport play, others
ad libs Dodd drew up in the huddle. "Our high school principal sat next
to Neyland, who was still sick," John Dodd said, "and Neyland told him
he'd never seen one of those plays before. Bob just let the rest of 'em do
what they wanted in their blocking positions. He won the game on his
own."

"I made up some plays," Bobby Dodd said. "Neyland didn't like it.
He'd say, 'Boys, they better work.' He didn't have any sense of humor.

"But I'm a starter from then on," Dodd said. "I played well enough.
Neyland couldn't get me outta there. He didn't particularly like me,
'cause, remember, I was going to take Hug and go to Vanderbilt."

Years later, talking about Dodd, Neyland told an Associated Press
writer, "He'd run them [plays he'd made up], and the first chance he'd look
toward the Tennessee bench and laugh. We never knew exactly what to
expect when Dodd was calling signals."

Florida managed to score twice, but twice missed their extra points.
The Gators lost the game 13-12 and, they argued, their trip to Pasadena.

And argue they did. The game was played on a wet, muddy field, and Florida angrily charged the Vols had watered it down to slow down the Florida offense. Had they?

"I don't think so," Dodd said. "I don't see how it would have helped us."

The outcome certainly helped Georgia Tech. Instead of Florida, Tech was invited to the Rose Bowl, squeaked past Cal and Wrong-Way Roy Riegels, and won the national championship. Indirectly, Bobby Dodd may have helped put Georgia Tech in a Rose Bowl after all. Imagine that.

Tennessee finished the 1928 football season with a 9-0-1 record, and then basketball began. "I liked basketball even better than I did football," Bobby Dodd said. "Basketball was a lot of fun to practice, and you played more games. Much more fun than football was, except during the game on Saturday."

In some ways, Dodd was suited better to basketball than football. Indoors, his lack of speed was less of a liability. "I loved the game," said Dodd, who would eventually become captain. And he cared for his basketball coach, Bill Britton, much more than he cared for Neyland.

"He was a good coach," Dodd said of Britton, one of Neyland's football assistants who came with him to Knoxville from West Point. "We had a lot of fun. He was very jovial, a very optimistic-type person. His philosophy kinda rubbed off on me a little bit."

As if Dodd needed to be any more jovial or optimistic. Away from athletics, and academics, Dodd enjoyed life in Knoxville immensely. He had two best buddies at Tennessee, a preacher's son named Stubby McClurken and an ex-athlete named Ed Corbett. The trio could usually be found together after football practice. After enduring the draining drills that Neyland prescribed each afternoon from two-thirty to five, Dodd would meet Stubby and Ed for dinner at a place called the Original Sandwich Shop.

At the Original, Dodd was anything but. He would invariably order a couple of glasses of milk. Or soup. Or a bowl of milk and several slices of toast, and soak the toast in the milk before eating it. Or milk shakes. Or desserts. Any food that was soft and wouldn't hurt his teeth—the custom he'd developed in Galax and still follows today. ("I'm the only man in America today over 60 who still chews his milk," Dodd said.)

After dinner, it was time to do something. Together. "If one of us had a date, the other two went along even if they didn't have a date," Dodd said. "That was not uncommon then. Whatever one of us wanted to do, the others did it. If we wanted to go to a picture show [silent movies were just giving way to talkies], we'd do that, or we'd go to Mary Hill's house or the girl I went with, Mary Neal Slatery, and listen to records. Nobody had a car then during the Depression, so we'd rent a U-drive-it to go out to one of the girls' houses and split the bill."

Mary Neal Slatery was a gorgeous local girl from East Knoxville, and two years behind Dodd at the University of Tennessee. When she first met him, though, she was still in high school. She was also dating his buddy Paul Hug.

Through Hug, she met Bobby Dodd. "Then I started dating him," said Mary Neal, now Mary Neal Culver but still living in Knoxville. "Oh, he was fun. He knew *everybody*.

"He was such a popular guy," Mrs. Culver said. "Oh, I felt like I was on top of the world when I went out with him. He was just so friendly. And, of course, he was a football player and was well known. But he was real friendly. It hadn't gone to his head."

So why did they stop going out, the beauty and the best-known and most popular man on campus? "He had other girls," Mrs. Culver said. "I wasn't the only girl. He had a girl come here from Kingsport. Oh, yeah, he had lots of girls."

During the day, Dodd spent most of his time—when he wasn't on the football field and when he should have been in class—at a local landmark called the E and E. The Ellis and Ernest Drug Store. It was on the corner of Stadium Drive and West Cumberland, where the University Center now stands. If the E and E was a way station for most students, it was a distraction for Dodd and his cronies. "We'd all meet at the drug store," Dodd said. "They had these booths, and we'd get to laughing and telling stories. It was time to go to class, and I'd say, 'I don't want to go.' I hadn't looked at the books and didn't know what they were talking about anyhow.

"So sometimes we'd cut class, and then I'd go across the street."

Across West Cumberland to another of his hangout-and-hustle spots. A miniature golf course. "Putt-Putt golf," Dodd said. "It was a big fad then."

Fueled by milk and/or milk shakes, Dodd would put on his Kingsport High baseball cap, stroll up to the Putt-Putt, pull out a putter, and do what he's always done best: beat somebody in a sporting game of chance.

"I'd play for money—a quarter for 18 holes," Dodd recalled. "And I'd stay on that golf course till my buddies got back from class. Sometimes, I couldn't find anyone to play with."

If not, it was usually because the word was out. "Even in ping pong," said Tom Siler. "He'd beat anybody. He was really happy-go-lucky, but he was a deadly gambler."

His gambling winnings supplemented the $40 a month scholarship. But that wasn't enough for room and board, and Dodd ended up borrowing about $400 from the school. But, in 1929, he yielded an enormous return on Neyland's investment.

By the start of that season, Dodd was firmly established as the starting quarterback. The Flaming Sophomores had all returned and opened with three easy victories, including a 52-7 destruction of a Mississippi team that had lost by just one point to the Vols in 1928. Then came the Alabama rematch, this time at Tennessee.

It was a scorching Saturday in Knoxville and, as usually occurred between top teams, the game developed into a defensive standoff. Dodd frequently punted on first down in hopes of better field position. At one point, an exhausted Vol guard named Hobo Thayer asked Dodd to run a couple of plays, so Hobo could catch his breath before running downfield to cover another punt. (Hobo and his teammates must have done as exceptional a job of covering punts as Dodd did placing them; for the 1929 season, opponents returned Dodd punts for an average of less than a yard).

Late in the fourth quarter, Tennessee led 6-0, but 'Bama was driving. On fourth down and goal, though, the Tide was stopped short. "They screamed," Dodd said, "they thought they were in." The Vols stopped them six inches short of the goal line.

In the huddle, Dodd told McEver, "I'm gonna fake a punt and pass to you in the right flat." After taking the snap, though, Dodd, standing in his end zone, couldn't find McEver. No matter. "I already knew what I was gonna do anyway," Dodd said. "Throw it out of bounds. Hell, they couldn't penalize me enough to hurt.

"So I threw it out of bounds, and Alabama hollered, 'Grounding the pass, grounding the pass!' So we were penalized half the distance to the goal line." Three inches to the three-inch line.

In the huddle, Dodd looked up and laughed at the Tide, told McEver to flare into the flat again, then threw the ball away again. This time, Tennessee was penalized an inch-and-a-half to the inch-and-a-half line. The Alabama defense was furious; some players flung their helmets onto the turf.

"I probably should have taken a safety," Dodd said in retrospect. Instead, he quick-kicked, punting on third down and out of bounds at the 'Bama 45. Two plays later, the game ended. Tennessee had beaten 'Bama again, 6-0. Many years later, Freddie Sington, Alabama's all-American tackle, said, "We had a better team than Tennessee that year, but Dodd just beat us himself. He had us so mad at him, we couldn't play football."

The next year, intentionally grounding the ball in one's own end zone became a safety.

Neyland's staunch defense shut out the next four opponents as well, routing Washington and Lee 30-0 and Auburn 27-0, obliterating Carson-Newman 73-0, and then defeating Vanderbilt again, this time in the mud at Shields-Watkins Field, 13-0. Perhaps it was the thought of losing to the dreaded Commodores, but Neyland stepped completely out of character that Saturday in hopes of victory.

The General and his staff devised a hidden ball play. "The only time in my whole career they did anything like this," said Dodd. "They said, 'Take the ball and fake it to McEver on a weakside crossbuck.' I'm supposed to fake that ball to McEver, put the ball in my lap, and I'm supposed to back through the line of scrimmage."

Standing in his den, Dodd demonstrated: bending his knees, taking the imaginary snap, spinning 180 degrees until his back was to the line, bending over the ball and then slowly backpedaling through the line.

"I almost tripped over a Vanderbilt guy," Dodd remembered. "He didn't know I had the ball, and I didn't see him." Eventually, Dodd turned, faced the goal line, and ran down the right sideline to score.

Usually, it was Hackman and McEver—Hack and Mack, the Touchdown Twins—who did the scoring for Tennessee. They were so celebrated, the E and E and other local drug stores served a Hack and Mack sundae. Dodd and McEver also endorsed Swan's Bread, posed for a photo for an advertisement, and were paid for it. In those days, there was no such organization as the NCAA, no sanctions against college athletes for posing for sorority charity calendars, much less endorsing products.

The following week against Shipwreck Kelly and Kentucky, though, Tennessee could score only once. And for the second consecutive year, Kentucky tied Tennessee, this time 6-6, again depriving the Volunteers of a perfect season and possible Rose Bowl bid.

The teams struggled in the bitter cold and swirling snow of Lexington, as well as in a hail of penalties. The snow had started the previous evening and continued throughout the game. The Volunteers had no gloves and poor shoes. Straw was dumped near the benches, and substitutes and coaches used it to cover their feet and legs.

Kentucky outplayed Tennessee in the snowstorm, but the Vols nearly won anyway. Late in the fourth quarter, Hackman told Dodd in the huddle, "Just throw me that damn ball, and I'll catch it anywhere. And if I don't, I'll eat my shirt."

"He knew I couldn't throw it," Dodd said. "The thing weighed a ton. Can you believe they only used one ball the whole game in those days? You can imagine, it had gotten fat—the ball was rounder in those days—and wet with ice on it. I'd just as soon have thrown a shot put. But I said, 'OK, I'll throw it to you.'

"So I heaved it out there to him, and he went down the sideline. We thought he scored, and Neyland rushed in our dropkicker specialty man."

Dodd's pass to Hackman was good for 41 yards and, initially, the officials ruled Hackman *had* scored. So Neyland sent in his dropkicker, Charlie Kohlhase, at fullback. The officials, though, scraped away the snow and discovered Hackman stepped out at the six.

"So we ran a play and didn't score, and Neyland was afraid if he left his kicker in there—who wasn't a good back—we wouldn't score," said Dodd. Neyland pulled Kohlhase for Paul Heydrick. Hackman then scored, but the rules forbade Kohlhase from re-entering. With Dodd holding, Heydrick attempted the extra point.

"I got it down pretty good for him," Dodd said, "and he kicked it pretty good but didn't get enough height on it, and it went under the crossbar. Couldn't get it over. So the game ended 6-6. We thought it cost us the Rose Bowl. We were definitely in the running."

In the season finale the following week, Tennessee took out its frustration on South Carolina 54-0. It was the seventh shutout for Tennessee in ten games. Only Centre, Ole Miss, and Kentucky had scored on the 1929 Vols, who outscored the opposition 330-19. McEver scored 130 of those points—including 33 against South Carolina—to lead the nation in scoring. For the second straight year, Tennessee finished 9-0-1. But for the second straight year, the Volunteers missed out on the Rose Bowl.

After the season, Bobby Dodd and six of his teammates were chosen to play in a new all-star game involving players from the Southern Intercollegiate Conference (the forerunner to the Southeastern Conference). The seven Vols were members of the north squad—composed of the northernmost members of the S.I.C.—in the north-south charity game.

The game was played in Atlanta on New Year's Day, 1930. It was the first, and only, time Bobby Dodd would play a football game on Grant Field. It was also the first Scottish Rite football game for the benefit of the Scottish Rite Children's Hospital.

"We were all put up at the Biltmore Hotel, which was then the showplace of the South," Dodd said. "You could charge stuff to your room: food, haircuts, manicures. Some guys charged a lot. When the game was over and they settled up, they found out that Scottish Rite was not gonna make any money. These guys from all over had charged so much.

"That's when they switched the game—Coach Aleck's idea, I think—to have the Tech freshmen play the Georgia freshmen, and everybody pays. Even the officials paid to get in." And still do.

During that game Bobby Jones, the great golfer, saw Bobby Dodd play football. Dodd's punting technique particularly enthralled Jones. He later said that Dodd's leg motion while punting was as nearly perfect a golf stroke as he ever saw, and that his swing "culminated in a whipping motion as the foot swung into the ball for a perfect carry-thru."

Dodd continued to play basketball and baseball at Tennessee. Once, after a baseball game against Maryville, after Dodd had tripled with the bases loaded, Bob Wilson, the sports editor of the *Knoxville News-Sentinel*, mentioned "Dodd's Luck" to him.

"I used to think I was lucky, too," Bobby Dodd said. "But I've changed my mind. There must be some skill in it. I'm too consistent for it to be called luck all the time."

Dodd continued to luck out academically as well. Said Dodd, "My sister and brother used to say that they [Tennessee] would send my mother notices that said, 'Your son Robert is on probation.' About two weeks later, when the football season or basketball started, they'd send another one that said, 'Your son Robert is off probation.'

"They said I was always on probation when a sport wasn't in season. It wasn't that I couldn't pass. I could pass. I just didn't like studying. Worst thing was, I cut so many damn classes."

Bobby Dodd, all-American.

Chapter 4
Lanky, Languid, All-American

EACH SUMMER, DODD returned home to Kingsport to stay with his widowed mother and to work various jobs. One summer he worked loading bags of cement; another working 12, sometimes 14 hours a day in a drug store. For that job, Dodd earned $75 a month, decent Depression wages.

One year, Dodd got a job at the Kingsport Press. He drove an electric cart loaded down with school textbooks, transporting them from area to area in the mill. It was the most time Bobby Dodd had ever spent with textbooks. On weekends, he played baseball on the mill team.

One June, friends persuaded Dodd to enter the city of Kingsport tennis tournament, played on the clay courts of the Kingsport Country Club. "The first time I ever played tennis," Dodd recalled. "I had seen it and hit the ball a little bit, but I'd never really played."

Dodd played tennis ambidextrously, as his brother John did. He never bothered perfecting that bothersome backhand; he just switched the racket from his right hand to his left and swatted another forehand over the net.

"Being the competitor I was, the first match I chased down everything they hit," Dodd said. "Just hit it back over the net, don't make mistakes, don't go for winners, just keep the ball in play." Just as he plays tennis today. Just as he coached football at Georgia Tech: no mistakes, no penalties, no turnovers, keep the ball in play, play field position, wait for the opposition to make a mistake, and then capitalize.

"I won that first one, and then I practiced for the next one. Never tried to hit winners—back in those days, you didn't try to hit winners, just hit the ball back over the net. I came up to the semifinals, and I drew a boy who had played tennis in college at North Carolina. He was about 30, but he could still play. I knew I was gonna have trouble with him. But I ran that ball down and he kept trying to hit winners and he made errors. And I beat him.

"Then in the finals, I drew a boy who'd played a little bit at Ohio State. He was supposed to be the big tennis player in town. He had strokes. Did

51

this [Dodd flicked an imaginary forehand with his wrist], did this [he flicked an imaginary backhand]. And I beat him. I won the tennis tournament. And while this was going on, they were also having a bridge tournament. That was big stuff then. That was when bridge just became popular, and everyone wanted to play."

And naturally, Bobby Dodd and his partner, Clinton Minnich, won the bridge tournament, too. Not because they were accomplished bridge players. They understood the format, and Dodd understood cards.

"My daddy'd taught me all about cards: setback, five hundred, poker, blackjack," Dodd said. "I knew all the con games—my daddy taught me how all the games at the carnival are crooked—and I knew everything there was to know about cards."

About bridge, he knew this: "The first night we played, I realized you could take advantage of the scoring system. If I double you, all the points are doubled, whether you win it or I do. If you re-double, they're doubled again. So what it means is, if the scores are doubled, they might be 500 instead of 150. I win 500, you win 500. But if you 500 against me and my partner, it doesn't take anything off of my score. It just means you've got a big score."

By using his double and re-double system, Dodd and Minnich won the tournament. All the good bridge players in Kingsport wanted to learn their system. Dodd remembers, "They said, 'Oh, we want you and Clinton to come play with us.' Funny thing was . . . we didn't know a doggone thing about the game, 'cept I knew about the scoring: double and re-double every damn thing."

In the summer of 1930, Bobby Dodd played some semipro baseball in Logan, West Virginia, with Gene McEver. On July 26, during a game at Appalachia, Virginia, McEver rounded third base and fell. He severely injured his right knee. It would be weeks before the Wild Bull tried to run on that knee again.

The advent of the 1930 football season brought an optimism as high as the Hill itself on the Tennessee campus. The Flaming Sophomores were now seniors, and there was considerable underclass talent. The interest in Tennessee football was so great and the profits so high—Tennessee now grossed more than one hundred thousand dollars annually at the gate—that the capacity of Shields-Watkins Field had been nearly tripled, from 6,800 to 17,860.

As in previous years, the season started smashingly with decisive victories over Maryville, Centre, and Ole Miss. Wearing a knee brace, Mc-Ever resumed practice in hopes of playing against Alabama. On the Tuesday before 'Bama, however, after carrying once off tackle for 15 yards, McEver was hit from the side. Hit in the knee. He lay on the grass, screaming and writhing in pain. His season was over.

After McEver reinjured his knee on Tuesday, both ends, Hug and Fitz Brandt, also suffered knee injuries and missed the Alabama game. Their absence hurt Tennessee badly.

Down in Tuscaloosa, the Red Elephants waited expectantly, recalling their narrow defeats the previous two years. Curiously, Coach Wallace Wade started his second team against Tennessee. When Dodd, on the Vols' second possession, moved them to the 'Bama 13, Wade hurriedly inserted his starters, and the Tide held. John (Hurry) Cain and Flash Suther scored for Alabama, and the lead remained 12-0 late in the first half.

"They were just wearing us out," Dodd said. "I was having trouble trying to complete a pass, because they were rushing me. Hackman could throw the ball farther than I could, but he wasn't a passer. He could just heave the ball—he threw it like a shot put—could just throw it a mile. So I said, 'Hackman, you throw the ball and let me go out as the receiver.' "

Hackman took the snap and scrambled in the backfield, giving Dodd time to slip downfield undetected. "I went out in the wingback position," Dodd said. "I went down, and I'll be daggone if I'm not in the end zone and there's no Alabama man there. I don't know where they went, I wasn't that fast. And Hackman threw me that ball, and I wasn't nervous. My Lord, you know me, I was just gonna take the ball like this and catch it for a touchdown.

"That ball hit in my hands and went right on through. Felt like a shot put. It's heavy as it could be. Wasn't wet, just a heavy ball, and I didn't bring it in to my body. And I dropped it."

Hugh Faust, one of Dodd's teammates, would later recount, "Dodd came into the dressing room. Tears streaked down his face. He berated himself like you never heard. He called himself everything he could think of. I never saw him so upset, before or since."

Alabama would score again in the third quarter, on Happy Campbell's touchdown. Three times in that period, Tennessee drove within the Tide 10 yard line but was stopped each time on downs. Hackman finally ran one yard for the Vols' only touchdown. Dodd, one of five Volunteers who played all 60 minutes, completed 11 of 17 passes for 163 yards, but that wasn't sufficient to prevent the first defeat for Tennessee in 34 games, since a 20-3 loss to Vanderbilt in the penultimate game of the 1926 season. Tennessee had lost more than a game, though. It had lost yet another chance at a Rose Bowl bid.

The following weekend, Tennessee reverted to form. The significant event that day, however, was not its 9-7 win over stubborn North Carolina. It was the misfortune of a young football coach named Mack Tharpe, and the ultimate good fortune of Bobby Dodd. Tharpe was an assistant coach to Bill Alexander of Georgia Tech. Alexander assigned Tharpe to drive up and scout the Tennessee game with North Carolina, Tech's next opponent. Tharpe headed out for Knoxville early Saturday morning.

"Mack drove a little ol' Ford as fast as it could run," Dodd said. "He's heading up through Cartersville and ran it off the road and into a cornfield. By the time he got it towed out and got up to Knoxville, the game was over.

"The game had just ended. We were walking into our dressing room, just as Mack was coming in. He saw Neyland, told him who he was and what had happened. Neyland didn't want to really fool with him, so he said, 'Go over there and talk with my quarterback, he'll help you.'"

Bobby Dodd and Mack Tharpe sat on the bleachers and talked about North Carolina for two hours. Dodd told him everything he knew about the Tar Heels and their unusual system.

"A lot of people back in those days didn't stunt, like, the end would go in here and tackle loop outside," Dodd said. "Most people weren't doing that then, but North Carolina was. We'd had a hard time, could only beat them 9-7. I told Mack what they were doing, and he thanked me profusely and then left. And I didn't think any more of it."

When Mack Tharpe returned to Georgia Tech, he gave his boss more than a scouting report. He gave Alexander a recommendation. "I think he said I was the smartest quarterback he'd ever seen," Dodd said, "and Coach Aleck should hire me."

For the remainder of the 1930 season, Dodd and Hackman literally carried the Volunteers through the schedule. In his first two varsity seasons, Dodd had been content to handle the ball, pass it, punt it, and play a little defense when necessary.

As far as carrying the ball, one Knoxville newspaperman, who wrote under the byline "Chips," wrote of Dodd's sophomore and junior seasons: "This lanky quarterback took the same attitude as President Coolidge—he did not choose to run."

That all changed his senior year, after the injury to McEver.

His Tennessee teammates called him ol' Dodd and Dodger, for Dodd's ability to dodge defenders, often pump-faking with the ball while running toward them. Certainly, it wasn't Dodd's speed that caused tacklers to miss him. Even Herman Hickman, who would become an all-American tackle in 1931 and later head football coach at Yale, could outrun Bobby Dodd. Hickman weighed three hundred pounds.

"Dodd, the Tennessee player, looked in street clothes before a game almost like a youngster fresh off the farm," sportswriter Malcolm Johnson wrote. "Lanky, languid, a gait something like you get from following a plow.

"On the field, he appeared about the same. His pants hung loose at the knees, halfway down his legs. He was almost sloppy—until he got his hands on the ball.

"With that football, Bobby Dodd was a magician."

Johnson described Dodd's throwing motion, how he would pass "from the shoulder, flip it." And, unlike almost every quarterback of his day, how seldom Dodd blocked.

Greasy Neale, the late coach of the Philadelphia Eagles and Pittsburgh Steelers, was once talking football during lunch with Temple University coaches Hal Williams and Josh Cody. Neale was stressing the importance of speed when Cody said, "If you get a back who's a good actor, you don't have to worry if he's slow. Bobby Dodd was one of the greatest backs I ever saw, and I don't think he could run a hundred in 17 seconds. With a football, Dodd was the greatest faker that ever lived.

"I saw him go 60 yards one day, and he never moved faster than a dog trot," continued Cody. "He had long fingers and could almost wrap them around a football. Every few yards, he'd lift that ball as if he were brandishing a knife—always faking a lateral. Every time he faked a lateral, the tacklers started for the receiver. Bobby would trot by them.

"When you act like that, you don't need speed. He could do anything with a football."

Then Josh Cody began describing the most celebrated play Bobby Dodd ever made. The victim was Vanderbilt, in that 1930 season, victimized by a player who would wobble all about the field, in all directions, from sideline to sideline, from the line of scrimmage toward his own goal line before completing the play.

The play came three weeks after Dodd had met Mack Tharpe following the North Carolina contest. Two weeks after a 27-0 shutout of Clemson. One week after a 34-0 sleepwalk over Carson-Newman. In the latter game, all the Tennessee reserves played. Meanwhile, Dodd and the rest of the starters went to Atlanta with Neyland to scout their next opponent, Vanderbilt. They saw Vandy edge Georgia Tech 6-0. The following Saturday in Nashville, thousands of folks saw the play that guaranteed gridiron immortality for Bobby Dodd, the player.

The buildup for the game was considerable. Tennessee and Vanderbilt had each lost to Alabama, but were otherwise unbeaten. The Vols and Commodores were bitter rivals, and they were two of the best teams in the South. But only one team had a Bobby Dodd.

Edwin Camp, the long-time sports editor of the *Atlanta Journal*, wrote under the byline "Ole Timer." Herewith is the lead to, and excerpts from, his story on the Tennessee-Vanderbilt game, played in Nashville on

November 16, 1930.

"Lanky, languid, disdainful Dodd—Bobby Dodd of Tennessee, defeated Vanderbilt 13-0 Saturday afternoon before 24,000, the largest crowd in Vandy's history.

"It was Dodd who destroyed a hard-fighting and skillfully prepared team. The touchdowns were scored by Buddy Hackman, and in twice crossing Vandy's goal, the stocky, blond halfback showed skill of a high order. But it was Dodd and his abnormal mentality, his magnificent physical equipment, and his nerve of cold steel that made them possible, and sent Hackman on his way to glory."

Without Dodd, Ole Timer wrote, Tennessee would be "a fair team, full of fight," but would have lost to Vanderbilt by three touchdowns.

"But Tennessee tallied twice, because of the incomparable coordination of the brain, toe, and good right arm of Dodd. He is, as Kipling said of another hero of combat, the past pluperfect prestissimo of football."

Ole Timer then described Dodd's extraordinary accuracy, punting out of bounds at the Vanderbilt four-yard line and setting up the first touchdown for Tennessee.

"Standing ten yards back of the line of scrimmage [standard for the time, unlike the 15-yard drop punters take today] on his 27, Dodd punts out of bounds on Vandy's four. Lyendecker, the smashing tackle, is on him as he kicks, but Dodd gets it away with direction, as though he had willed the ball to the spot 69 yards away."

A shanked Vanderbilt punt went out of bounds at the Commodore 22. "On the first play," Ole Timer wrote, "Dodd falls back to pass. He waits eternally—a sloppy, shoddy, slothful figure. Two ends and a back are in, or headed for the end zone, every one of them covered by a Vandy back. But Hackman is not.

"Hackman has gone somewhere, perhaps for a drink of water or a chew of tobacco. Suddenly Hackman appears at about the center of where the scrimmage began. Dodd snaps out of his languor, his inane introspection and rifles the ball into the grasping hands of Hackman. No one is within 15 yards and he runs for a touchdown."

(Regarding his "rifle arm," Dodd now says, "My rifle was like the last shot out of a Roman candle. I got the ball to the man, but I didn't have a rifle arm.")

In the third quarter, with Tennessee still leading 6-0, the Volunteers took possession on their 20. "Two plays net nothing," Ole Timer wrote. In the huddle, Dodd had called the play: "Fake punt and pass to the left end."

"I faked, dropped back to pass, and I can't find my left end," Dodd said. "I don't know whether he got held up on the line of scrimmage or someone knocked him down. But I can't find him."

Here are two accounts of what next transpired, Bobby Dodd's and Ole

Timer's. First, Dodd:

> So they're coming in on me, rushing the quarterback. Now, I was a pretty good quarterback; I could dodge. So I dodged the people coming in on me. I scrambled over here—couldn't find anybody. But I'll stay up as long as I can.
>
> And they chase me over there and I reversed my field. Back then, nobody did that—you didn't see that zig-zagging around like [Fran] Tarkenton did. I did that a couple of times, losing ground all the time. Got back to about the five-yard line.
>
> All of a sudden, I see Hackman, standing by himself on the line of scrimmage. He's not a receiver, he's been blocking for me, but I threw it to him. He picked up our blockers—all the Vanderbilt people were on my side of the field—and he went 80 yards down the sideline.

Now, Ole Timer:

> Lyendecker and a couple more break through and swoop at him. Back and to his left Dodd retreats, like a crab being menaced. He gives ground slowly as he can, until he reaches the east sideline and the five-yard stripe.
>
> He can retreat no further, so he wheels toward his goal line and starts running—toward the west. He gets away from the angry mob milling around him, though he goes into the end zone to do it. He runs with a long, loping stride until he gets back to his 10 and—mind you—within 15 yards of the *west* sideline.
>
> Then he shoots a pass. It whines, I fancy, like a Minie ball [a Civil War projectile] as it cuts the air. Hackman, Dodd's mental affinity, is standing on the 20. He takes the ball in and sets out for the goal 80 yards away. Thayer, Derryberry and Saunders encircle him and run convoyage from midfield on. Kohlhase dropkicks the point and the score is 13-0.
>
> And nothing Vanderbilt can do thence on alters it by jot or tittle.

That day, Dodd punted six times into the wind for an average of 32 yards per kick, eight times with the wind for a 46-yard average. That's 14 times for an average of 40 yards. Neyland forgave him, though. (The

General always wanted his punters to kick the ball precisely 39 yards, no more, no less, and high in the air. That combination of distance and height would allow the Volunteers sufficient time to run down field, cover the punt, and prevent any substantial return.) Several of Dodd's punts, in addition to that 69-yarder, were downed or went out of bounds inside the Vandy ten.

Dodd carried the ball nine times for 39 of Tennessee's 67 yards rushing. He completed 7 of 12 passes for 159 yards and two touchdowns. He was sacked once for an eight-yard loss and twice was called for intentional grounding. He intercepted two passes and returned one 21 yards. His yardage gained (at that time even interception returns were counted) against Vanderbilt was 212 yards—all but 14 of the 226 total for Tennessee.

Ole Timer concluded his game story that day by declaring Bobby Dodd the greatest southern football player ever.

Thirty-six hours later, apparently enough time for reflection and perspective, Ole Timer wrote another column: "I should like to second my motion, with the amendment that no greater football player ever lived. There could have been no better."

Ole Timer rattled off some remarkable names, including Jim Thorpe, George Gipp, and Red Grange. "But," he declared, "never have I seen the equal of Robert Dodd, the Bristol mountaineer."

Edwin Camp revealed one reason he traveled to Nashville to cover the Tennessee-Vanderbilt game. "I wanted to see if this Dodd stuff was a myth, or perhaps a sort of infectious hysteria." Ole Timer had seen Dodd play once before, in that S.I.C. north-south all-star game the previous January in Atlanta.

"He had punted and passed and blocked extremely well, and he had slouched around picturesquely," Camp wrote, "but I couldn't accept that charity affair as any test. I wanted to see him under as hot a fire as ever could be spurted at him from 11 flame throwers directed by a master strategist.

"Finally," Camp admitted, "I thought the boy had been the beneficiary of a unique sequence of luck. I couldn't believe what I had heard."

He believed now. "Was ever such a record made by a football player?" Camp asked after recounting Dodd's exploits and total offense against Vanderbilt. "I never heard of anything near it.

"But figures do not give you the picture. He was hounded as relentlessly as ever a star was. . . . He took plenty of punishment. . . . He was more like a wraith, a slouching, shambling ghost. Reach for him and he isn't there. He is just one inch away, indolently and disdainfully fading from the touch of flesh.

"The man is inhuman."

("Ole Timer," Dodd said, "he could really write.")

The love affair between sportswriters and Dodd—an affair that flourished at Georgia Tech—was just beginning to bloom. Of the Vanderbilt game, Blinkey Horn, the sports editor of the *Nashville Tennessean*, wrote: "Major Bob Neyland may be coach of this triumphant Tennessee tribe on Monday, Tuesday, Wednesday, Thursday and Friday. But Bobby Dodd is coach on Saturday.

"Tennessee not only outplayed Vanderbilt but Bobby Dodd outsmarted them. A fellow like that is wasting his time playing football. He thinks so many minutes ahead of the other gent that he ought to be selling coal to the devil.

"In times of stress, he invented plays. In times of stress his poise was rugged as Gibraltar. There's a fellow who would not bat an eye if he had money in twenty thousand banks, and they all busted in his face at once." The ultimate Depression accolade.

Like Ole Timer, Blinkey was captivated by Dodd, calling him "one of football's immortals . . . the gawky young gentleman whose name is Bobby Dodd—the quarterbackingest party the Southern Conference has ever seen."

The great game against Vanderbilt, which inspired such glowing praise, ironically left Dodd with an empty feeling. "I hated that we beat Vanderbilt three years, and I had a part in two of them," Dodd said. "I had a great love for Vanderbilt, still do. Great respect. But I had to win for Tennessee. I never did gloat over it. I never liked playing against Vanderbilt, and that I had a part in beating them."

This was the Bobby Dodd whom "Chips" wrote of before the next Tennessee game, against Kentucky: "No finer sportsman or cleaner young man than Dodd ever dug a cleated hoof in the sod."

In their traditional Thanksgiving Day affair, Tennessee finally beat Kentucky, which had tied the Vols twice and at least once deprived them of a trip to the Rose Bowl. Tennessee concluded the season with a 13-6 win over Florida in Jacksonville, a game which further enhanced the notion that Bobby Dodd had one of the most inventive football minds ever.

Neyland later recalled, "We were moving down the field nicely, and all of a sudden a play started that none of us had ever seen before. Everybody on the bench stood up to see what was coming off, and none of us could find the ball. Finally, Skeet Mayer, the center, came up off the ground with it and started down the sidelines all by himself. He was in a wide open field, loose for a certain touchdown, but slipped in the sand and fell down. We were ahead, so I took Dodd out and asked him where he got that play. 'I just happened to think of it,' he said, 'so I told the boys about it during a timeout and we decided to use it.' "

By now Dodd was an enormously popular figure in Knoxville, one of heroic proportions. Indeed, Bones Barrier, a Tennessee classmate and a friend of Dodd's, composed a poem entitled "Our Bobby," in which the Tennessee quarterback might as well have been Sergeant York. A few lines:

> *And who is it looks like a bald graven image*
> *While mighty lines charge in bone-crushing scrimmage,*
> *Who looks neither worried, nor hurried, nor scared,*
> *Who never gives quarter, nor wants to be spared?*
> *Our Bobby.*

Bobby may have been a "baggypants" hero on the gridiron, but "Gawky" Dodd (as one Knoxville newspaper had called him) cut a more stylish figure on campus and around town, tooling about Knoxville in his famous Ford "Flivver." He got it from a car dealer whose son, Charlie Kerr, went to college with Dodd. It was a four-door sedan without a roof, and Mr. Kerr had painted it orange and white, with "UT" in a few prominent spots.

"We'd drive it to school every day, if we could get it started," Dodd said. "We had to push it a lot. But that was big stuff to have that car. Nobody had a car back in those days, and everybody wanted to ride in my Ford, all painted orange and white.

"With no roof on it, if it rained, we got wet. I didn't even try to put a roof on it. Would've cost more than the car cost."

The car, Dodd said, cost him $20. "Or maybe Mr. Kerr gave it to me."

Colorful, friendly, and a bona fide hero, Bobby Dodd was a popular subject for the media. One Knoxville newspaper interview conducted after his senior year described his football philosophy—the innate understanding of competition that would help shape the tenets of his coaching career, and his success, at Georgia Tech.
Some excerpts:

> All this talk about smartness and psychology is good stuff, but it's the old frame of mind and poise that counts most. . . .
> Psychology will beat you in the long run. You can win with it sometimes, but in a tight place, some other guy is going to "out-psychologize" you. It doesn't pay to be too smart. You're riding for a fall when you get that way. . . .
> I try to start out just like a boxer feeling out his opponent. I feint around with several ploys, keeping close note on how certain plays go or fail to go. Then, when I'm in a scoring spot, I've got a pretty good idea which of our pet touchdown plays will work. . . .
> You've got to figure out what they're expecting and give them something different. . . .

I try to study closely every man on the team until I think I know just how much I can depend on him. Then you don't have to waste time and downs trying to find the right man for the play you're going to use. . . .

My advice to quarterbacks is to study possible situations revolving around your plays ahead of time and then have several solutions available for use when the time comes. Don't wait for circumstances and then try to depend on your quick thinking to get out of trouble.

The last excerpt became one of the staples of Dodd's coaching philosophy and game preparation.

Tennessee finished the 1930 season 9-1. In three years, the Volunteers had played 30 football games and lost just one, compiling a 27-1-2 record. There would be other Tennessee teams under Neyland who would be even more successful, but none as exhilarating as Bobby Dodd and the Flaming Sophomores of 1928.

Twenty-five years later, before a testimonial dinner in his honor, Neyland told the members of the 1928 Vols, "The '28 team probably was not the greatest team, but it was the most colorful. And it gave me more thrills than any of the others that I have ever coached."

And despite all their differences, Neyland eventually called Dodd "the greatest competitor I have ever coached."

By Christmas of 1930 Dodd began to get national recognition as well. In the December 27 issue of *Collier's*, the national weekly magazine ran an article on the all-American college football team as selected annually by one of the most famous sportswriters in history—Grantland Rice. Rice named 13 players to his all-American team, including a utility lineman and five backs. One of those five was six-foot, 180 pound Robert Lee Dodd.

Rice wrote:

There were two quarterbacks this last season who were far in front of the parade, acting as directing field marshals with other useful accomplishments. They were Carideo of Notre Dame and Dodd of Tennessee.

Carideo, a magnificent blocker and defensive back, was practically a seasoned coach upon the field. Dodd of Tennessee, for all-round performance, was on a par with Carideo and in some ways ranged beyond him. Both were smart field generals; both were fine kickers and blockers; and both were cool under fire.

Dodd was a better passer, possibly the finest passer of the year, and Carideo was a slightly better all-around defensive back. [Among the various categories in which Rice rated players, Dodd received a 95 in passing to Carideo's 80.] For example, Dan McGugin of Vanderbilt rates Dodd as "another Benny Friedman." Having faced him for three years, McGugin says he is one of the great quarterbacks of football history. Dodd, like Friedman, could hit a receiver in the head at 35 yards, moving at full tilt. He knew when to pass, how to pass, and where to pass.

For two such outstanding performers, two such rare contributors to team strength and to all-round football value, there is room enough on any All-American team.

"I sure am one lucky boy," Dodd said when told he was an all-American. "I still don't see how they happened to pick me." He does now.

His selection was fundamentally a concerted effort involving coaches Wallace Wade and Dan McGugin and the Ole Timer, Edwin Camp. "One reason I've always been very fond of Coach Wade is that he was one of the men that got me on the all-American football team," Bobby Dodd said. "Also Dan McGugin of Vanderbilt. I don't think Neyland had anything to do with it.

"I wasn't a great football player. But I was under a good coach, and I played well against Vanderbilt and Alabama, and they [McGugin and Wade] bragged on me-so much that they, I think, got me on the all-American team."

McGugin highly recommended Dodd to Rice. So did Wade, who had said before the Alabama-Tennessee game Dodd's junior year, "I respect McEver and Hackman, but I fear Dodd."

Years later, reflecting on Dodd's remarkable performance against Vanderbilt in 1930, Ole Timer wrote: "His play that day won him All-American, and that was in the era when football fame lay primarily in the East and West and we southerners were regarded as bush leaguers. But Dan McGugin, whose heart Dodd broke that day, and the oversigned [Ole Timer] went to bat for him with no little guile and know-how, and between us we sold him to the guy who had the say-so."

Grantland Rice. There was no television back then and few, if any, sportswriters saw all the great players play each season. So all-American selections were greatly influenced by recommendations from prominent coaches like McGugin and Wade, and writers like Camp. Ole Timer had just one problem with Dodd's all-American honor.

"If Dodd was a halfback, your present narrator was a Greek wrestler," Camp wrote. "Dodd couldn't run for beans, was slow as molasses, and at that time an apparently anemic and undernourished stripling."

Dodd's football career as a player was over. Basketball season began again, and Dodd, a starting guard, was also captain his senior year. But before that, an Atlanta man named L. W. "Chip" Robert summoned Dodd to Atlanta. Mr. Chip, as Robert was known, was a Georgia Tech alumnus, star halfback and captain of the 1907 team, and by 1930 a wealthy Atlantan and member of the Georgia Tech athletic board.

Robert, Tech football coach William Alexander, and professor Anthony Armstrong, then faculty representative at Tech, composed the search committee for a new assistant coach. Actually, they wanted more than just a new backfield coach. They were hoping to find Alexander's eventual successor.

Robert selected his criteria carefully, mindful of recruiting concerns, which were changing at Georgia Tech. He recalled later, "We were really looking for a solid southern boy with southern temperament who could know and deal with southern boys. We wanted to recruit from Georgia and surrounding states and not be having to go up to New York and Pennsylvania to get football players.

"We had made a careful study of Dodd while he was starring at Tennessee. We had ascertained that he was a very delightful boy, unsophisticated, and with a great personality. We figured we'd better get after him because if Neyland was half as smart as he was supposed to be, he would nail him down himself."

Indeed, rumors circulated that Neyland was going to sign Dodd as an assistant, after earlier rumors suggested Wallace Wade, who had left Alabama for Duke, wanted to hire Dodd and bring him along to Durham. Around Christmas time, Robert phoned Dodd and said he had a vacancy to fill. Don Miller, one of the Four Horsemen of Notre Dame and later Alexander's backfield coach, had left the Flats.

"They didn't have but three coaches back then," Dodd said. "The head coach, backfield coach, and line coach. You coached both ways then, coached the same boys."

Robert invited Dodd to come to Atlanta for a dinner meeting at his home during the Christmas holidays. Alexander was not present; he was in New York at a National Coaches Association meeting. Robert, Mr. Chip, at that time Mr. Tech, the leading Tech alumnus of his era, had the authority to hire Dodd in Alexander's stead.

The more they talked, the more certain Robert was that Dodd was the right man. He offered Dodd the job and a salary of three hundred dollars a month. Dodd inhaled, gulped, and said, "I never expected to make that much money in my life."

"That was big money then," Dodd says now. "That was during the Depression. I was very flattered and very interested in making three hundred dollars a month. I told Mr. Chip that I would do it, but that I was gonna finish the basketball season. And the day after the season ended, which would be in a tournament here in Atlanta, I would come to work for Georgia Tech on the basis that Mr. Chip said he would pay me a bonus of six hundred dollars, if I would come and coach spring practice.

"I had never seen six hundred dollars and never expected to see it, and I jumped at the chance of coming here."

Dodd and Robert shook hands. Dodd returned to Knoxville with his bonus, most of which went toward paying off debts he'd accrued there. And after losing in the Southern Conference tournament—to Georgia Tech, of all teams—Bobby Dodd remained in Atlanta and went to work at Tech the next day.

Now, more than 56 years later, he's still at it.

Tech's New Coaching Staff Walks Into the Picture!

The 1931 Georgia Tech coaching
staff. From left to right, Roy
McArthur, Mack Tharpe, Coach
Alexander, and Bobby Dodd.

Chapter 5
The New Assistant Brings Razzle Dazzle to the Flats

THE FIRST THING Bobby Dodd did after moving to Atlanta was buy an automobile from a former Tech guard named Joe Westbrook. "Bought me a $250 car," Dodd said. "A Ford convertible. Second-hand, of course."

The next thing Bobby Dodd did was wonder what in the world he'd gotten himself into.

Surely, this could not be the genuine Georgia Tech. Not the Tech of John Heisman, the renowned coach at Tech from 1904 to 1919, the stern taskmaster who once said, "Better to have died as a small boy than to fumble the football," who won the national championship in 1917, who once went 33 games without a defeat, and later had a trophy named after him.

Not the Tech of William Alexander, the Old Man of the Flats, whose 1928 Tech team also won the national championship and then edged Cal in the 1929 Rose Bowl.

No, Bobby Dodd found a different Georgia Tech team when he came to town in 1931. "We didn't have many players," Dodd said. Bodies, yes. Players, few. A halfback named Wink Davis, then a sophomore, was the top player at Tech in the early '30s. "We had one or two other good players," Dodd said. "Bob Tharpe. But otherwise, our third string at Tennessee was better than the first string at Tech."

For that, Coach Aleck could be faulted, and admired.

In 1919, after World War I ended, William Alexander returned to his job at his alma mater. He had attended Georgia Tech in hopes of later becoming a doctor and, on the Flats, served as a doctor of sorts and trainer to the football team.

Alexander was not a good football player. He served as unofficial captain of the scrubs for four years. But he had a keen football mind and eventually became a scout for Heisman while still an undergraduate.

Academically, Alexander struggled at Georgia Tech, but, as in football, he stubbornly persisted. He went through several courses twice and took six years to graduate. Upon graduation, Alexander taught mathematics at

Tech and became an assistant to Heisman. In 1919, after Alexander returned to Tech from military service, Heisman left Tech to coach at his alma mater, the University of Pennsylvania. Alexander was popular with the players, who wanted him to succeed Heisman. They got their wish.

In 1920, the young coach made some immediate changes, changes that pleased his players and would later affect the coaching philosophy of Bobby Dodd. He shortened the number of practice sessions and reduced the number of rough scrimmages. (Heisman had even ordered his team to scrimmage full-tilt on Fridays, the day before games, and in 1919, Tech once practiced into the early evening in the faint glow of car headlights.)

Most importantly, Alexander stressed that practices and games should be fun. His players loved the notion and loved playing for him.

Alexander's offense was more methodical than Heisman's. He stressed the kicking game, an improved defense, and the benefits of playing a national schedule. "If you've got to lose," Alexander reasoned, "lose before a big crowd and bring a lot of money home." (Bobby Dodd would later preach the flip side of that financial coin: If you've got to play, beat *anybody* at home before a big crowd and make a lot of money.)

Alexander was an immediate success. His first three teams were Southern Conference champions, winning 23 while losing only to Pittsburgh, Penn State, Navy, and Notre Dame. In fact, Alexander's teams did not lose to a southern team until falling to Alabama in 1924.

After a few mediocre seasons the Jackets lost but once in 1927, to Knute Rockne's powerful Notre Dame Fighting Irish, tied Dan McGugin's Vanderbilt team, and shared the Southern Conference championship.

And in 1928, Georgia Tech won everything, beat everybody. The Jackets won all nine regular-season games, including a 33-13 thrashing of an Alabama team that Bobby Dodd and the rest of the Flaming Sophomores of Tennessee had barely beaten by two points. Tech's slimmest margin of victory was 12 points that season. The Yellow Jackets were the undisputed Southern Conference champions. Many considered them national champions as well.

After the Rose Bowl, Tech was a unanimous number one. Although edging Cal by just 8-7, Tech dominated the game. Roy Riegels, of course, dominated the headlines the next day and the lore of the game ever since. (When Riegel's wrong-way journey with a recovered fumble prompted the Yellow Jacket substitutes to leap to their feet and roar in disbelief, Alexander admonished them, "Sit down, all of you. He's just running the wrong way. Let's see how far he can go." He went to the Cal one.)

As Riegels ran, the preeminent sports announcer of the era, Graham McNamee, screamed into the radio microphone and over the air, "What's the matter with me? Am I going crazy?"

A couple of years later, a lot of people were asking the same question about Bill Alexander.

The remnants of Tech's 1928 national champions plummeted to 3-6 in 1929, then 2-6-1 in 1930, including a 55-7 humbling by Florida. In response, in disgust, Alexander resorted to the extraordinary. He simply, stunningly stopped awarding football scholarships.

The 1928 squad left a mixed legacy at Tech—the pride of a national championship but a reputation for rowdiness and poor discipline. The players weren't obeying Alexander's rules, and in 1929 and 1930 they weren't winning anymore. "Coach Aleck got mad and just quit giving scholarships," Dodd explained.

"After two or three years, he started back giving loan scholarships," Dodd said. "You give back the money when you finish playing at the school. A lot of the good boys didn't want to do that. They could get a scholarship at another school. So we didn't get choice football players through the early 1930s."

Dodd's first season on the Flats, 1931, was a terrible year for Tech and the new assistant coach. Tech's record was a dismal 2-7-1, the worst season since 1902, when Grant Field didn't even exist. For Bobby Dodd, though, the on-field futility couldn't compare with the pain in his heart. Shortly before the season opener, his mother died. Dodd left Atlanta immediately and drove to his sister Ruth's home in Nazareth, Pennsylvania. Susan Viola Dodd had died from a malignant tumor. She was 53. Bobby helped escort her body back to Kingsport, where she was buried beside her husband.

Back in Atlanta, Bobby Dodd's debut as an assistant coach was a 25-13 win over South Carolina. The season went abruptly downhill from there, however, and concluded with losses to Georgia and California.

"In 1931 we were very weak," Dodd said. "The '30s were bad, real bad. The early '30s and early '40s were the only times Coach Aleck was in trouble."

In football and financial trouble. Supporters grumbled about Alexander's scholarship decision and the subsequent decline in football at Tech, but Dodd insists that Alexander was never in any real danger of losing his job. The financial health of the Georgia Tech athletic department could not be ignored though. It was gasping for breath and existing on its very own life-support system: Bill Alexander.

"The athletic department went broke in 1931," Dodd said. "They had no money to pay us. Coach Aleck paid me out of his own pocket. Me and George Griffin [another assistant coach]. We had to have money to live on and we'd go see him each month and he'd pay us our three hundred dollars. It took a few years before the athletic association got out of debt."

For Bobby Dodd, the most fortunate thing about that abysmal 1931 season occurred one Saturday night after a football game. A Tech fraternity was having a dance at an old dancehall across Peachtree Street from the Fox Theatre. That night, a Tech player named Tarzan Lackey introduced Bobby Dodd to Alice Davis.

Not that they needed any introduction. Alice, an Atlanta girl, was a striking beauty. "She was very popular with the players," Dodd said. Alice was the sister of Wink Davis, the sophomore halfback whom Dodd coached. Another brother was a manager for the football team.

"I was a Tech girl *long* before Bobby was a Tech man," Alice said. "You know, if you live in town and never go away to school, you're available. And I was available. And loved it. Had a great time."

Bobby Dodd was also in the public eye and in demand. "Back then, a new football coach came to town, everybody knew him," Alice said. "Bobby was very popular with all the girls."

"If you had an automobile and coached football like I did, it didn't matter how you looked," Dodd said. "You could get dates."

Neither Alice nor Bobby lacked for dates. In fact, although they danced several times the night they met and enjoyed each other's company, they didn't go out again until the following spring. By then, Bobby Dodd was already an extremely well-known young man about town. Well-known and well-liked.

Especially with his players. "He was very, very popular," recalled his brother-in-law, Wink Davis. "Just a jolly, well-met fella. Bobby was young and Jack Cannon, our line coach, was young. But Cannon [an all-American from Notre Dame] was sort of a rough guy, and any time he tried to show us something, Bob Tharpe [a tackle and future captain of the 1933 team and Georgia Tech Hall of Famer] could always do it better."

Whereas no one could outdo Dodd, from the moment he stepped onto the gridiron during spring practice of 1931. "He was just like one of us," Davis said. "He kicked and played and acted just like one of the fellas rather than one of the coaches. But he knew what he was talking about when he got down to telling you what to do and how to do it.

"He was just a natural athlete. He'd always have these punting contests between kickers before practice, see who could kick out of bounds nearest the goal line. He'd win 'em all. Same way with passing contests. And he always wanted to bet. He'd bet you milk shakes on anything. He'd bet you in a punting contest or passing contest. He would even bet you which sparrow sitting up on the [power] line would fly first."

That fall, Dodd made it perfectly clear that he knew his football. "He came up with a lot of different things," Davis said. "When we came out of the game or were going in, he would always point out something you could do better. I didn't always have enough gumption to get it done, but he was always trying to help you."

When Bobby Dodd began coaching at Tech, he lived in the now-defunct downtown Atlanta Athletic Club on Carnegie Way. It was one of the first of several private Atlanta clubs he would join and he loved it. He paid only $50 a month for rent, but more importantly, "They had a cheap poker game down there, and pool tables."

Dodd grew to like even more the affiliation the Atlanta Athletic Club had with the East Lake Golf Club, the home club of the great golfer Bobby Jones. Members of the AAC had golf privileges at East Lake.

"I played golf out at East Lake nearly every day that I wasn't coaching football," Dodd said.

Bobby Dodd had played some golf before moving to Atlanta, but in Atlanta, he embraced the game with a passion bordering on obsession. Three young Tech golfers eased Dodd's indoctrination into the game: Berrien Moore, Scott Hudson, and Charlie Yates, who would become a national collegiate champion and British amateur champion. All three lived near East Lake, which Hudson's stepfather ran. This threesome got Dodd so interested in golf, he made it a foursome.

"Golf was very competitive, and I loved the challenge," Dodd said. "I didn't do any gambling with them that I remember of. If I did, it was very small, because this was during the Depression see, and nobody had any money.

"But then I found out that a group about my age was playing out at Brookhaven Country Club—that's the Capital City Club, associated with the downtown club. Short and easy to play, but beautiful. I heard from some of my buddies that they were out there gambling. They talked me into coming out there, and I got interested in gambling on the golf course.

"I played for about 18 years. I gambled, and I was like the Mexican on the tour, [Lee] Trevino. We wouldn't tee off unless we had at least a $25 or $50 bet. I played there from then on. I didn't go back to East Lake. I wanted to be in the gambling crowd.

"Eventually we got to playing for big money, and it was fascinating because we were playing for more than we could afford."

In 1932, Dodd's second year at Tech, football was also fascinating. Although the Jackets finished 4-5-1, the games were usually close, with the worst defeat in the finale, a 27-7 loss at California. But that was understandable. Georgia Tech took the train from Atlanta to Berkeley, a five-day trip.

"A great trip," Wink Davis still calls it. "Right near everybody had the flu. It was -40 degree weather when we went through the Continental Divide. When we stopped, everybody who wasn't already sick got out."

Ralph McGill of the *Atlanta Constitution* accompanied the team to Berkeley. McGill and Alexander were great friends. "He and Coach Aleck would get in that drawing room—we always traveled by train—and they'd get themselves a jug of whiskey, and those two would drink and tell stories," Dodd said. "I just had to sit and listen to 'em."

College football teams traveled a little differently in those times. The only wide bodies on road trips were linemen, not L-1011s. After playing in Berkeley in 1932, the Yellow Jackets took a train down the California coast to Los Angeles. There, they boarded a boat that would carry them through the Panama Canal and, eventually, back to the East Coast.

When Dodd came home from that California trip, he came home to Alice Davis. They weren't married yet, but they were now dating regularly, if not exclusively. A typical date?

"Something active," Alice said. "Bobby bowled a lot. We were always doing something."

They went to the movies at the Fox for free, a perk for Dodd; the theater manager was a former football player at Tech and let them in. Afterward, of course, they would drive over to the Varsity on North Avenue, a block from the Tech campus.

"That was the big thing in Atlanta," Dodd said. "After a movie or a dance, go to the Varsity and get something to eat and drink and visit."

Dances were very popular then, and according to the customs of the time, fit right in with Dodd's love for competition.

"Oh, Alice was the most popular girl on the dance floor," Dodd said. "You had to get in line to break on her. You couldn't take three steps with some of 'em like her. You'd put your arm around her and take a few steps, and somebody'd say: 'Break in, please.' "

Could Bobby Dodd dance? "Real good," smiled Alice. "Still can."

"Oh, no," Dodd demurred. "She's a good dancer. I'm a country two-stepper. We still try to dance the same now, 'cept we're not quite as good at it."

"Can't last as long," Alice said. "I could last forever. Not now."

Dancing was a vice—one of several—that was frowned on by Alice's father. Herbert Davis was strict and principled. "Her daddy was against dancing, didn't want her out there hugging some boy," Dodd said.

"I'm a little ashamed that he felt that way," Alice said. "But he thought it was indecent."

In the summer of 1933, Alice Davis got herself a different dancing partner. Bobby Dodd was away for awhile, visiting his sister in Pennsylvania. So Alice started dating Ed Hamm, a former Tech track star who won a gold medal at the 1928 Olympics. In 1933, Hamm lived in a two-room house near East Lake, a house he shared with . . . Bobby Dodd.

"I almost lost her to my best buddy, my roommate," Dodd said. "When I came back from Nazareth, I just let him keep going with her and I started going with somebody else. We finally got back together. I forget how."

"Ed went to California," Alice said.

"But anyway," Dodd said, "it never did upset either one of us very much."

Pause. "At the time it did," Alice said.

"At the time, it did," Dodd agreed. "Oh, yeah. When I found out they were going out, I didn't like it. I didn't see any sense in her going with him, and for him asking her for a date. When I got back, I just said, 'Well, let it be that way, I'll go find me another girl.' "

"And I'll tell you," Dodd said, "in Atlanta, you could find a lot of 'em. There were a lot of pretty girls in Atlanta. Oh, Lord, a jillion of 'em. It didn't matter if *you* were pretty or not. I didn't have any trouble getting dates."

Dodd had more trouble that fall on the football field. Tech was much improved from 1932, but the record hardly reflected it. The Jackets improved a scant half-game, from 4-5-1 to 5-5. "We lost some at the end of games," Wink Davis said. "Flukes." They lost five games by a total of 15 points, including two one-pointers and two three-pointers.

After the 1933 season Bobby Dodd was invited back to Knoxville to coach and play in a charity all-star game. The Great Smoky Mountain Classic, they called it. Dodd's north team won 7-0, and as the victorious coach, he received a sterling silver trophy in the shape of a football, which was to be awarded annually to the winning team. Since that was the one and only Great Smoky Mountain Classic, Dodd still has the trophy on display on his windowsill in his office at Georgia Tech.

Before the game was even played, however, Dodd won something even more valuable than a sterling silver football, and something that only added more credence to that burgeoning phenomenon known as "Dodd's Luck."

Dodd: "They gave away a new Shevalay [Chevrolet] automobile. It was a drawing between the players and coaches of the two teams. They lined 'em up and a guy held a hat, and each player would walk by and take a card. They had a lot of other prizes, too, but the Shevalay was the big prize. The rest of 'em was a suit of clothes, a hat, a tie, or something. And each one would go by and open his little envelope and see if he won anything or not.

"Being the coach, I was last. Hackman, my buddy, was right in front of me with McEver. And Hackman, when it got down to him, there wasn't but two left, for me and him. He reached down under and took the bottom one, because he thought that maybe they'd framed it up for where ol' Dodd here would win. That's what he told me. He said, 'I figured, boy, that last one down there would be for ol' coach.' You know, they were kinda stacked in line.

"So he reached down and he told me, 'I took that bottom one.' And he got a tie or a shirt or something. And I took the last one there." Big smile. "Shevalay automobile. Brand new Shevalay automobile. Of course, they all said I was lucky anyway, and said, 'That damn Dodd's Luck, he's lucky, he's the luckiest guy in the world.' "

Several months later, in Atlanta, at the 1934 Chevrolet show at the Peachtree Palace, Bobby and Alice Dodd happily accepted the title to their new Chevy. It made a perfect wedding gift.

Shortly after the 1933 season, Alice Davis and Bobby Dodd had announced that he would soon be Wink Davis's brother-in-law. "We were keeping it a secret," Alice said. "Nobody was supposed to know we were getting married. And with Bobby coaching Wink, we didn't want to get married during the season."

Neither Bobby nor Alice remembers when and where—and by whom—the marriage proposal was made. They decided to marry just a week or two before doing so. There would be no big wedding ceremony or reception. "Those were hard times," Alice said. They would be wed in her parents' home, with her family and just a couple of friends present.

And just what did Alice Davis think about becoming Alice Dodd? "I'll tell you what my brother thought," she said.

"What'd your brother think?" Dodd asked.

"He was afraid," Alice said, "that I was marrying a gambler."

"Oh, that's right," Dodd said. "I forgot about that."

"They were real nervous about it," Alice said. "The boy cussed, you know."

"You see, her brother'd listen to me out on the football field," said Dodd. "I'd bet these players all the time I could beat 'em doing so-and-so. I could beat 'em kicking. And beat 'em walking on my hands. Beat 'em at everything. And, 'course, I coached the baseball team. I'd give 'em money to eat on, and then we'd go to the pool room. I'd shoot 'em for the money I gave 'em for food, and I'd have to loan it back to 'em.

"Oh yeah, I loved to gamble. And I'd bet on anything."

"We were kinda straight-laced in my family," said Alice.

"But I used to tease Mrs. Davis," Dodd said. "She was a perfect Virginia lady, and she was afraid Alice was marrying a low-life gambler from somewhere up in the mountains of Virginia that came from nobody."

"And he took a drink, see," Alice said. "Nobody in my family ever took a drink."

"Oh, no," Dodd said, "they're teetotalers. Your mother would have a glass of wine at festivals, like Thanksgiving."

"Not till she got older," Alice said. "But when we were coming along, you didn't consider having alcohol in the house. Not even medicinal."

Despite their differences in upbringing, Bobby Dodd and Alice Davis went through with their wedding plans. The ceremony was set for the afternoon of Wednesday, December 6, 1933, in her parents' home at 259 11th Street. The night before her wedding, Alice Davis did something slightly unusual. She went out on a date. With another guy.

"See, all that time, you weren't just going with one fella," Alice explained.

"I think I had a late date with you," Dodd said to his wife, "and you had an early date with one of those Tech boys."

"Um-hmm," Alice agreed. "We were keeping it a secret. Nobody's supposed to know we're getting married."

Anyone who read the December 6 edition of the old *Atlanta Georgian* knew their secret, though. That day, the newspaper ran a wedding announcement headlined, "Cupid Outruns All-American." Beside photos of the couple, the subhead read, " 'Bobby' Dodd and Atlanta Girl Wed."

The ceremony was as unconventional as the courtship. The Reverend Richard Orme Flinn, pastor at the North Avenue Presbyterian Church, which the Davises attended, performed the ceremony. He brought along his wife.

"And the preacher and his wife both cried," Alice remembered. They were not tears of joy. "They thought I was gonna marry their son. We had a lot of tears at our wedding."

The Flinns had hoped Alice would marry their youngest son, Billy. "Her mother would have just been thrilled to death if she'd married Billy Flinn instead of me," Dodd said.

"Or her Sunday school teacher's son," said Alice. "Either one of those would've been all right."

After the ceremony, and the crying, were over, Mr. and Mrs. Bobby Dodd hopped in their car and headed off to New Orleans for their honeymoon.

For two days, Bobby and Alice sampled the pleasures of Bourbon Street and the rest of the French Quarter. On Saturday, Bobby Dodd took his bride of three days to a football game. They drove from New Orleans to Baton Rouge, to watch Tennessee lose to LSU 7-0. He was already preparing her for life as a coach's wife. To her credit, not once did Alice wonder if this was what the minister meant when he mentioned "in sickness and in health."

As far as "for richer and poorer" was concerned, though, the newly-weds were already familiar with those terms. Too familiar. "We had no money anywhere in sight when we got married," Alice said.

"So I had to borrow three hundred dollars for us to go on our honeymoon," Dodd said. "I remember well, three hundred dollars, 'cause the banker didn't want to loan it to me."

A Tech assistant coach came to Dodd's financial and marital rescue. Mack Tharpe. "You know, the one who ran into the cornfield on the way up to the Tennessee game?" Dodd said. "Mack heard me talking about it and fussing about it, and Mack said, 'C'mon!' And he took me down to the Trust Company of Georgia and he introduced me to a guy named Mose Turman."

Mack Tharpe could never have known how prescient he would be when he said, "Mose, this boy Bobby Dodd's working at Tech and he's gonna be there a long time." Tharpe told Turman what Dodd's salary was, that he was getting married, and didn't want anyone to have to co-sign for a loan.

"I'll loan him the money," Mose Turman said casually.

"So he loaned me the three hundred dollars," Dodd said. "That was 54 years ago, and I still do business with Trust Company of Georgia 'cause that guy loaned me money. And I won't switch off. They've tried to get me to other banks many times, and I won't switch off, 'cause that meant more to me, the fact that he's the one guy who would trust me and loan me that money."

Home from their honeymoon, the Dodds settled into their apartment at 2855 Peachtree Road. Their adjustment to marriage was much easier than the continued adjustment of Georgia Tech fans to football in the 1930s.

The nineteen thirties were a relatively dismal decade for Tech, and its nadir was the 1934 season. The Yellow Jackets won their opener 12-7 over Clemson and then lost their last nine games. Many of the losses were lop-sided, but the most intriguing was a narrow defeat that nearly wasn't played at all.

In the fourth week of the season, Tech traveled to Ann Arbor, Michigan, to play the University of Michigan. Neither team was very distinguished, although the center and captain for Michigan, Gerald Ford, would later assume another position of authority in the White House.

Dodd said, "We went up to Michigan, and I'd heard all about Fielding

Yost's point-a-minute teams in the early 1900s, and about their big stadium. But I never heard a word said until we got to Michigan that they even had a black boy on the team. I doubt that we even knew it, 'cause you didn't scout teams from another part of the country like you do now.

"But we got up there, and I heard Coach Aleck fuming around that they had a black boy named Willis Ward and that we couldn't play against them. And I never had thought about it, whites playing against blacks. I'd never gotten into that, didn't ever enter my mind. We didn't play against blacks, weren't any blacks on any teams in the South."

In that era, of course, the South was officially segregated. Bobby Dodd had never coached against a college team that had a black player. He'd never played against any blacks at Tennessee. "In high school, I didn't ever think about it. But I heard Coach Aleck and them fussing, and they were very disturbed about whether they were gonna play the game or not."

On Friday afternoon, Alexander began a smoldering debate with Yost, who was also the athletic director at Michigan. Alexander told Yost that Tech could not play against an integrated team, that the white population back in Atlanta wouldn't tolerate it, and that Alexander feared for the safety of his team when they got back home if Willis Ward played.

Initially, Yost was inclined to bench Ward for this game. The Young Communist League at Michigan found out about Yost's plan, though, and began demonstrating. By Friday night, when the Yellow Jackets were housed outside of Ann Arbor in a Ypsilanti hotel, hundreds of Michigan students made the eight-mile trek to the hotel and demonstrated outside the building. Students were also planning what would become known in the 1960s as a sit-in. The plan called for hundreds of students to sit down on the field in protest if Ward couldn't play.

Alexander resumed negotiations with Yost. Over a bottle of whiskey, the two men talked, and debated, and argued. "They argued way into the night," said Dodd. "Coach Aleck flatly said, 'We cannot play the game against a black man. We could not go back to Atlanta.' "

Finally, Alexander and Yost struck a compromise. Willis Ward played right end for Michigan. If Michigan benched Ward, its star player, Tech would bench its right end, a fine player named E. H. "Hoot" Gibson.

"In doing that, it would be a fair trade-off," Dodd said. "Finally, we went out and played the game."

There were no demonstrations the next day, following a joint announcement Saturday morning. Yost said Ward had "volunteered" to sit out, and Alexander said Gibson would reciprocate. Voluntarily, of course.

The quality of the game was as miserable as the weather, which, combined with the poor records of both teams, helped limit the crowd to one-third capacity. The crowd and the game itself disappointed Dodd. "It was probably as poorly played a game between two major college teams as I've ever seen," Dodd said of the 9-2 Michigan victory. "There were no incidents in the game. It was just poorly played."

Hoot Gibson's disappointment, of course, was far greater. "Gibson was very bitter," Dodd said. "He never did seem to get over it in later life. Was always bitter at Coach Aleck and Tech for benching him for a black boy, trading him for a black boy. He was kinda cocky, with a chip on his shoulder, thought he could whip anybody. He didn't like that idea at all."

That 1934 season was as unexpected as it was awful. "A shocker," Dodd called it. Indeed, that 1-9 mark is the second worst record in the 82-year modern history of Georgia Tech football. Tech's 1935 varsity was so atrocious that it lost the lone scrimmage against the Tech freshmen team. "After that," said Bill Jordan, then a freshman end at Tech, "Coach Aleck didn't let us play the varsity any more."

"Starting the next year, though, our football fortunes started improving," Dodd said. "Not drastically, but better in 1935-6-7-8, until we finally came up with that 1939 team."

By then-relative Tech standards, the four-year period from 1935 to 1938 was a statistical success. From that 1-9 abomination in '34, Tech improved to 5-5 in 1935 (including its first victory over Georgia in seven years), 5-5-1 in 1936 and 6-3-1 in 1937. But it wasn't just how Tech did. It was how Tech did it. With a lot of Razzle Dazzle.

A decade later, when Bobby Dodd became the head coach, Georgia Tech was alternately ridiculed and envied because its football practices occasionally resembled volleyball practices. Periodically, Dodd would permit, yea, encourage his team to play volleyball, using a football as the volleyball and the crossbar of the goal post as the net. But in 1935, Georgia Tech football *games* resembled volleyball games. And rugby matches. And pickup basketball games. And touch football, too—anything but conventional football warfare. Naturally, that was also Bobby Dodd's doing.

Tech had finally recruited some talented athletes who would not only play football well, but basketball as well. Both ends on the football team, Bill Jordan and Ed Jones, were also outstanding basketball players. The quarterback, Fletcher Sims, also played both sports well. Indeed, all three would help Tech win the Southeastern Conference basketball championship in 1936.

Since Tech had several football players who played basketball so well, Bobby Dodd convinced Bill Alexander that their football team should simulate basketball. "We started doing more of what you might call a forward lateral," Dodd said. "We would send the ends down about 10 yards and turn 'em around, face the quarterback. And the quarterback would throw it in there to 'em. And one of 'em [Jordan] was about six feet, seven inches. He could go up too."

In contemporary football terminology, the pattern Bill Jordan ran is called a curl, similar to the old buttonhook. Tech called the pass play 61 Spot. "I'd go down and catch a little spot pass," Jordan said, "and lateral it off to anyone."

And he meant anyone. "We'd have a wingback or a center go by him, and he'd lateral to him," Dodd said. "Yes, the center. Say the right end, he goes down here and catches it, and the center, he comes right down the line. Now, the center didn't run with the ball long; he took the lateral, and then he pitched it out to the wingback. And we were the cleverest that you ever saw at doing that, and we got to where we could do it real good."

"We played Alabama one year—1936, in Grant Field—and I think we had about 17 laterals on one play," Bill Jordan said. "But it was called back, and I was the culprit. I made the first lateral forward. The referee saw it, but everyone else kept going. About everyone touched the ball, and we went down and scored a touchdown. They called it back, but Coach Dodd, he encouraged that sort of thing."

But not forever. "A right funny thing happened," Dodd said. "Everybody wanted to get the lateral, all the linemen. So instead of going downfield blocking, they were all chasing the ball carrier, wanting that lateral. So we actually had to give it up, because we couldn't get any downfield blocking. All the guards and the center and everybody wanted to get the lateral and wanted to carry the ball.

"But we did it there for two, three years, and we were called the Razzle Dazzle Team and got a terrific reputation for doing it."

In instituting the Razzle Dazzle, Dodd called on his own experiences as a player. "I did it because I was a basketball player, and I was also a football player, and I realized that these guys could do it," Dodd said. "My favorite pass was where the ends go down about 12 yards and turn around and face the passer. I always said that's the toughest for the defense to knock down, because they're facing the passer, they're not going away from the ball. And if you got big ends, it's just hard to knock down that ball.

"We developed that, and we went from that into hiding the ball in 1939."

They could hide the ball, but they couldn't hide the curriculum. Recruiting for Georgia Tech had become even tougher. In 1936 the University

Board of Regents took away the commerce department—the business major—and ruled that it would be taught instead at the University of Georgia in Athens. Many football players at Tech had majored in commerce. Not only did this business background qualify them for good jobs on graduation, but it also gave them a reasonable course of study in which they could make passing grades and remain eligible to play football.

"They took the only easy course we had where we could put a weak student," Dodd said. "Coach Aleck couldn't do anything about it. There was too much Georgia influence on the board of regents and in state government."

Having lost its commerce department, Tech started losing some good football recruits to Georgia and other schools. Of those athletes who chose to come to Tech anyway, more struggled academically than had previously done so.

After the 1937 season, when Tech finished 6-3-1 for its best record since that national championship season of 1928, Bobby Dodd grew increasingly eager to become a head coach. This desire, however, didn't diminish his enormous respect, admiration, and love for Alexander.

"He was a great guy and could handle people really well," Dodd said. "If he said, 'Go ram your head into that wall,' you wouldn't ask any questions. You'd go ram your head into that wall."

But after that one winning season in 1937, Bobby Dodd decided he wanted to become a head football coach. Georgia Tech's head football coach.

"I felt like I was ready to be a head coach at that time," Dodd said, "and I felt Mack Tharpe and I were ready to take over the team."

The two discussed this with Alexander, who was also the athletic director at Tech. "But Coach Aleck was not quite ready to retire at that time," Dodd said.

"He started getting a little bit sick in those years, but he wasn't real sick like he was later. Later, we had the real good '39 team and I guess that kinda pepped him up for staying on."

In 1937, Bobby Dodd stayed on, too, as an assistant coach. His ascension would take much longer than he envisioned.

Lining up a putt with Bob Hope.

Chapter 6
Ramblin', Gamblin', and Hot Magic

DODD SEEMED CONTENT as an assistant coach, however, as long as he could find outlets for his competitive drive. So Bobby Dodd continued to play games. He played baseball, volleyball, ping pong, and football. At Tech he often ran the scout team (an Alexander innovation) in addition to the touch games during and after practice. His love of play was infectious, and the Atlanta newspapers caught the fever, frequently featuring photographs of his antics.

With the exception of football photos taken during and after Georgia Tech games, Bobby Dodd was never more photographed than he was on the golf course. Any golf course. As dearly as he loved his wife and his football, golf—and gambling on golf—became Bobby Dodd's unbridled passion.

Through golf, Bobby Dodd would become fast friends with Ol' Ski Nose. Whenever Bob Hope was on the road to Atlanta, he would play golf all around the town, as he still does everywhere he travels. Hope would play at East Lake (where he played many times with Bobby Jones), at Capital City, anywhere he could play a round and play around. A few times, good buddy Bing Crosby was in town and played with Hope. But usually, Hope's foursome would include Bobby Dodd.

"Bob Hope Loses Golf But Wins Repartee" the headline in the *Atlanta Journal* read. The story below chronicled a match pairing Hope and an Atlantan named Morton Bright against Dodd and one Johnny Bulla. The previous year, when Hope was performing at the Fox Theatre, Dodd had beaten him on the links, and Hope sought revenge.

Hope and Dodd posed for a photo on the first green at Capital City, getting down on their hands and knees and lining up Hope's putt. During the match Dodd sliced a tee shot into the gallery and Hope announced he could make money selling Band-aids to injured spectators. This, of course, was just long-term preparation for when Hope would start playing golf with former Michigan center Gerald Ford.

On number seven, a low-flying Army aircraft buzzed the crowd. Hope, of course, accused Dodd of arranging the pilot's flight plan, as part of a scheme to rattle Hope's nerves. Whatever, it worked. Hope and Bright broke even with Dodd and Bulla when Bulla three-putted the 18th. Individually, Dodd again beat Hope, this time by two strokes on the front nine and one coming in, and won their separate side bet.

Bobby Dodd played one of his most celebrated and publicized rounds of golf in July 1938. Not only did the *Atlanta Journal* and *Constitution* cover the match, but both players wrote numerous advance stories on what the *Journal* billed as "a freak golf match."

Bobby (One-Club) Dodd and Chick (Two-Club) Ridley would play at the Capital City Club. Dodd would use only a spoon, a three wood; in practice, he had holed out from a trap with it. Ridley, a former state golfing champion and the golf pro at the Piedmont Park municipal course, would use just a long iron and mashie niblick (two and eight irons). He'd already used them to shoot an 86 at Capital City.

Dodd had played in this sort of match several times before. As usual, there was money involved, a one hundred dollar bet. Pretty big money for the late 1930s. Dodd arrived attired in a gray Georgia Tech sweatshirt and a pair of grimy brown pants. Ridley donned a straw hat and an old, ill-fitting polo shirt that accentuated the paunch in his stomach. About one hundred people followed the match, including several reporters and photographers, Alice Dodd, and Coach Aleck.

On the 18th, Ridley hit his drive to the edge of the green, laid up to within two feet, and sank the putt for a par three and a one-stroke victory. Dodd shot 44-40—84 to Ridley's 83.

A gracious winner, Ridley said, "I wouldn't have believed it possible. I had a big advantage over him and should have beaten him at least four or five up. But I never had a harder job winning a match."

Two weeks after the "One-Two Club" match, the *Atlanta Constitution* sponsored a two-club tournament at Piedmont Park. This time, Dodd used two clubs but again failed to win. In the qualifying, however, Dodd did shoot 76, holing out with a chip shot on number 18 for an eagle.

As entertaining, humorous, and publicized as matches such as these were, Bobby Dodd's most memorable moments on the golf course were not recorded, at least not for public consumption. Some may have been played on public links but were still private affairs. Most were conducted on private courses, in the company of other men who liked their golf as Dodd did: with something riding on it.

Bobby Dodd had his regular golf cronies. "All these people, their families, were well-to-do," Dodd said. "Belonged to Capital City Country Club out there. They're the ones I played with the most. Even during the Depression, their families had enough money where they could belong to these clubs, and get by. But they were all just like I was, out working, not having been out of school long, and some of 'em were having a tough time making a living.

"We played every Saturday and every Sunday. Sometimes, we'd even meet at six in the morning and play till eight o'clock, time to go to work. We'd get these big money games and get involved with somebody we thought we could win some money off of, other than our crowd.

"And it became kinda an obsession with us. We became kinda addicted, I guess, to gambling. Golf is a good gambling game, and I loved to gamble. I must have inherited that instinct of competitiveness and gambling from my daddy."

Dodd also knew instinctively that to be a good gambler on the golf course, you had to get your bets right. "Now it was hard to get a fair bet out of Bob Hope. That rascal drove a hard bargain on the first tee. He was always trying to get an edge. But I always got at least a fair bet. I had sense enough to know how good I could play and based my game on what I knew I could do. In golf, like in football, you've got to do everything you can to help yourself before you put the ball on the tee."

At that time, Dodd was still making his three hundred dollar monthly salary at Tech. On weekends, on the links, he might play $25 Nassau, maybe $50, sometimes even $100. A third of his monthly income. "I couldn't have done it if I hadn't been winning," Dodd said.

Dodd did not confine his golf and gambling to Atlanta, though. Like his buddy Bob Hope, Bobby Dodd was often on the road with his other buddies, to Alabama, to Florida, to North Carolina, wherever the action might be.

Of all their destinations, Highlands, North Carolina, was the favorite. "About seven of us would go up," Dodd said, "and we'd play golf all day, and we'd play poker at night. Same crowd that played golf played poker. One ol' boy from Montgomery I liked named Bert Evans. Ol' Bert and I played a lot."

Through golf, Dodd made the acquaintance of a character from Nashville named Titanic Thomas. No one knew why he was called Titanic, but everyone knew his act. "He was a known gambler," Dodd said. "He'd go from town to town and try to hustle people. He came to Atlanta one time, and he had a buddy of his who was on the pro circuit. He was a pro golfer, and a good one, and he could stand on one leg and play real good golf. See, he played a lot like that, he practiced.

"Titanic was always getting a bet that the pro, playing on one foot, could beat the best golfer you had. Now my daddy taught me, 'Don't fool with gamblers you don't know.' And I didn't know how good this guy was. He was on the circuit, I knew that. He couldn't get me to bet on him. He got some of the others to bet on him, and they lost their money.

"But one cold day Titanic was out there at Brookhaven, and he had on his topcoat. Went down to there, a long topcoat. And he was trying to get

a bet. He said 'I bet you I can beat you, and I'll just keep on my topcoat.'
Now I wouldn't have played the pro like that, but I knew Titanic was not
that good, and I said, 'You can't beat me in that topcoat.'

"And so we went out, and I beat the hell out of him. A guy like that,
though, he'll make a bet with you to get you started, and then he'll make
another bet with you, and the first thing you know he'll double the bet,
and he'll beat you. They're sharp, you know. They're con men, and I know
con men. Hell, I was damn near a con man myself.

"So when I won from him, I took his money and that was it."

All this sounds terribly Runyonesque, but it was not very conducive
to stable personal finances and balancing a household budget on an assistant football coach's salary—and not knowing how much of that salary
you could depend on each month. As much as she knew her husband
loved his golf and gambling, Alice Dodd was not exactly enamored of the
idea.

"She probably despised it, but she never really fussed at me about it,"
Dodd insisted. "She let me run my life, I let her run hers. She knew this
was something I just had to do."

The 1938 season had been nothing more than a 3-4-3 curiosity. In
November, the Yellow Jackets endured three consecutive ties—14-14 with
Alabama and then back-to-back scoreless exercises in frustration with
Florida and Georgia—before going to Berkeley and losing to Cal 13-0. But
in 1939 that all changed.

The pinball looniness of the Razzle Dazzle was still a vivid memory,
but in 1939 Dodd and Georgia Tech refined the Razzle Dazzle with preci-
sion and panache. Dodd realized that those Yellow Jackets were not
physically equipped to overpower people. Instead, they would have to rely
on guile. Alexander gave his blessing. The result was the college football
equivalent of baseball's hidden ball trick, an offense that was a smashing
success and widely, wildly popular.

Even today, nearly a half-century later, Dodd gushes at the memory.
"My kids loved it," Dodd said. And so did he. The principals in that sleight
of hand single-wing attack were a little tailback named Johnny Bosch,
blocking back Buck Murphy, a trio of wingbacks named Billy Gibson, Earl
Wheby, and Bobby Pair, and Howard Ector, the senior fullback and signal
caller.

"Back in those days," Dodd said, "nobody really specialized in hiding
the ball and lateraling the ball. But we did it, and we became a very colorful

team. Now, that wasn't Coach Aleck's nature at all, that was my nature. Coach Aleck was conservative: Play defense, kick the ball, let the other team have it, and play more defense. That's the way he believed in winning. But we got him around to playing this way. If we had the material, we could win like this. But we didn't always have the material, so we got beat some."

In 1939, they played, and won, like this.

In the single-wing formation, Tech would employ either a balanced or unbalanced line, either right or left. The center would snap the ball to Ector, the fullback, who would then turn his back to the line of scrimmage.

Usually, Ector would spin and hand off the ball either to Bosch, the tailback, or to one of the wingbacks. Off of that, Ector had numerous options. He could pass, fake, reverse, or spin completely around and carry the ball himself up the middle of the line.

"But the big play was the end-around," Dodd said as he jumped to his feet to demonstrate, "where Ector would take the ball and the wingback came around, and he faked the ball real good to the wingback, and the tailback went out here like he's gonna lateral to him but then Ector slipped the ball to the end, Bob Ison. And the only people we pulled were the two guards, the first guard to block the end and the second guard to block the halfback.

"The fake was real good because everybody went away from the play. We ran the wingback reverse so well, they didn't realize who had the ball. We did a good job of handling the ball. Ector was real good at that."

During practice, Dodd stood on the defensive side of the ball, posed as a linebacker. "When the wingback went by Ector," Dodd said, "I wanted them to be so good that I couldn't tell which one of 'em had the ball. And I'm coaching 'em, you know, and I know the play and everything. But I wanted 'em so clever, I couldn't tell which one had the ball. And they got to where they were very clever. I'll tell you, you couldn't tell. We did it so well that you couldn't tell which one had the ball."

Tech quickly developed a reputation as the most clever ballhandling team in the country. After barely losing its opener at Notre Dame 17-14, Tech won seven of its eight remaining regular-season games. The only other loss came on a freak play to a powerful Duke squad, 7-6. Bosch, attempting a quick kick with Tech leading 6-0, kicked the ball right into the backpedaling right guard's rump. Duke recovered deep in Tech territory, scored, and kicked the extra point for the victory.

The Jackets blanked 'Bama 6-0 and nipped Auburn 7-6 with their legerdemain, which some called "Hot Magic." Dodd's ploy was fun to play, fun to watch, and often productive. It is difficult to determine when Hot Magic was at its hottest and most magical, either against Kentucky or later in the Orange Bowl against Missouri.

"Against Kentucky," Dodd said, "we faked the ball so well that our end went by the Kentucky halfback, and he was looking the other way. He was *looking the other way!* They had a picture in the Atlanta papers."

The photo captured Ison running the end-around for a 60-yard touchdown. Ison was running past a Kentucky defensive back, who was looking the other way. He was looking at another Jacket carrying out a fake, even though one of his teammates, a linebacker, was screaming at him and pointing toward Ison.

"And here's Ison with the ball going by him," Dodd said, chuckling. "Damnedest thing I ever saw."

At least until Tech went to the Orange Bowl. The opponent there was Missouri. A well-known Atlantan, Forrest Fowler, was a Missouri graduate. In college, Fowler had played football and roomed with Don Faurot, who was the head coach at Missouri. Faurot had asked his old roomie to scout Georgia Tech. Fowler did so and stressed this point: "You've got to stop one thing. You've got to stop the end-around. If you don't, they'll score on you."

"And wouldn't you know it, we get in the Orange Bowl and we ran 54 yards on the end-around," Dodd laughed. "And they laughed about it and said Forrest didn't do a very good job of scouting us because Bob Ison still ran our end-around 54 yards for a touchdown. The end-around was just great."

If Fowler was prophetic, Ted Husing, who would call the Orange Bowl play-by-play on the radio, was pathetic. He was also mightily embarrassed. Husing was a famous sports announcer, one of the most accomplished and respected announcers of his era.

"He was big time," Dodd said. "But Coach Aleck and everybody told him, 'You better come out and watch Georgia Tech practice or you're not gonna know who's got the ball.' He said, 'Oh, pfff.' He was real blasé. 'Oh, I've watched a lot of teams play. I won't have any trouble.' He was out playing golf and didn't come to watch us practice."

Husing should have spent less time on the links and more time at practice preparing. When the game began, Hot Magic burned Ted Husing. From his booth in the Orange Bowl press box, what transpired below must have looked like an enormous electric football game, players buzzing in every direction.

"During the game, they say he was terrible," Dodd said. "Now we didn't hear him 'cause we were coaching, but they say he was just terrible. He'd have the wrong man with the ball, and when he discovered who really had it, he'd say he lateraled it to that guy. He covered up for himself the whole game that way. They say he was terrible, but since it was on radio, nobody outside the stadium ever really knew."

Indeed, when Georgia Tech, trailing 7-0, ran an end-around, Husing was describing the muddle in the middle of the line. That's where he was searching for the ball. Ison, meanwhile, was running 54 yards down the sideline for the tying touchdown. The Jackets struck again on another act of deception—wingback Earl Wheby scoring on a reverse—and ultimately upset Missouri and its star, Paul Christman, 21-7.

The triumph of the skill people gave Tech a record of 8-2, its best since 1928. It also gave Bobby Dodd another nagging itch. An itch to be his own man, his own boss. In March of 1940, Dodd returned to Florida, this time to Gainesville to meet with University of Florida officials about becoming the head football coach of the Gators. On March 28, Dodd was quoted as saying, "I am very much interested in the job and would like to have it if we can get together on terms. It depends on how much salary there is in it, what kind of assistants I could have, and what kind of arrangements can be made about scholarships."

Dodd wanted at least a three-year contract, although he preferred a five-year deal. "But I'd sign for three years if the terms are right," Dodd said. "If I had not made good in that time, I don't think they would have to ask me to leave. I would want to go myself."

He never got the chance. When he returned to Atlanta, Dodd went to see Alexander. "I had accepted the Florida job," Dodd recalled, "but Coach Aleck wouldn't let me take it. When I told him I was going to Florida, he said, 'The hell you are. Your place is at Georgia Tech. Now, get out of my office.'"

With a flip of the back of his hand, Alexander gruffly dismissed Dodd—while retaining him—and shooed him out of his office. And that was that. Alexander told Dodd he couldn't leave Tech, and he didn't. "I had the Florida job for one day," Dodd said. Alexander knew what Dodd and everyone else already knew: that Dodd would eventually succeed him. He just needed to be a bit more patient. And if Alexander told Dodd to be patient, he would.

Of that, Alexander was certain. But just in case, Alexander did something while Dodd was interviewing at Florida. He took Alice Dodd out, and together they selected and purchased a new house for the Dodds. It was a lovely Dutch colonial, white with black shutters, on Polo Drive, just across the street from the first fairway at the Ansley Golf Club. The $4,800 price tag was steep for 1940, and Dodd put another $1,200 into renovation. But the house was attractive, well-constructed, and in a good neighborhood. The Dodds moved out of their last apartment, on Juniper

Street in Midtown, and onto Polo Drive. There, they lived happily for 18 years.

Although Dodd had resolved his future—resolved to bide his time—and his family was now living in a comfortable home, the satisfaction of the 1939 season was fleeting. Ector graduated in the spring of 1940. Without him, and with the country about to go to war, Tech slid back again. Sharply and quickly.

After winning two of three to open the 1940 season, Tech lost six straight games. Even a 13-0 victory over California left the Jackets a dismal 3-7. The next fall was only slightly better, and then only because Tech scheduled nine games, not ten. The Jackets went 3-6, and football on the Flats again went flat.

The early 1940s were hard years. World War II may not have been fought on American soil, but its effects rippled through every aspect of stateside life. A generation of young men went to war, and many never returned.

Of the 33 players on the 1939 Georgia Tech team, 32 served in the war. Nine were killed in combat, as was Dodd's old friend, assistant coach Mack Tharpe.

Ironically, though, when the United States went to war, the football program at Georgia Tech was an indirect beneficiary.

"Forty-two, '43, and '44 were war years," Dodd said. "We had the advantage over a lot of schools in our section 'cause we had the Navy V-12 program (a naval training program). If you had the Navy V-12, you got a lot of boys. They sent 'em in from other schools. We got some good boys from Alabama—football players—and some from Clemson. And we had good football teams, those of us who had the Navy V-12."

Tech was one of four southern colleges offering the program, the others being Duke, Tulane, and Vanderbilt. "Actually, the four best academic schools down here had it," Dodd said. "Notre Dame had it, too, and a lot of schools up East. But that was the only thing that turned things around for us."

Dodd was never drafted into military service. "It looked like to start with that I was gonna be drafted," Dodd said. "But every time it looked like I would be, they changed the draft law to where I was exempt because of my age and my children."

In the summer of '42, Bobby Dodd was 33 years old and the father of two. A daughter, Linda, had been born in 1937 and a son, Bobby Jr., in 1941.

The draft board decided that a 33-year-old father's place was in the home. Plus, Dodd was needed at Georgia Tech, and not merely to teach wingbacks how to run the reverse.

"In addition to the Navy V-12 program we had a lot of Army boys sent in too," Dodd said. "The Army wouldn't let their boys play football, but we—the athletic association, Coach Aleck and myself, and one or two of his assistants—were responsible for exercises, playing volleyball, going through the obstacle courses.

"They had assigned that to us, and I had classes all day, teaching Army boys, playing basketball, gymnastics. I could run the obstacle course faster than anybody I had except one boy. They were the worst-shape guys you ever saw. There was a lot written about what horrible shape the American boy was in when we got into World War II. Well, he was in terrible shape.

"None of 'em were taking any exercise. They couldn't chin themselves twice, a lot of 'em. Just horrible shape. I was thirty something years old, and I could do things better than 99 per cent of my class could do.

"The war really helped Coach Aleck. We got a lot of good boys through the Navy V-12 program. Also, a lot of kids wanted to come to Tech because they'd be deferred if they did."

So they came, and thousands saw Tech conquer. In 1942, Tech won its first nine games. The second was a surprising 13-6 upset at Notre Dame, in which Tech unveiled a phenomenal freshman running back named Clint Castleberry. Freshmen were eligible during the war years and although Castleberry looked like a freshman (he weighed less than 160 pounds), he performed with the grace and skill of a senior. Against Notre Dame, Castleberry ran for the first touchdown and threw for the second, and decisive, score.

During his lone season on the Flats, Castleberry rushed for 466 yards and averaged 8.5 yards per carry. He was a daring, fearless punt returner. Against Navy, Castleberry intercepted a pass and ran 95 yards for a touchdown. He led the Jackets to those nine victories but was hurt by the end of the season. So were several other Jackets, and Tech played just 14 players against the great Georgia team of Charley Trippi and Frank Sinkwich. Georgia easily won the game 34-0 and a Rose Bowl bid. Tech received its first invitation to the Cotton Bowl, where the Jackets threw three incompletions from the Texas three-yard line in the final seconds and lost 14-7.

And then Clint Castleberry was gone forever. He enlisted, and during a combat mission his plane vanished over the Mediterranean. His body was never found.

"He'd have probably been an all-American for three years and been the greatest back in Georgia Tech history," Bobby Dodd said of Castleberry. "He was that good. Small, 155 pounds, bowlegged. Looked like a lot of backs you see today. Kinda like the basketball player Spud Webb, except a little bigger. Could move quick.

"Unfortunately, he played in the single wing and never got to play in the T-formation. He should've been with his talent. He was a wingback, and you don't get great plays from the wingback position. But he could catch the ball, run the ball, and play defense."

The late Jim Luck, a member of that '42 team, who would become the winningest baseball coach in Tech history, wistfully described Castleberry as "a star on the horizon . . . he was here, he made things happen, and then he was gone."

Midway through Castleberry's only season at Tech, Alexander had suffered a heart attack. The heart condition was publicly minimized, but Alexander had actually had a coronary occlusion. He also suffered from a disease of the gall bladder. With Coach Aleck bed-ridden, Bobby Dodd assumed interim control.

Dodd was well prepared, and well armed, for this moment. He had a dominant Tech team, unlike the 1940 and '41 squads. He had the players with which to work, and he even had the poor-mouth sound of a wary head coach. Prior to his first game as interim coach, Dodd gravely warned, "Kentucky may be on the verge of breaking out all over Grant Field with their best game of the year. They can give us fits unless we are at our best."

Right. Tech won 47-7.

The day before meeting the next opponent, Alabama, Dodd said, "I'm going out to see Coach Aleck tonight and ask him to move over. This coaching business has got me down." Alexander didn't budge and neither did Tech's defense. That 7-0 shutout of Alabama, coupled with the victory over Kentucky, prompted United Press International to name Dodd—technically still an assistant—as Southeastern Conference coach of the week.

Dodd coached the final two regular-season games against Florida and Georgia. Doctors advised Alexander to quit coaching, but he refused. Ordered to limit his physical activity and observe a strict diet, Alexander returned to the sidelines for the Cotton Bowl. By then, he'd already finished as runnerup to Georgia's Wally Butts as SEC coach of the year. Who finished fourth in the balloting of conference coaches? *Assistant coach* Bobby Dodd.

By then, Dodd had already instituted Friday volleyball games to enliven the light workouts the day before a game. He was still engaging his players in kicking contests, still punting to perfection, and winning milk shakes off players like Pat McHugh, Jim Luck, and Jack Helms. Dodd was still playing plenty of golf, where the stakes were a bit higher, and also a regular game of poker, where the stakes were higher still.

The poker game was quite different from the old ten-cent, low-rent games Dodd played at the Atlanta Athletic Club in the 1930s. "During World War II, we started playing a big poker game down at the Capital City Club," Dodd said. "About once a week. During the war, you know, everybody thought, 'Oh, I may get killed next week, I may have to go in the service.' So everybody was gambling big back in those days. We were gambling big on the golf course, we were gambling big playing poker.

"So we had this poker game once a week, playing two, four, six dollar poker. Most of the same crowd that played golf were in the poker game. And it got to be pretty big. You could win as much as four or five hundred dollars on a good night, a real good night."

Frank Broyles, a kid from Decatur who would play for Dodd, become one of his coaching disciples, and then create a football dynasty of his own at Arkansas, never forgot the tenets of football Dodd taught him, or the fantastic tales of the Capital City Club poker game.

"There was one guy who played in the poker game who would lose a bunch of money each year to Coach Dodd and the others," Broyles said. "But he didn't seem to mind, because he was rich and could afford it. He got to become good friends with Coach Dodd, and he learned how to play poker."

Said Dodd, "You know on the Coca Cola bottle, it's got C-O-C-A C-O-L-A standing out on the bottle? That's his grandfather's handwriting, so you *know* he inherited money. He was a loveable character, with a great personality, and is still a good friend of mine, but as a poker player, he wanted to dance every dance—just couldn't sit out a hand, and he lost to everybody, not just me."

Bobby Dodd smiled at the recollection. "I won a lot of money playing poker during the war years."

In 1943, Tech split its first six games before winning its final five to finish 8-3. In the Sugar Bowl, the Jackets overcame an 18-7 halftime deficit. Rallying around tailback Eddie Prokop and a slow sophomore fullback named Frank Broyles, Tech edged Tulsa 20-18. With that Sugar Bowl appearance, Georgia Tech became the first team to appear in all four major bowl games. Alexander had taken the Yellow Jackets to the Rose in 1929, the 1940 Orange, 1943 Cotton, and 1944 Sugar.

The wartime football renaissance continued on the Flats in 1944. Bolstered yet again by the Navy V-12 program and by such superb underclassmen as Broyles, George Mathews, and Dinky Bowen, Tech again finished

8-3. The Jackets opened with five consecutive victories before losing at Duke. Later they rebounded from a 21-0 shutout at Notre Dame to rout Georgia for the second straight year. They lost the rematch with Tulsa, however, this time in the Orange Bowl, 26-12. It was the last game William Alexander ever coached for Georgia Tech.

After returning to Atlanta, Alexander informed the Tech athletic board that he was finally retiring, finally listening to the insistent pleas of his family and physicians. He would remain as athletic director but would be Coach Aleck in name only. His health wasn't good, but Bill Alexander knew he left his football program in very good hands.

In June 1945, three hundred grateful Tech supporters attended a banquet in honor of the Old Man of the Flats. Alexander had retired after 25 years as head coach with a record of 134-95-15. He'd been the first coach to take a team to all four major bowls. He'd won a national championship. And he'd taken the torch from John Heisman and carried it high and nobly before passing it on. For that, those three hundred in the banquet hall and thousands more were very, very thankful. Of this, Bill Alexander was certain: Bobby Dodd would be an even more successful head coach than he or Heisman.

"Bobby was a great football player himself, something we were not," Alexander told those who honored him that evening. "And in addition, he had a flare for the game, is a fine strategist and . . . he's lucky."

Bill Alexander was a very smart man.

He was also the man Bobby Dodd admired most. In 1954, Dodd—by then orchestrating the most glorious age in Georgia Tech football history—wrote a book entitled, *Bobby Dodd on Football*. It was a technical, instructional book aimed at high school and young college football coaches. The dedication read:

"In memory of William A. Alexander. The finest man I have ever known."

"Coach Aleck was like a daddy to me," Dodd says now. "He kinda thought of me as his own son. He was a kinda dominating person, and he wanted to control me like he would his son. But he loved me and wouldn't let me leave Tech."

Bill Alexander left Bobby Dodd much to emulate, the most important of which Alexander dwelled on at his testimonial dinner. Alexander stressed that it was his players' welfare, not his won-lost record, that should matter most to any coach. To this day, Dodd's concern for his players remains the hallmark of his half-century at Tech.

"I really enjoyed my years under Coach Aleck," Dodd said.

All 14 of them. But in 1945, after serving Alexander faithfully if not always patiently for 14 long seasons, Bobby Dodd finally became the head football coach at Georgia Tech.

The new head coach, 1945.

Chapter 7
After Fourteen Years, Head Coach At Last

"AFTER 14 YEARS, I knew enough football to be a head coach," Bobby Dodd said. "I felt like I was ready to be a head coach about 1937, but Coach Aleck wouldn't let me go to Florida. So I knew I was gonna be the head coach at Georgia Tech. I just didn't know when."

In addition to the Florida job, Dodd had had several other inquiries and some outright offers. Nothing of financial substance, though, that could pry him away from Alexander, Tech, and Atlanta. College football and the coaching profession were quite different then.

"Under normal conditions today, somebody would've offered me two or three times my salary at Georgia Tech, and I would've gone to another school," Dodd said. "I was contacted by a million schools, by quite a few when I was still an assistant and young head coach, and then more as a head coach. But as an assistant in those days, you didn't get the credit like they do now. People didn't know you like they do now because of TV and the media. So I wasn't given the credit outside the Atlanta area that you would normally get as a top assistant coach."

So he stayed on for the simplest and best of reasons. "I was crazy about Atlanta," Dodd said, shrugging in explanation. "I married an Atlanta girl; her family was all here and they were all Tech fans. I was happy here, real happy. I was playing golf, loved to play golf, had a lot of good golfing buddies. Belonged to all the nice clubs here: Capital City and East Lake and Ansley, almost all but the Piedmont Driving Club.

"I was just having a good life. And I didn't have any responsibility because back in those days, the head coach took all the responsibility when we got beat. Coach Aleck never pushed it on his players; he certainly didn't push it on me and the other assistants. I was making fair money for the time, not big money. But I was winning playing golf, and I was getting along pretty good.

"And I liked Coach Aleck, although I wanted him to let me run more of the football team, and he wouldn't do that, except when the game started, then he'd let me do about anything. Anyway, I was satisfied enough to where I stayed here longer than I normally should have. Yes, I should have started coaching about 1937, '38, or '39. I should probably have taken the Florida job. I expect I would have had pretty good football teams down there and maybe made a name for myself early. Then I probably would have moved on like most coaches do.

"As it was, Coach Aleck finally decided to quit after 1944. He'd been sick. And it was a bad year for me, the worst year he could have chosen, because we'd been getting the war boys, the Navy V-12 boys, the heart of our program. And that ran out. At the same time, our boys who'd been in the war hadn't come back yet. So 1945 was one real bad year for football material."

Nevertheless, Bobby Dodd became the head coach at Tech at an annual salary of $8,400, or $700 a month, according to state auditing figures. At Georgia, Wally Butts's base salary was $8,166, but a subsistence allowance, Oil Bowl bonus and contingencies, and a percentage of concession and program sales raised that to $14,746. Dodd didn't have many perks in his contract, mainly because he didn't have a contract.

Then again, Bill Alexander never had a contract when he coached, either, and he lasted 25 years. So why should Bobby Dodd fret over the lack of a contract? Such an oversight might even work to his advantage. "Just go to work every day," Dodd said. "It'd be hard to fire someone who just comes to work every day."

And besides, Tech would treat Dodd well. Well, make that reasonably well. "I never had to ask for a raise," said Dodd, who never did sign a contract. "But I never got overly paid, either."

Dodd had poor football material with which to debut, but from the very beginning, he had the media solidly on his side—and no unrealistic expectations on the other side. "When Bobby Dodd comes out with his first team as head coach," one sportswriter wrote, "he can feel that he does not have to win a championship or a bowl bid to keep his job. On the contrary, he may feel he is beginning another 25-year regime with the best wishes of everybody even remotely concerned."

Bobby Dodd was only the third coach at Georgia Tech in four decades. As stable as Tech's program was, however, Dodd didn't resist change. Indeed, his first decision as head coach was to scrap the single-wing for the revolutionary T-formation. That move was born as much out of desperation as keeping up with the Joneses and ahead of the Neylands of college football.

Dodd recalls the change this way.

"If I hadn't done it, I doubt if I'd have won over one or two football games playing the single wing. I knew it was the coming thing in football, and I wanted to be ahead of the crowd. And I was.

"The big thing was, you did not have to have the great blocking in the backfield with the T. We didn't have anybody hardly block anybody. We were faking or in motion or handling the ball, and we didn't have to have blocking. In fact, I sold a lot of small backs on coming to play for me. I'd say, 'Look, you don't have to block. All you have to do is either fake running with the ball or carry the ball, or be in motion.' And they loved that.

"Up on the line of scrimmage, it was what we just called kind of a brush block. It's always one-on-one. We rarely double teamed like you did in the single wing, where you had two men try to turn one defender. We didn't try to turn people much. We just kept 'em where they were. We just blocked right up in their face and held 'em there, and the ballcarrier ran right by 'em. You can't do that in the single wing. In the single wing, they snapped the ball back to you and everybody on the defense saw who had the ball, and it was 'There he is. Here he comes.'

"In the T-formation, the quarterback's got the ball and he's either giving it to somebody or faking it, but he may pitch it back to a guy going way out here. So we freeze a lot of people, and fool a lot of people. So, the T-formation had a lotta things I liked, a lotta things."

Dodd had examined the T-formation for a couple of years, but to install it, he imported Ray Ellis, a veteran high school coach from Madisonville, Kentucky. Dodd can't recall who led him to Ellis. "They knew I was hunting for a man who knew the T-formation, and there weren't many people playing it," Dodd said. "They said he was coaching the T-formation up in the little town of Madisonville, Kentucky, and that he'd been coaching it for I don't know how many years, and he'd been whipping those other schools around him with the T with no better football players in Madisonville than those schools he's playing against. I thought that was a good recommendation. And then I found out he'd picked up the T from George Halas's outfit [the Chicago Bears].

"I called Ray and he came down to Atlanta, and I hired him on the spot," Dodd said. "I don't think it took any dickering around. I just said, 'I want you as my coach to put in the T-formation. You'll be the offensive man.' Back in those days, you didn't have but three coaches."

The third coach became Dwight Keith, from Boys High School in Atlanta. Curiously, Keith, like Ellis and Dodd, was a backfield coach. "We didn't really have a line coach," Dodd said. "We didn't do much line coaching so far as techniques were concerned. But we did get a lot out of those kids. They played hard for us. We did a good job on the T-formation."

A particularly good job, considering that Bobby Dodd's first starting T-formation quarterback was the second-string center the previous season. Ed Holtsinger, a senior, lived out every backup lineman's dream. He rose from the slop and obscurity of the trenches, and from the hard pine anonymity of the bench, to breathe freely the lofty, heady air only T-formation quarterbacks inhale.

"I couldn't find anybody else," Dodd explained. "I was looking for a quarterback who could handle the ball well, fake the ball, was good with his hands, could throw a short pass. I didn't care about any bombs. If he could throw 15 yards, that's all I wanted, but Ed could only throw the ball about 10.

"But maybe because he was a center, he had pretty good movement, pretty good agility. So we chose Holtsinger, but I don't know how in the world we ever picked him out."

As he would for all of his quarterbacks, Dodd made life simple for Ed Holtsinger and his teammates. As much as Dodd adored the trick play and the element of surprise, he always kept the rest of the game plan simple.

"We hit the dive play, nothing but the old dive play, the halfback straight ahead in the straight T," Dodd said. "We would put a man in motion. We didn't set flankers in those days, but we'd put a man in motion. We threw the little flare . . . they throw it all the time now in pro football, where the right halfback will just belly out and the quarterback throws to him behind the line of scrimmage. We called it the flare, or the banana, 'cause he ran a banana curve."

Tech used the flare and the running pass often, and with great success. "George Mathews was the greatest running pass thrower I have ever coached," Dodd said. "We faked that dive play and we pitched that ball back to Mathews, and you couldn't tell if it was a running play by the way he acted or the way we blocked. We stressed, 'You block just like it's a running block.' The defense would come up and our end would get behind that halfback and George would hit him for a touchdown or for a long gain. That's how we won as many games as we won.

"We didn't have many plays, didn't need many. Just execute 'em. All faking; the blocking on the line of scrimmage was simple. And so we got along good. As the years went on, we added more and more to the T-formation. Got more complex, did more things with it."

Initially, though, Dodd had to teach the rudiments of the T to his players. That nurturing process began in the spring of 1945, during one of Bobby Dodd's least-favorite football activities: spring practice. The weekend before his first practice as head coach, Bobby Dodd, naturally, played golf. That Monday, he stepped into the brilliant sunshine and onto Rose Bowl Field, the Tech practice turf. Dodd wore navy blue sweatpants, a white T-shirt, and low-cut black football cleats. The new head coach and his two assistants were the first three men on the field.

After calisthenics, Tech lined up in several variations of the single wing before switching to the T. "The new regime had started to work," Joe Livingston wrote in the *Atlanta Journal*.

Later during that first practice, Bill Alexander made a quiet, unobtrusive entrance. He watched awhile and informed the press that spring practice was expected to last six weeks. "Or," Coach Aleck said, "until Dodd gets tired."

Ed Danforth knew, however, that Dodd would need every one of those six weeks. Surveying the sad scene before him, and bemoaning the loss of the Navy V-12 program, the sports editor of the *Journal* wrote: "Coach Dodd's first squad would be enough to make him turn golf professional were it not for the fact that most of the teams his team will play are likewise depleted in undergraduate power."

That fall, Tech returned to practice with 39 varsity players donning mustard-colored jerseys while another 42 B-teamers dressed in red. Characteristically, Bobby Dodd spent a lot of time that first fall practice session working on punting drills.

As fall practices go, Dodd's went rather quickly. Classes had already begun. No two-a-days for three weeks in August back then. "Only one workout a day can be held owing to the heavy scholastic work carried by the squad," the *Journal* announced. "Most of the other conference schools manage two a day now."

"We were all under a lot of pressure in 1945, with the Navy program and long classes and long labs," said Paul Duke, the center and captain of Bobby Dodd's first Tech team. "And it was a quick change with Coach Aleck getting sick and Coach Dodd coming in."

The players saw a marked difference between the two men. "Coach Aleck got very upset at me his last two years because he knew I had a lot of potential but didn't do a lot of things right," said Duke, who hadn't played high school football until his senior year. "He was real strict. We all loved Coach Aleck, but he was very strict.

"We had a great love for Coach Dodd. All of us who played were so different, but we all believed in him. If he asked me to jump through that window now, I'd do it. I don't know why."

Perhaps because Duke remembers how, during his first two awkward seasons, he'd stay out after practice, working for an hour, sometimes an hour-and-a-half on the fundamentals everyone else mastered in high school. Out there working with him each day after practice was an assistant coach named Bobby Dodd.

"He had a way of instilling confidence in us. He could gauge talent and had a way of challenging us in a positive way. He kept inspiring us rather than pushing us. And it worked."

Dodd always did things at his pace. Frank Broyles recalled that as an assistant Dodd had been "loose, have a good time. The same philosophy he had later as a head coach."

Loose and informal—one of the guys. George Mathews was astounded when he reported to the Flats as a freshman in the fall of 1944 and encountered his backfield coach. "I can see Bobby wearing his blue sweat-suit," Mathews said. "It was just an unheard-of thing to me to have the coach so intimate with us." Once practice started and calisthenics were done, Dodd gathered his backs around him and said, "OK, Broyles, you take whoever you want and I'll take who's left, and we'll beat you."

Beat you in touch football. Bobby Dodd used touch football games as practice drills. Naturally, Dodd played, and usually won. "This is after the season opened," Mathews said, still incredulous. "We're playing *Duke* the next week.

"Bobby," George Mathews said, "was one of us, one of the team."

Touch football wasn't the only touch Dodd brought to the head coaching job. Once the 1945 season began, Dodd stopped scrimmaging. He did not want his players worn down, much less injured, in practice. If an injury was inevitable, let it inevitably occur during a game.

It was a revolutionary concept, anathema to most coaches, but an idea Dodd adhered to throughout his entire career. Even Coach Aleck was skeptical at first, however, and the local media was unimpressed with the new ideas and the returning talent.

By the 1945 season opener against Carl Snavely's North Carolina team, the prognosis at Tech was decidedly guarded. In a preview, Ed Danforth wrote in the *Journal*, "The Georgia Tech line is big and slow, the backs can run but there's no passing game." For that era, that was a thorough scouting report.

"We didn't know how good North Carolina was," Dodd said, "'cause this was the opening game for both of us. You didn't hear anything back in those days. You didn't know whether they had a great team or a poor team, but he didn't know what we had either. I knew what we had. I knew we didn't have much."

The opener was at Chapel Hill. On Friday morning, 19 Georgia Tech football players left Atlanta by train for North Carolina, chaperoned by Ray Ellis and the trainer, Davis Sandlin. The 18 Navy V-12 players could not leave their station on the Tech campus for more than 48 hours, so they caught a 7:20 train Friday evening, along with Dwight Keith and Dodd, and didn't pull into Chapel Hill until mid-morning Saturday. Those players immediately ate an early lunch and warmed up one hour before kickoff.

Just before Bobby Dodd's first team took the field, a telegram was delivered to the Tech locker room. It came from Bill Alexander. "Real Knute Rockne stuff," George Mathews recalled. The telegram was read aloud:

"This is the first time in 25 years that I won't be on the sidelines. But I want you to know that Coach Dodd is a better coach than I was. He was a better player than I was. And he was a quarterback and understands offense better than I did."

Outside, there were twenty-two thousand spectators baking, not basking, in the searing sun in Kenan Stadium. Wrote Ed Danforth: "It was hot enough to make a desert Arab yell the Moslem equivalent of 'uncle.'"

Dodd watched his team receive the kickoff, stall, and promptly punt. Bob Davis, a hulking sophomore tackle, kicked the ball high and far beyond the Carolina punt returner. It traveled 59 yards to the three yard line, field position that led to Tech's first touchdown. After a Tar Heel punt and Jack Peek's 12-yard return to the Heel 25, it took Tech just three plays to score. Holtsinger ran for three yards and passed to Peek for seven more. Then Dodd unveiled the running pass, this time to the left, and the left-handed Peek hit Bill Busbin in the end zone for the first touchdown of the Bobby Dodd era.

It was a play especially installed for that game. It quickly became 13-0 on the next North Carolina possession, when Dodd's Luck manifested itself for the first time for Bobby Dodd, head coach. During a trick play, as the Carolina backfield shifted on the center snap, the ball rolled back toward the goal line. One Heel tried to pick it up but was hit and fumbled, and the ball rolled into the end zone where Walt Kilzer recovered for the second Tech touchdown.

By halftime, however, North Carolina had regrouped and taken a 14-13 lead. After another short Tar Heel punt, Tech drove 33 yards to score, George Mathews running the final two to put the Jackets back up 20-14. By the fourth quarter, the game became an exercise in exhaustion and attrition. Sandy Sandlin, the Tech trainer, rushed onto the field during timeouts and doused his players, already soaked with perspiration, by pouring buckets of cold water over their heads.

On what would be its final drive, Carolina punted on third down, hoping for better field position. Jack Peek wisely signaled for a fair catch but was tackled, and the Tar Heels were penalized. Tech took over at the Carolina 26 and ran out the clock for a 20-14 triumph, the first for Bobby Dodd.

"Bobby Dodd's debut was a notable success," Ed Danforth wrote. "His team was better prepared for a tough game and had a wide enough variety of plays to score the deciding touchdown. They looked like a tough bunch coming from behind in the third quarter, and they'll be hard to beat from now on."

The following Saturday, Dodd's official head coaching debut in Grant Field started joyously. A crowd of thirty-five thousand—three thousand above capacity—somehow squeezed into the stadium for Tech-Notre Dame. The crowd included Bill Alexander—sitting in the stands for a Tech opener for the first time in a quarter-century—as well as three thousand servicemen who paid a reduced admission of 50 cents. Tech had vowed no servicemen would be turned away, and kept its word. Service-men sat on temporary seats erected for this game, as well as on the grass behind the north end zone.

The roar of that crowd shook the old cement horseshoe when Tech scored first. Ed Holtsinger exposed the Notre Dame aggressive pursuit when he ran eight yards on a naked reverse for a 7-0 Tech advantage. "What would happen," Ed Danforth mused the next day in print, "if a cockney threw a rock into the midst of an Irish peat-digging detail? Well, they did. The Irish came back from the shock of that initial touchdown and poured it on."

Notre Dame had superior talent, especially in its passing attack, and scored easily and constantly. Stan Krivak, a highly decorated fighter pilot home from World War II, successfully drop-kicked four of six extra-points and the Irish prevailed 40-7.

"We just got beat by a better team," said Bobby Dodd, who would never be one to alibi.

The third game, against Howard, figured to be a rout. The roster printed in the game program revealed Howard had only two players who weighed more than two hundred pounds. That was not all that unusual for the time, though. (Neither were two advertisements in the program, one extolling a "Scarlet Nectar" ice cream soda, made with four scoops of ice cream for just 17 cents. The posh Piedmont Hotel was also advertising room rates from $2.50 to $8.)

Dodd played the reserves most of the game, and Tech coasted to a 43-0 victory.

The next week in Baltimore, Tech faced a bigger, stronger Navy team. "We have no complaints," Bobby Dodd said after his team's 20-6 defeat. "Our boys played the kind of game a coach appreciates."

Dodd grew even more appreciative, especially of his quarterback. Trailing Auburn 7-6 at halftime, Ed Holtsinger threw a 79-yard touchdown pass to Kilzer, then returned an interception 35 yards for the clinching score in the 20-7 Tech victory. A 14-6 loss to Duke in the mud in Grant Field evened the Jackets' record at 3-3. Dodd again started his second team, this time against Tulane, and again routed a weaker team 41-7.

Against LSU, Georgia Tech scored with five minutes remaining for a 7-6 lead. On the ensuing kickoff, LSU was downed at its 10. But the rules of the day required incoming players to report to the referee, even substitutes who played only on the kickoff team. One Tech player had failed to report, so after being penalized five yards, the Jackets re-kicked. Short. From his 25, Bill Montgomery returned it to the Tech 39. Y. A. Tittle could only move the Tigers to the 20, but Gene (Red) Knight kicked a 39-yard field goal that barely cleared the crossbar with a minute to play. Tech lost 9-7, but Dodd never lost his composure. Afterward, he never mentioned by name the Tech player who had failed to report. The press never reported it, either.

Next up, Clemson. "We had gone down and beat Tulane pretty good, but Tech didn't even scout us," said Frank Howard, Dodd's old college adversary from Alabama who, by 1945, was coaching at Clemson. Indeed, Dodd again chose not to start his first team, hoping to rest up his starters for the season finale against Georgia and use his backups to beat Clemson. This time, the strategy backfired.

Although Dodd resorted to all of his starters by the second quarter, Clemson held a 14-0 lead at halftime. A Clemson tailback named Marion (Butch) Butler scored both touchdowns, the first on a one-yard plunge, the second on a 19-yard end run which, *Atlanta Constitution* sports editor Jack Troy wrote, badly fooled Tech: "Tech's left side missed him completely as Butler did an adagio dance to get across the double stripes on a naked reverse."

That Butch Butler was in a Clemson uniform at all was a tribute to Frank Howard's ingenuity and persistence. "Well, you see, back in 1945, Charley Trippi got out of the Army—the war was over—and the Army caught so much hell about discharging him that they kept the other boys in there," Howard said. "Well, Butch Butler was stationed down there at Fort Jackson, just sitting on his butt, doing nothing. Well, that's the way all of 'em did when the war got over. But I called the ol' general down there and told him that he had one of my good football players, and I needed him. He said, 'Coach, I can't give him a discharge, but I'll give him a 45-day leave.' "

In return, Frank Howard gave the ol' general a bottle of real fine ol' Scotch. "The best," said Howard, who then looked at the schedule.

"I started at the last game of the season and counted back 45 days," Howard said. "Butch was in shape when he got here, and he just played. And I remember one thing about him, it kinda made him mad that Tech didn't even scout us at Tulane. We looked pretty good. So Dodd started his second team against us, but when he put in the first team, they did even worse than the second team. And I remember Butler going by him at the half and saying, 'Well, Coach, I reckon you'll start that second team again. But leave that first one out there, they're easier to go against.' "

Tech closed to within 14-7, but Clemson scored again for a startling 21-7 victory. It was the first Clemson victory over Georgia Tech since 1936, and only its second since 1907. The 1945 game was the beginning of a long, lopsided, but colorful—and sometimes off-colorful—rivalry between Bobby Dodd and Georgia Tech, and Frank Howard and Clemson.

Against Georgia, another enormous crowd strained Grant Field. This time, thirty-four thousand—two thousand above capacity—squeezed in. For the first time, season ticket sales had extended beyond the 30-yard line on the east side of the stadium. Game tickets then cost $3.60, and scalpers were getting $30 for two tickets. The huge crowd was featured in the *Atlanta Journal* the next day in an aerial photograph that also showed all the parked cars that had lined up early on Techwood Drive. This was years before the invention of the transistor radio, much less the battery-powered television with a one-inch screen. So hundreds of chilled Tech and Georgia fans huddled in their automobiles an hour before kickoff, listening intently to the Army-Navy showdown.

The Army-Navy game started at one-thirty. For years, kickoff at Tech was always two-thirty. Games weren't televised then and starting times weren't whimsically switched to accommodate the great god TV. It was bourbon-and-blanket weather that cold day in Grant Field, and an even greater chill, a hushed silence, came over the crowd whenever the public address announcer would give an Army-Navy score. Those updates provided much more suspense than did Georgia-Georgia Tech.

Before the game, one Bulldog fan warmed himself by working on his second flask. He also waved a pair of one thousand dollar bills and offered to take Georgia and give six points. He had no takers. Even Bobby Dodd knew, maybe better than anyone else.

"My boys looked better in practice Wednesday, but they still were not sharp," Dodd had said before the game. "They are simply burned out, but we are trying to reach the heights one more time."

Tech's reach hardly exceeded its grasp. With Charley Trippi throwing three touchdown passes and scoring once, Georgia easily won 33-0. The Bulldogs had to punt but twice. Tech only crossed midfield twice, and not until the third quarter.

"They beat us," Dodd said afterward, "and they beat us the way we were afraid they would."

And with that, Bobby Dodd's first season as head coach ended.

Georgia Tech finished with a record of 4-6. It was a losing season, an insult Bobby Dodd would suffer but once more in the next 21 years. Years later, Dodd would call his debut "a disappointment," particularly after the previous three seasons. Now, though, Dodd says, "The first year was a success, considering the material."

Some others weren't pleased. An anonymous package arrived at Dodd's home on Polo Drive. When his wife opened it, she found six football game programs. Programs from each of the six games Tech had lost in 1945.

There was also talk around town that Dodd was a fine assistant coach, but perhaps not head coach material. A Tech fan of the day, Joe Byrd, recalled telling his uncle, Scott Candler, "Bobby will make a good head coach, but he'll find it tough filling Coach Aleck's shoes."

Said Uncle Scott, "That's what everyone said when Aleck succeeded Johnny Heisman."

"I'm sure I got some criticism, but it wasn't like it is today," Dodd said. "The newspapers didn't come out and cut you. There wasn't TV. I didn't get the public criticism. Certainly, I didn't get any over at Tech. People over there, didn't anybody fuss at me about that, not even Coach Aleck."

Paul Duke remembers the refrain he heard after the 1945 season.

"Coach Dodd had a lot of alumni that were down on him. About 15, 20 came to me after the season, 'cause I was the captain, and kept asking me a lot of questions. From February till the following September, the alumni were talking about Coach Dodd, analyzing him, asking questions. Asking about his system, if he could do it. Was he ever late to practice, and what have you. Coach had a style of never coaching us too hard; he always had that. That was very different from Coach Aleck; he scrimmaged us hard.

"Plus, there was all that golf and gambling. Coach was kind of a playboy—real nice but not very serious—and the golfing and gambling, the alumni didn't like that. That was OK as an assistant coach, but not a head coach.

"They were just asking too many negative questions."

So Paul Duke decided to do something positive for his coach. He decided to return to school in 1946 for his fourth and final year of football eligibility, even though he'd already earned a mechanical engineering degree and worked for nine months as a sales agent. "I just came back to help Coach Dodd, that's the only reason I came back," Duke said. "We all loved him so, and we wanted to see him do well."

Duke returned to Tech against the advice of Bobby Dodd. "Coach Dodd, to his eternal credit, did not want me to come back," Duke said. "He said, 'If you're not gonna coach and not gonna play pro football, go out and get yourself a job.' He was thinking what's good for me."

Duke was thinking of what was good for his coach. So Duke returned to the Flats, got a second degree in industrial engineering, and became an all-American. He also became part of an exceptional group of football players, many now home from military service.

"I had a bunch of men coming back from the war years," Dodd said, smiling, "and we had a real good football team."

Those men included Frank Broyles, the slow single-wing running back who would now thrive as a T-formation quarterback. Halfback Pat McHugh returned to the Flats, as did a fine guard named Bill Healy. It was Dodd's job not only to hone all these talents, but also to help them coexist and, ultimately, to thrive and succeed.

There were two distinct groups. There were the hardened World War II veterans, many in their mid-20s, married, some four, five, even six years in the service and, consequently, out of football shape. And there were the college kids, many pimple-faced teenagers, single, just a year or two out of high school.

"It was a little cliquey at first," admitted George Mathews. Most of the veterans lived in inexpensive, military housing at Dobbins Air Base in Marietta, 20 miles north of Tech. "They'd ride back and forth together in cars and have a lot of time to talk about things," Mathews said. One topic of conversation: Bob Davis, a senior tackle, was the captain, while Mathews, just a 20-year-old junior, was alternate captain. Dodd had chosen them at a football banquet following the previous season.

"Some of the veterans didn't like that," Mathews said. "They thought one of them, an older guy, should be captain."

"You had the emotional stress and combat training of the old-timers, and then these young kids, new to Tech," Paul Duke said. "Coach Dodd had to make it an extra-warm environment to get these two groups together. And he did it. We didn't have two factions. Everybody was together."

Dodd used his personality and presence, as well as his unique practice techniques, to hasten the team's coalescence. "He was one of the few coaches in the country to get these veterans, who were out of shape, back in shape," Duke said. "He did it by making it fun. Instead of having wind sprints, we had races where we cheered each other on. And it was genuine.

"We played touch football, too, and the coaches played with the players. We'd cut up and play and laugh. And he'd bet us milk shakes, and give someone two milk shakes if they did something right. He was phenomenal."

Yet he was also a somewhat different man—or at least a different coach, in one sense—than he had been in 1945. After one game in 1945, Dr. Rufus Askew, the Georgia Tech team doctor, threw a party at his sumptuous home on Habersham Road. The guest list included some friends, Dodd and his staff and their wives, and the married Tech players and their wives. George Mathews was there.

"Out on the porch, Dr. Askew had a big chest, like an old pirate chest," Mathews said. "He opened it up, and it was full of champagne. Bobby didn't say no, so we all had some champagne. After awhile, we were all dancing around in our bare feet, listening to Trippi kill Kentucky."

The Monday after Dr. Askew's party, Tech, as usual, held a brief, light workout in sweatsuits. Then Dodd read a list of players he wanted to see immediately after practice. "All the players who'd been at the party at Dr. Askew's," Mathews said. "Coach Dodd told us, 'I had nothing to do with what happened the other night. If it gets out, I could lose my job.'

"To my way of thinking, Bobby was never as close to us as players again."

It was not that Dodd no longer cared for his players. He just had to care for them a bit differently now, on another level. As a head coach. "He had to grow up pretty fast," Mathews said.

If Dodd's outlook was more mature in 1946, so was his football team. "That was the first year I had some football players," Dodd said. "We had a lot of good football players back from the war. I knew I had a good football team."

Dodd also knew he had his ideal T-formation quarterback in Frank Broyles. "A natural T quarterback," Dodd called Broyles. "If you ever wanted to see me as a football player, see Frank Broyles and Billy Lothridge (Tech's quarterback in 1962 and '63 and, like his coach, an all-American in his senior season).

"Both of 'em knew football real well and both were real slow. But all three of us could play football. All three were fine punters, all three were fine passers, all three knew football."

All three also had exceptional supporting casts. In the 1946 opener, though, that wasn't enough for Broyles, Dodd, and Tech. The Jackets opened at Tennessee, against General Neyland, Dodd's former coach. Much was made of the confrontation.

"I was supposed to be his star pupil, and I was coaching against him," Dodd said. "I knew what he was gonna do. With Neyland, there was nothing fancy, just sound, fundamental football. Intercept passes, play the kicking game, sound defense, field position."

Tech outplayed the Vols that Saturday, but Broyles threw two interceptions, and each led to Tennessee touchdowns. His first pass of the game was high, wobbly, intercepted, and returned to the Tech 11. From there, Tennessee scored. Later, George Balitsaris went 58 yards with the second interception for the deciding touchdown. Near the end of the game, the Vols took three intentional delay-of-game penalties and then a safety to preserve their 13-9 win.

Although Dodd dearly wanted to beat his former coach, he returned to Atlanta somewhat pleased and highly optimistic. "We played a terrific game," he said, "and I knew I had a good football team."

This good: the Yellow Jackets won their next eight games. After easily dispatching VMI and Ole Miss, Tech traveled to LSU. It was a historic journey. When a Delta DC-4 carrying 39 players and the coaching staff took off from Candler Field, it was the first time Georgia Tech had ever flown to a game. The starting lineup, all wearing coats and ties, posed beside the DC-4 before departing. The seven linemen stood on the ground, with Broyles on the first step and his backfield on the upper steps leading to the plane.

Once in Baton Rouge, the Yellow Jackets made more history. They became the first team to frustrate an opponent into saying, in effect, "Turn out the lights, the party's over." Then, as now, Tiger Stadium on a ragin' Cajun Saturday night was a pit, the pigskin equivalent of the LaBrea tar pits.

LSU was unbeaten, Y. A. Tittle was the quarterback, and it was homecoming. Naturally, the Tigers took Tech too lightly. Sam Lyle, who played for LSU (and later became an assistant coach for Dodd), admitted the LSU coaches "grossly underrated" Tech, while the Bayou abounded with bowl visions, Orange or Rose.

Trailing 7-6 at halftime, the Jackets preempted the planned, postgame fireworks celebration. They exploded. Mathews went 44 yards to score on a trick play hastily designed for LSU, Dinky Bowen scored on 34 Trap, another play installed for the game, and then Tommy Carpenter intercepted Tittle at the LSU 35 on the final play of the game. Carpenter raced down the sideline, headed for a certain touchdown, but as he neared the goal line, an LSU athletic official disgustedly threw the light switch, casting the stadium into darkness. "And then," Johnny Bradberry wrote in the *Atlanta Constitution*, "the late war was replayed."

Fireworks, flares, and the rockets' red glare set the sky afire. The noise was deafening. Carpenter had scored, but after the two teams fumbled about in the darkness, trying to locate the ball and line up for the extra point, Dodd agreed with the referee's suggestion to forget the point after, settle for a 26-7 upset, and get out of there alive.

A huge crowd packed Grant Field the next week for Auburn. Temporary bleachers were built on the running track encircling the field, but tickets were still at a premium. Perhaps that's why that Saturday, Pat McHugh, a fleet running back returned from the war, was standing outside the stadium shortly before kickoff, dressed in his game uniform, in his stocking feet, trying to scalp his tickets. Instead, McHugh almost got arrested.

"I think Pat talked his way out of it," Mathews said. "He must have, because he played. But that was pretty uniform, players selling their tickets."

Often, Dr. Askew, the team doctor, bought tickets from many players. "A lovable guy," Mathews called the good doctor. "I know he didn't sell them, not for what he paid for them." For a $3.60 ticket, Dr. Askew paid $25. (There were no college rules preventing athletes from selling their complimentary tickets at that time, but the police did try to prevent ticket scalping at the games.)

"If we'd been playing for Notre Dame, you could've gotten more than that," Mathews said. "We were the only game in town, and the war was just over, and there was plenty of money."

Also on sale outside Grant Field that day were game programs. They included an ad for Philip Morris cigarettes, in which the Philip Morris bellhop demonstrated the signals used by football referees. Four times that day, the referee threw both arms up overhead to signify Tech touchdowns in a 27-6 victory.

There followed a landmark triumph for Bobby Dodd. Wallace Wade had returned to Duke that fall from the war, but the Blue Devils had temporarily fallen from grace. Tech ruined Duke's homecoming with a 14-0 whitewash in the mud. On the train back to Atlanta, Bill Alexander told Frank Broyles, "That's the first time in 30 years I've seen Wallace Wade get beat by the kicking game."

Twice coming out of the huddle, Broyles had lined up at left halfback instead of quarterback, taken a direct snap, and quick-kicked Duke into oblivion. The two quick-kicks led to both Tech touchdowns. Tech was dressed in white uniforms, all of which were muddied except Broyles's. Having passed, handed off, and quick-kicked, Broyles was never knocked down into the mud. Only the knees of his pants were soiled, from kneeling in the huddle to call plays.

Bobby Dodd, though, felt even more cleansed than did Broyles. And never mind that this had been the fourth straight Duke defeat. "I always had great respect for Wallace Wade," Dodd said. "And when we won that game, I knew then I was a good football coach. Afterward, Wallace Wade was very gracious. I was much more in awe of Wade than Neyland."

Dodd was not alone. "Wade was quite a fellow," said Dodd. "His players said they'd walk across the street rather than pass him. Once, at a reunion they had at Alabama, when he walked in that room, everyone put out their cigarettes. After they've been out of school 10 years, they're all hunting for a place to put out their cigarettes when Coach Wade walked in the room. He must have been something." Must have. One of those ex-players hunting for a place to put out his cigarette was Bear Bryant.

Navy was the opponent for homecoming. This was not one of the Middies' better years, but as Ed Danforth noted, "For a team that had lost five games in a row, they appeared disgustingly healthy." The crowd was healthy, too, with thirty-two thousand people at Grant Field a full 25 minutes before kickoff. Some fans were in their seats an hour before game time while others circulated outside, where scalpers surreptitiously sold tickets, wary of Pinkerton guards.

A two-story goat, covered with yellow jackets, adorned the front of a Georgia Tech fraternity house. Above was a prediction: "Billy Bites More'n He Can Chew." The new Tech mascot was unveiled that day: a remote-controlled airplane, which buzzed and harassed Bill X, the Navy goat. "It flew perfectly," wrote Ralph McGill, "sounding not unlike an annoyed yellow jacket."

It was a gorgeous Atlanta afternoon in the anxious, excited city. "A gay-in-spots city," McGill called it. Many homes hosted noon football breakfasts. Navy brass and braid were prominent at many of those pre-game parties. "And by no means were all the scrambled eggs on the buffet table," said McGill.

111

In Grant Field later that day, they played a glorious football game. Navy, leading 20-14, drove to the Tech seven late in the day. But fullback Wild Bill Hawkins was hit by Johnny McIntosh, and the ball flew into the arms of George Mathews. Aided by Jack Bills's block at midfield, Mathews raced 95 yards along the east sideline for a touchdown. Dinky Bowen's point after gave Tech a 21-20 advantage with 2:30 left. Then, after Pat McHugh returned an interception 61 yards to the Navy six, Broyles passed to George Brodnax for the 28-20 final.

"Not everybody was able to stand as the band played the national anthem [then a post-game tradition]," wrote Ed Danforth. "It was a finish that left them limp in the aisles."

Of Mathews's run, McGill wrote that Paul Revere's ride was "dull as ditchwater compared with the mad gallop of George Mathews, who had just proved that fact is stranger than fiction."

The facts as supplied by Tech line coach Bob Woodruff, who peered into the press box after the game and announced, "By the grace of luck we didn't deserve."

Dodd's Luck. But not totally. Or as William Tucker of UPI wrote: "Although Coach Bobby Dodd of Georgia Tech is thinking of opening a blacksmith shop with the surplus of horseshoes that developed in his victory over Navy, you can't deny the fact that he had the right man for the right moment."

There followed successive victories, easily accomplished, over Tulane 35-7, and Furman 41-7. As usual, Grant Field was full. A choice season ticket in the west stands cost $24, and the Grant Field aristocracy in those west stands roared their approval of George Mathews's performance against Tulane. After the Green Wave tied the score at 7-7 in the second quarter, Mathews ran 52 yards for a touchdown and passed 29 yards for another.

"George Mathews was the smartest football player on the field of any player I ever coached," Bobby Dodd said. "He knew more of what was going on on the football field. He was thinking out there all the time. It looked like he was always in the right place at the right time—that's smartness.

"He let a Georgia boy catch the ball once up here [Dodd held his hands overhead] and he just reaches up and snatches it out of his hands. He knew he was gonna do it."

Dodd said Mathews could do one thing better than anybody he ever saw in college football. "He was the best man at throwing the running pass that you ever saw. We used it a lot, had great success with it because nobody on the field knew if George was gonna throw the ball, except the quarterback and me. George would run from left to right, make it look like a run, and then he'd jump in the air and throw it."

Neither Mathews's running nor passing was needed against Furman. Dodd played his first-stringers only briefly; the second- and third-teamers were mainly responsible for a 34-7 halftime bulge. After the fifth Tech touchdown in the third quarter, Dodd sent his starters into the locker room to shower up and dress. The reserves finished out the game. During most of that time, the crowd kept chanting, "To hell with Georgia."

By now, Tech was 8-1, Georgia 9-0. Already, Bill Alexander said that this 1946 Tech team was as good as his '42 squad, which went 9-2 and which he designated as the best team in Tech history. Georgia, though, had something much more potent: Charley Trippi.

A crowd of fifty-five thousand, the largest football crowd ever in the state of Georgia at that time, came to Athens. Another ten thousand were turned away. Those inside saw the Man—as Trippi was called—in motion.

Ralph McGill described him as "a ten-ton truck, fully loaded, and going at top speed, able to turn and twist like a jeep."

Trippi turned and twisted for three touchdowns, including a 66-yarder that immediately followed the only Tech score. He also passed for a fourth touchdown to give the Bulldogs a 35-7 win, their first undefeated, untied season since 1896, and a Sugar Bowl date opposite North Carolina and Charlie "Choo Choo" Justice.

Tech was going bowling, too. To the young Oil Bowl in Houston, the forerunner of the Bluebonnet Bowl. The Yellow Jackets were invited because many affluent and influential Tech engineering graduates lived in Houston and worked in the oil business.

While his team practiced back in Atlanta, Dodd flew out to Houston to attend to some Oil Bowl preparations. He was delayed in returning, however. Dodd was being courted by Baylor University to replace Frank Kimbrough, who'd resigned as head coach after a losing season.

Dodd ultimately turned down Baylor but recommended his line coach, Bob Woodruff. Woodruff would get the job and take along Frank Broyles as his backfield coach. Dodd also gave a prompt refusal to Vanderbilt, searching for a new head coach after Red Sanders left Nashville for Los Angeles and UCLA.

In the Oil Bowl, Tech was to play St. Mary's of California. Oil Bowl officials met the Yellow Jackets at the airport with three hook and ladder trucks. The Tech players piled onto the fire engines and off they went, careening through Houston, the sirens wailing, until they were dropped off in style at their hotel.

"From that point on," said Paul Duke, "it was the best bowl any of us ever went to. The whole week was fabulous."

The weather on game day was not. A crowd of twenty-two thousand turned out but didn't dally when rain fell and the temperature dropped to 34 degrees, turning the rain to sleet. "A miserable day," Dodd remembered.

"One of those Texas northerners blew in there."

St. Mary's was led by a tiny, elusive Hawaiian named Herman Wedemeyer. Like the old Tech Razzle Dazzle teams of the 1930s, the Galloping Gaels liked to haphazardly lateral the ball. But on this day, they had no chance.

After falling behind, St. Mary's tried to pass the wet football. Tech intercepted eight passes, Pat McHugh returned one 75 yards for a touchdown. The Jackets threw for three scores and won decisively 41-19 to finish the season with a 9-2 record.

The Oil Bowl was a minor bowl, but noteworthy for a number of reasons. It was the first bowl success for Bobby Dodd, who would become known as the bowlmaster. It prolonged Frank Broyles's bowl streak; Tech went to a bowl in each of the four seasons he played on the Flats. Later, as an assistant to Dodd, Broyles would go to six more bowls in six years, for a remarkable string of ten bowl appearances in each of his ten Tech football seasons.

The Oil Bowl was also important because it proved something to some others about Bobby Dodd. "That was the first time people believed I was gonna be a good football coach," Dodd said.

After the 1946 season, the west stands at Grant Field were torn down as part of a stadium expansion plan. The west stands were reconstructed closer to the field and built much higher, to expand the capacity to forty thousand. A sparkling new press box was added, the largest in the South, with seating for three hundred media people. During the 1947 season, that new press box and those enlarged stands were badly needed.

In the off-season, there was another important addition to the scenery at Grant Field. After Bob Woodruff left for Baylor following the Oil Bowl, Bobby Dodd needed a line coach. He called his old Tennessee teammate, Herman Hickman, who by then was coaching at Yale. Hickman still ate an enormous amount. He reached an agreement with Dodd that a new line coach would cost Dodd a country ham. So Hickman recommended a younger Volunteer, a lineman named Ray Graves who had gone on to play for the Philadelphia Eagles.

The Tech dressing room after beating Georgia 7-6 in 1949. Flanking Dodd on the front row are Ray Beck (60), Ewell Pope (18), Tom Coleman (36), and Morris Harrison (28).

Chapter 8
Good Teams in the Late Forties—
and the Drought Begins

WHEN THE 1946 SEASON BEGAN, Ray Graves replaced Woodruff, but Dodd still needed someone to take the place of Frank Broyles, who had been named the all-SEC quarterback ahead of Y. A. Tittle of LSU and Charlie Connerly of Ole Miss. Yet as much as Dodd valued Broyles, his departure didn't overly worry the head coach. Dodd had too many other players returning to the Flats.

"The '47 team had more speed and more savvy—smarts—than any team I ever coached," said Dodd. "I had a lot of speed and a lot of intelligence, so we could change a lot of things during games."

For openers, Dodd also had a mission: Tennessee. More precisely, Neyland. "I don't have any love for Tennessee," Dodd says today. "I played for them, but Neyland and I were never very close."

(In 1964, Dodd was elected to the National Football Foundation and Hall of Fame, based on his performance at Tennessee. He has since tried unsuccessfully to change his Hall of Fame designation from Tennessee all-American player to Georgia Tech coach. "All I want to do is be associated with Georgia Tech. Tennessee doesn't mean that much to me anymore. I was only there four years. And besides, I think I'm a better coach than I was a player.")

Neyland and Dodd were not very close on September 27, 1947, either. "One of the greatest games ever played," Dodd said, grinning. "Everything we did was right. We just killed Neyland's team. I called 'em off."

The final score was 27-0. It could have been worse, but not for Bob Neyland. It was the worst defeat in Neyland's 16-year coaching career and would stand as his second-worst ever (exceeded only by a 43-13 thrashing by Ole Miss later that year). It was the first time a Neyland defense had ever surrendered four touchdowns in one game, three of which were scored by George Mathews. And it was no accident.

Georgia Tech had had four weeks, its entire fall practice period, to prepare for Tennessee. Like Dodd, Ray Graves was intimately familiar with Neyland's offensive and defensive schemes. Offensively, there was never anything deceptive about the Vols, at least when Bobby Dodd wasn't playing for them.

To help prepare Tech, Graves took a crayon and made rough sketches of Tennessee's two favorite plays, number nine (an end sweep) and the famous number ten (the off-tackle play). Graves's defense did its math homework diligently.

"They schooled us so well," George Mathews said, "that when Tennessee came up to the line, we, in unison, screamed, 'Here comes number nine!' The Tennessee team claimed that we mischievously learned their signals. But we had just been prepared so well, we knew what they were going to run. And we just smashed them."

For that game, Graves suggested a play the Eagles had run in Philadelphia. "We called it a 'flip pass,' " Graves said. It was basically a toss sweep to the left, with the entire left side of the Tech line pulling out to block. Dodd was skeptical about the prospects of the play, but agreed to use it with this stipulation. "Bobby said, 'If you give me a dollar for each yard we lose on the play, I'll give you a dollar for every yard we make on it.' "

Two of George Mathews's touchdowns came on the flip pass. After the second one, Graves said, Dodd turned to him and muttered "The bet's off."

Sports editor Walter Stewart wrote in the *Memphis Commercial-Appeal* the next day:

"Employing a meat-cleaver as more conventional types would apply a comb, Robert Dodd got into his old master's hair this breeze-winnowed Saturday afternoon and removed the scalp right down to shoe-top level. When the wreckage, sporting an orange and white motif, was swept up by a gallant squad of salvationists, it was learned that Georgia Tech had notched 27 points while Tennessee (playing the role of innocent bystander) had garnered none at all.

"It was the rowdiest treatment ever suffered by Gen. Robert Neyland and it is sad to note that it was caused by a man the Tennessee touchdown tycoon had once nurtured to his breast—even taught to play football. Man's inhumanity to man is a text which will undoubtedly be favored in Knoxville pulpits Sunday along with that line dealing with a serpent's tooth and the keenness thereof."

Stewart went on to note that "Dodd struck with a weapon only slightly more complicated than the innards of a submarine. His assault was delicately balanced and deadly as a guillotine."

F. M. Williams was a bit more succinct: "The pupil taught the teacher a thing or two about football at Grant Field Saturday."

And the pupil loved it. Ralph McGill watched Dodd closely during the waning minutes:

"He was coatless in blue shirt and red tie and grey pants and tan shoes.

A grey brim hat shadowed his eyes. But the smile on his face was such as the angels have when they look over the rim of Heaven and see a sinner saved. The smile on his face was like a small boy served extra ice cream and cake."

"That was a big game to me," Dodd said. "I'd beaten my coach, who'd beaten me the year before, and I'd beaten him decisively. In fact, they got bitter because this was Neyland's worst defeat in history, and he didn't like it a damn bit. They claimed the officials down here in Atlanta were on our side, but there wasn't anything to that. They were just mad 'cause they got beat. I remember I told Neyland after we'd seen the films that the officials had made good calls. He said, 'Well, when they were throwing the flags, it looked like they were enjoying it.

"But that was the start of a good football team."

Perhaps a great football team. Georgia Tech won its first five games handily, shutting out three opponents and allowing just 13 points. Then Duke came to Atlanta, arriving by train the morning of the game. The Blue Devils were also undefeated, but a far more conventional, traditional team than Tech. As Ed Danforth put it:

"Tech goes to work and suggests one of these slinky jobs right out of *Vogue*. Duke will remind you of your Aunt Emma, who wore common-sense shoes and long ones in winter, but who could cook a batch of biscuits so light they had to be wrapped up in a napkin to keep them from rising right up off (pronounced 'off'n') the plate."

Surprisingly, it was the team in *Vogue*, not Aunt Emma, which was better suited to the Saturday rain in Grant Field. Jim Still's first-quarter touchdown pass to a diving George Brodnax was all the slinky scoring Tech needed for a 7-0 win.

"We had four great players hurt in that game," Bobby Dodd recalled. They were Frank Ziegler, Lewis Hook, Jack Griffin, and George Mathews, who broke his right ankle. "That team," Dodd said, "would have gone down as one of the great teams at Tech if we hadn't got those four players hurt."

As it was, Tech still dared to be great. Without the four injured starters, the Yellow Jackets managed to squeeze by Navy 16-14. But against Alabama, they were victimized by the passing of Harry Gilmer, who passed for one touchdown, scored another, and beat Tech 14-7.

In 1947, the loss of four starters debilitated a team even more than it would today. Football was still an iron-man exercise then, basically one-platoon football in which players performed on both offense and defense. The absence of Hook and Ziegler, the two Tech linebackers, was particularly noticeable against Alabama's Gilmer, who completed 12 of 13 passes, several in third-and-long passing situations against backup linebackers.

"We were never the same team after losing those four," Dodd said. "Against Tennessee and Duke, we were a great football team."

After annihilating Furman, Tech still had enough manpower to defeat Georgia, finally. Without Trippi, the Bulldogs fell to Tech 7-0 on freshman halfback Red Patton's "running pass" to George Brodnax. Bobby Dodd had beaten Georgia for the first time.

With that victory, Tech was 9-1 and was invited to Miami to play in the Orange Bowl. "We had a great time down there," Dodd said. "That was when everybody started talking a little bit about my bowl preparation. I had the same philosophy for bowls during my whole career.

"I didn't scrimmage any. I didn't work 'em hard. We had a good time. We took the game seriously, though. When the time came to play the game, we were ready to play."

In the Orange Bowl, Tech met Kansas. George Mathews's ankle had healed sufficiently, and he played. The Yellow Jackets took a 20-7 lead after Still threw three touchdown passes, two to Red Patton and one to Billy Queen. Kansas, however, closed to within 20-14 and was inches from the goal line when Lynn McNutt fumbled on a quarterback sneak. Rollo Phillips recovered to preserve Tech's 20-14 victory, 10-1 record, and number 10 national ranking.

The 1948 season began as promisingly as had 1947. Georgia Tech won its first six games. After the sixth, a thorough 19-7 decision at Duke, Wallace Wade acknowledged, "Georgia Tech has the greatest team I have ever seen."

(For Dodd, that was a treasured compliment, if not an accurate assessment. It was Dodd, after all, who once said of Wade, "If we must lose to anyone, I'd choose to lose to Wallace Wade. When we have beaten him, Mr. Wade has always come over and congratulated us in a way that made us know he meant what he said. He has never blamed the weather or the field, the officials, or hard luck. He has never complained that he lacked material or that his players fell down on him. . . . You cannot grudge a victory to such a man.")

After the win at Duke, Dodd was named national coach of the week by UPI. Dodd told the wire service that at Tech, "We play on the theory that football should be fun. The boys make their own training rules and are responsible for enforcing them. No one checks them in at night."

Dodd also addressed his team's uniforms. He'd abandoned the traditional Tech garb—drab, mustard-colored jerseys—in favor of two color-coordinated combinations: blue shirts and white pants, or white jerseys with gold pants. "A well-dressed team has more pride and self-confidence," Dodd explained. "Those uniforms are worth about a touchdown a game."

Those uniforms, unfortunately, were of little help the last month of the 1948 season. This time, General Neyland got his revenge, stopping Tech's six-game winning streak with a 13-6 victory. A victory that meant so much to Neyland. After the game, the General called his players together in the locker room. With tears streaming down his face, Neyland told them, "I love every one of you cock-eyed bunch of fighting wildcats."

Tech would lose three of its final four games in 1948. The Tennessee defeat was quickly followed by a narrow 14-12 loss to Alabama. A 54-0 conquest of the Citadel hardly prepared Tech for what it would encounter in Athens.

The anticipation in Athens was great. The ticket demand, as usual, was so overwhelming that on Friday, the day before the game, Georgia coach Wally Butts ordered more stands built that afternoon. Every time a carpenter finished a new row of seats, one Jimmy Hayes in the McGregor printing office got a phone call with instructions on how to number the new tickets.

On the morning of the game, on the front lawn of the Sigma Alpha Epsilon fraternity house on the Georgia campus, stood an elaborate contraption of Rube Goldberg proportions. The SAE brothers had erected a replica of Wally Butts holding a bulldog on a leash. At regular intervals, the bulldog—accompanied by growling sound effects—would leap up and bite a replica of Bobby Dodd in the posterior. Thus bitten, Dodd would grab a rope and ring a miniature version of the Georgia chapel bell, which tolled only after Bulldog victories.

Late that afternoon, the actual Georgia chapel bell tolled for real. For Georgia outplayed the little Jackets 21-13 and left them with a 7-3 record and nothing to do on New Year's Day except recover from New Year's Eve.

"There were very few bowls then, not like it is now," Dodd said, "and only the big bowls were popular."

Soon, the big bowls would become a staple of life at Tech, just as little backs were already a way of life on the Flats. "We were playing with small backs back then, smaller than anybody else was playing with," Dodd said. Such backs as Billy Queen, Jimmy Jordan. "Little ones, 145 pounds, 150, 155," Dodd said. "But they could run, they were quick. We didn't have to block a lot of people. They did a good job of handling the ball, faking, freezing the linebackers.

"We couldn't stand slow football players," said Dodd, one of the all-time slowest great players. "We wanted fast guards, we wanted fast tackles."

Away from the football field, Bobby Dodd still wanted to live life in the fast lane. During his first four seasons as head coach, Dodd still played an inordinate amount of golf, bet an extraordinary amount of money at the country club and the poker table, and usually won at both games.

Dodd was a masterful putter, particularly on the putting green. In fact, Bobby Dodd's biggest golf payday took place *after* he'd finished playing a round at the Capital City Club one day. Like most golf clubs, Capital City has a putting green near the clubhouse, where you can practice putting before teeing off. This day, Dodd had just come off the course in a foursome that included a pro.

"He was a golf pro, on the circuit," Dodd said. "he was a long hitter, big fella, and could hit that ball a mile. If he'd had any kind of short game, he woulda been a real winner on the pro circuit.

"When we finished playing, it wasn't uncommon for us to go over on the putting green and start putting for money, sometimes more than we'd been playing for out on the course. And I was a good putter. I could out-putt Bobby Jones and he was a world champion. And that pro said, 'I'll putt you for $25 on nine holes.' I said, 'You can't beat me putting, you know I can putt. But I'll putt you for $25.'

"I won that. So, I don't know how the betting went, but he started doubling up—as losers do—playing for two hundred, three hundred dollars. Finally, he owed me about sixteen hundred dollars. We were putting for about four, five hundred dollars. He was doubling up and trying to get even, see. But I could out-putt him, and I knew I was gonna beat him. So I won it. Well, anyway, it ended up where he owed me either twenty-four or twenty-five hundred dollars. He said, 'I'll pay you Monday.' He's never paid me to this day.

"My short game was real good. And the crowd I played with—we all played about the same game. There wasn't too much difference. It'd really come down to the guy who could make the putt on the 17th and 18th holes. And I was a better putter than they were. I wouldn't choke up for money, and some of them would. I won a lot of money."

"Coach Dodd was the best putter in this part of the country," Frank Broyles said. "In fact, Bobby Jones once told me that if you put Coach Dodd on a putting green, he could probably out-putt anyone in the world. It didn't mean he could read the greens on the tour, but you just put him on a putting green with 18 cups and let him practice a couple of times, he'd beat anybody. He was an unbelievable putter in his time."

Dodd recalls one particular phone call from his secretary, Margie Bennett. "I was only making about twenty-five thousand then, but she told me that for the previous year, I had deposited sixty-nine thousand dollars into the bank," Dodd said. "The rest of the money was from golf and poker.

"I still played a lot of golf when I was first head coach. But I knew I was playing too much." Others felt that way, too.

There was growing concern in Atlanta—on the Flats, among Georgia Tech alumni and around town—over Dodd's public, extravagant gambling. It simply was not proper, did not suit the conservative Tech image to have the head football coach hustling some wealthy corporate honcho on the golf course. Certainly, William Alexander disapproved.

"Although Coach Aleck never told me not to do it," Dodd said, "I knew he didn't approve." Nor did other members of the administrative hierarchy.

After losing to Georgia to conclude the 1948 season, Dodd went down to Florida to fish, golf, gamble, and watch Georgia play Texas in the Orange Bowl. That was a momentous journey, and on it, Bobby Dodd's public life took two memorable turns, one right, one wrong.

The day before the Orange Bowl, Dodd and his two top assistants, Ray Graves and Ray Ellis, were coming into Miami.

As Dodd tells it:

"We were in my old DeSoto automobile that I had won in a golf game from an old guy who was an automobile dealer down in Barnesville, Georgia. And we had a small aluminum boat up on top. Didn't have trailers much back in those days, so you put your boat up top. We had been at Lake Okeechobee for four or five days, fishing hard. We had great fishing, had a lot of fun. We didn't take a bath. We were out in an ol' cabin and we didn't have a bath for five days. Just dirty as could be, and, of course, that ol' DeSoto automobile was dirty too, driving on those dirt roads back in there at Lake Okeechobee.

"On New Year's Eve, we head into Miami. We had reservations at the Seminole Hotel on Biscayne Boulevard, the main drag. And ol' Graves was driving. As we got to Biscayne, we could see there were a lot of lights on, but we didn't think anything of it. There had been a barrier up that blocked the road, but somebody moved it and left enough room to where an automobile could go through there. And ol' Graves didn't slow down a damn bit, just *wwwssshhh* right through there to Biscayne. And we made a left turn into Biscayne and there's a float back there behind us and a big float in front of us. We're right in the middle of the damn Orange Bowl parade.

"The boat's still up on top of the car, the car was dirty as hell, we were dirty as hell, and we couldn't get out of that parade. I've never been so embarrassed in all my life. The people on the sides of the streets were punching each other and asking, 'Who in the hell are they? What are they doing in there?' Graves was driving, and I was kinda cringing down here, and Ray Ellis was in the back seat laying down, staying outta sight.

"Ray Graves said, 'Coach, up there in the back of that Cadillac is the president of the Orange Bowl. You know him. Call to him and tell him to get us out of here!' So I let the window down and stuck my head out and I hollered to him up there, and he heard me. He turned around and said, 'Hey, coach, whatcha doin' back there?' I said, 'For God's sake, get us outta here!' He said, 'Oh, don't worry, soon as we get up to the reviewing stand, I'll getcha out.'

"We had to ride in that thing the whole way to the reviewing stand, must've been a quarter of a mile. We're driving just two miles an hour, with everybody looking at us. Most embarrassing thing you ever saw. When we got up in front of the reviewing stand, the judges didn't give us any prizes. But the Orange Bowl president hollered to one of the policemen and said, 'Help Coach Dodd get that car outta there.'

"The policeman thought it was funny, but we didn't. So he parted the crowd, and we pulled right up over the curb and in back of the reviewing stand. They had bleachers, and we pulled right in back of them and locked the car and ran across the street to the Seminole Hotel and upstairs. It was so embarrassing. I didn't even stop to thank the guy or see anybody that day. We just wanted to get to the hotel. Nobody would've believed that we got in that Orange Bowl parade the way we did. But we did. 'Course, it could've been worse. It could've been on national television."

A few days later Dodd met up with his friend Fred Hooper. Hooper, a wealthy man whom Dodd had often met in Montgomery, Alabama, to play golf, was by then a successful horseman in the thoroughbred racing industry. As such, he was living in Miami. More important to Dodd, though, Hooper was still a golfer and gambler.

"Fred and I, we were big buddies through the years, and we had a standing bet," Dodd said. "Wherever we met, at any time, we're gonna play for a hundred dollar Nassau. That's one hundred dollars on the first nine, a hundred on the second nine, and a hundred on the 18. So, if you can win all three of 'em, you win three hundred dollars. But you can take these fresh bets, and take another hundred dollars. If he gets two-up on me, I can say, 'All right, I'll take a fresh bet.' That means another hundred from here in.

"Well, we got out there, and I hadn't played any golf, 'cause I'd been coaching. And we got out there on his course—the Riviera Country Club—and he just beat the hell outta me. He won seven hundred dollars. I don't think I had that much in the bank. 'Course, I wrote him a check, and covered the check.

"And when I got through, I had a buddy named Charles Shepherd, who was following us around, probably betting on me, I expect. I put my golf clubs in the back of his car, and I never took 'em out. He said he carried 'em for about two years and didn't know what ever happened to 'em."

Charles Shepherd and his three brothers all attended Tech, and all became close friends with Bobby Dodd. They were ardent supporters of Dodd's football program, traveling to most road games and all bowl trips. The four brothers all worked in the family construction business.

"If I had a football player who needed a job in the summer, I just called up the Shepherds and said, 'I'm sending a boy out to you, he needs a job bad,' " Dodd said. "That's all I had to do. They put him to work on some construction project."

But the Shepherds never helped Bobby Dodd and Georgia Tech more than the day Charles Shepherd put Dodd's golf clubs in his car. "I never took 'em out to play again," Dodd said. "I decided that I was playing too much, I was head coach now and it wasn't good for the players to know that I was gambling for that much.

"And then," Dodd said, "I took up tennis."

In 1949, Tech got off to another fast start. The Yellow Jackets won four of their first five games. They survived against highly regarded Vanderbilt in the opener 12-7, yet Dodd was upset that Bobby North, his placekicker, missed both extra points. So Dodd called up two reserves, a guard named Earl Allen (both starting guards had been hurt against Vandy) and Peden Templeton.

Even in the infancy of two-platoon football, Dodd already specialized. "I want to develop an extra-point specialist who can devote at least 30 minutes daily to practice kicks," Dodd said. "North is a good kicker, but he does not have the time to devote to it as a specialist when we are working him at fullback."

The specialist found no work at Tulane, where Tech lost 18-0, the first time a Dodd team had not scored since the 1945 finale against Georgia. After winning its next three, Georgia Tech was inconsistent the remainder of the year.

After losing to Duke 27-14, Dodd returned to Knoxville. It was homecoming on the Hill and forty-five thousand spectators—the most ever to see an athletic contest in the state of Tennessee at that time—somehow squeezed into Shields-Watkins Field. Tennessee was a two-touchdown favorite, but Georgia Tech was inspired this day.

The aim of a pre-game, players-only meeting in the Georgia Tech locker room was clear: "Win this one for Coach Dodd." With Darrell Crawford, a sophomore from Kingsport, skillfully replacing the injured Jimmy Southard at quarterback, the aim was true. The Yellow Jackets stunned Tennessee 30-13.

With time still remaining on the clock, Dodd was borne across the playing field on the shoulders of his players, who lowered him so he might shake hands with Bob Neyland. The handshake completed, the Jackets again hoisted Dodd and carried him around the field and into the locker room.

"That was one of the most satisfying wins I ever had," Dodd said. "Tennessee was favored, and we had injuries, but we out-shrewded Tennessee.

"I knew what a fanatic Neyland was. He didn't like where you do anything unusual, like putting flankers out, putting three men out over here. He wanted you to line up normal.

"So I said, we're gonna split the weak side of our line and see what they do. If they start splitting with us, we'll run the quick dive play. If they don't, and they give us an angle block, we'll block down, and we'll run the sweep.

"And you know, it bothered those Tennessee boys so, my players said they were cussin' each other. They're fussin' at each other we got 'em so frustrated, and we played a helluva football game. That's one of the greatest, most satisfying games that I ever won."

So satisfying that in the locker room afterward, while hugging Darrell Crawford, Dodd shouted, "I want watches for each of these men who played today, and I want the score engraved."

The 1949 victory was the last Bobby Dodd would ever have over Bob Neyland. The Southeastern Conference was notorious for its scheduling wars, with each team trying to gain an advantage against its rivals, and Dodd and Neyland could not agree on the placement of their matchup. Dodd wanted to move the Vols earlier on the schedule to avoid the late-season gauntlet of Duke, Tennessee, Alabama, and Georgia, but Neyland wouldn't budge. Tech and Tennessee didn't play again until 1954, and by that time, Neyland had retired.

In 21 seasons, the General won 173 games, lost but 31 and tied 12 for an extraordinary winning percentage of .829. Neyland never won Bobby Dodd's affection, but Dodd always remembered, and coached by, the words Neyland wrote on a blackboard before every game Bobby Dodd played at Tennessee.

"Axioms, he called 'em," Dodd said. "I didn't know what that meant, but I knew what he was talking about: the team that makes the fewest mistakes wins. If the game is close, the kicking game will determine the outcome."

On August 18, 1953, a testimonial was held for Neyland at Cherokee Country Club in Knoxville. By then, Dodd had mellowed a bit toward his former coach and fierce rival. It was Dodd who thought to collect money from Neyland's former players to give their old coach a suitable keepsake. And it was Dodd who made the presentation to Neyland of an air-conditioned Cadillac. But it was Bear Bryant who murmured under his breath that evening, "Thank God the old guy finally quit."

After Neyland lost his last meeting with Bobby Dodd in 1949, Tech stumbled at Alabama, losing 20-7, but recovered to beat South Carolina and Georgia. For the second straight season, Tech finished 7-3 but bowl-less. That 7-6 victory over Georgia, however, would become a historical footnote. "That's a big game," Dodd still says. "The two teams were pretty evenly matched, and it was the first of my eight years that I dominated Georgia. I needed those eight years because a lot of times, I couldn't dominate Georgia. They were tough, boy, let me tell you."

In 1949, no one, especially Bobby Dodd, would have believed that Tech would whip Georgia, the state university with all its recruiting advantages, for eight consecutive years. The reign had begun for Tech, but over in Athens, they called it the Drought.

At the time, of course, Dodd couldn't know the reign had begun. Nor could he imagine the pain of the season to come—1950, one of the most trying seasons of his career.

"That '50 season was very disappointing to me," said Dodd. "I was ready to quit at the end of the season. I was very depressed."

"He was very down," said Alice Dodd. "It was just terrible. He'd come home wearing a gray suit, you couldn't tell where it stopped and he started. It was pitiful. He was so down, you didn't even want to tease him."

Suddenly, Dodd was having trouble recruiting players. The problem was partially academic. Several recruits couldn't qualify for Tech, and Dodd felt he was being badly beaten in the recruiting wars by Georgia, Alabama, and Tennessee. This was particularly significant, because, as substitution rules evolved toward the two-platoon system, college football was becoming a game of numbers, with larger squads and more emphasis on depth at all positions. Dodd was naturally worried that the increasing recruiting problems would limit his ability to compete.

In addition, injuries caused the Tech talent pool to come up dangerously shallow. "We knew we were in trouble," Dodd said, "and we ended up having a very poor year by our standards."

The poorest of years by Dodd standards. Georgia Tech lost its first two games in 1950, the only time that ever happened during Dodd's head coaching career. After a 33-13 embarrassment by Southern Methodist and 7-0 loss to South Carolina, the Yellow Jackets responded with a three-point decision over Florida and shutouts of LSU and Auburn.

"We had no business beating LSU," Dodd said. "How in the world we won down there I'll never know. We were weak and LSU was a better football team than we were."

LSU also realized that. But the day before the game, several LSU players watched Tech engage in its customary volleyball game during Friday practice. The Tigers left the stadium confident. Too confident. Saturday night, after Tech engineered a 13-0 upset, one LSU player sought to explain the inexplicable: "We were at least two touchdowns better. They were so loose and relaxed that we played that way, and they beat us."

That left Tech with a 3-2 mark, but the next month left Bobby Dodd dazed and disillusioned. The Yellow Jackets lost their next four games, the longest losing streak in Dodd's 22 seasons as a head coach. The losses to Bear Bryant's Kentucky team (led by quarterback Babe Parilli) and Duke were painful. A 14-13 upset by VMI on Grant Field was downright embarrassing. But Tech reached its nadir in a 54-19 humiliation administered by Alabama's powerful passing game. Those were the most points ever scored against a Bobby Dodd team. And it deeply wounded Dodd.

A season-ending 7-0 win in Athens was a salve for Dodd but not a remedy. Both Tech and Georgia, he realized, were weak that year. And Tech had had another losing season, finishing 5-6 for its second losing season in six years under Dodd. Although administrations, alumni, boosters, and the media were far more tolerant of losing football coaches back then than they are today, there was still some grumbling, some public criticism over Dodd's losing record. Also, the Jackets would not be playing in a bowl game for the third straight year.

Bobby Dodd knew all that too well. What he could not know, however, was two-fold:

He would never have to endure another losing season as head coach. And from the moment of that humbling loss to Alabama, Georgia Tech would not lose again for another 31 games.

None of that mattered, though, when the 1950 season finally, mercifully came to a close. Bobby Dodd called his brother, John, who was still living back in Kingsport and working as an accountant. "I told John I was either going to have to quit, or go to another school," Dodd said. "I was not getting enough football players to win."

He was not getting any younger, either. Dodd had turned 42 by the end of the season, but that was chronologically speaking. One can only imagine how much the stressful season had aged Dodd. Physically, he was tired. And philosophically, he was tired of the constant battle between academics and athletics at Georgia Tech. To Dodd, there seemed to be only one way out.

"I was thinking about going some other place," he said. "I was just depressed, really depressed. My Lord, I'd gotten humiliated on Grant Field by Alabama; all the home folks saw that.

"But I wouldn't have been a loser long," Bobby Dodd said. "I wouldn't have stayed in coaching if I was gonna be a loser. That wasn't my nature. I would've quit coaching. I wouldn't have gone through what some of these coaches go through today. Hell, I wouldn't have gone through what Bill Curry went through. My Lord."

Fortunately for Georgia Tech, Bobby Dodd changed the forecast dramatically after that 1950 debacle. "The sun came out," Dodd said, grinning. "Boy, it came out from behind a dark cloud."

But not until Bobby Dodd had to make the most painful decision of his life.

"The most depressing thing I ever had to do," Dodd said, "was to take Ray Ellis and Dwight Keith and tell them that there wasn't any place for them, really. And I had to let them go. Broke my heart to do it."

Dodd wanted—no, needed—younger and more knowledgeable assistants, coaches who could produce better football players, as well as improve Tech's recruiting. Ray Ellis and Dwight Keith were older, contemporaries of Dodd. They were also his good friends.

Furthermore, Alice Dodd's best friend was Dwight Keith's wife, Randa, and they were quite close to Martha Ellis. All three couples enjoyed each other's company, especially on Saturday nights after games, when they all met at the Dodds' for a steak dinner.

"We were all close back in those days," Dodd said. "When you only have a small coaching staff like we had, you become close.

"And when you get together on a Saturday night after getting beat on Saturday afternoon, you don't want to be around anybody but your coaching staff and their wives."

So the decision was excruciating, but necessary. And Dodd knew he had to make changes to regain a competitive edge.

There were actually three significant reasons that Bobby Dodd's outlook and Tech's performance made drastic improvements in 1951: he had a new staff of assistants, a new wrinkle to his offense (the belly series), and enough experienced players to take advantage of the two platoon system. The first of these changes was Dodd's revamped—and expanded—

coaching staff.

Dodd retained Ray Graves, who was a fine line coach and outstanding defensive coach. For the 1951 season, Graves installed the "monster defense" (the monster man was a roving, linebacker-defensive back hybrid). Graves had learned the monster, which was designed to stop the split-T, from Oklahoma's Bud Wilkinson.

On offense, Dodd brought Frank Broyles back home to the Flats. "Broyles was a big asset," Dodd said. "He was enthusiastic and a real good offensive coach."

It was Broyles, under Dodd's guidance, who introduced the belly series to Tech football. In the summer of 1950, Dodd returned to Chicago to serve as an assistant coach for the college all-star team. This time, one of Dodd's quarterbacks was a half-pint Houdini named Eddie LeBaron.

One day during practice, Dodd recalled, "Eddie and I were out there fooling around, which we'd do every once in a while. Hiding the ball, talking about different things. And he told me they had this play at Pacific which they got a lot out of, called the belly series. I said, 'Show it to me.' "

LeBaron demonstrated the belly series. Dodd was captivated. "He was clever as could be," Dodd said. "Just a great quarterback.

"Anyway, he showed me the belly series and I immediately knew it was good."

It was the kind of offensive attack in which Bobby Dodd would have thrived as a quarterback, relying on ballhandling, deception, and quick thinking. "The secret of it," Dodd said as he jumped to his feet to demonstrate, putting his hands together as if taking the snap from center, then pivoting to hand off, "was that the quarterback had the option at the line of scrimmage, either to hand off to the fullback coming up the middle or to pull it back and go wide. Sometimes, of course, he'd give him the ball, but the fullback's covered up by the line blocking, and the linebackers over there can't see if he's got the ball. And we blocked just exactly the same whether we're gonna give him the ball or not.

"And then if we don't give it to him, the quarterback takes the ball and he pitches it back to the halfback, who's gonna run wide. We would freeze the linebackers with the fullback fake and then pitch the ball. And we'd outrun 'em. I had speed galore. So we used the belly series, and we got a lot out of it."

A lot more out of it than Pacific had, even with Eddie LeBaron. For Dodd didn't just run the belly, he fattened it, expanded it. Pacific ran the basic belly play, Dodd recalled. "But we added other plays. We added what we called the inside belly. We rode the fullback and then we handed the ball right behind him to the halfback, hitting off tackle, right off of his butt. Instead of going wide, we went off tackle.

"Then we got to where we put men in motion. We found out whether they'd go with the man in motion; if they did, we'd go back the other way. We did a lot with the belly series."

Especially Frank Broyles, who may have done too much with the belly series for Dodd's liking. It was Broyles, a staunch believer in the belly who extolled its virtues at coaching clinics, who also wrote the chapter on the belly series in *Bobby Dodd on Football.*

"Told everybody everything we were doing," Dodd said, smiling. "I didn't like that. I didn't want everybody to know everything we knew about the belly series. But he and Graves, they wanted to make money. But we got a lot out of it before other people started copying us. And we did more with it and stayed ahead of 'em a little bit. By the time they'd catch up with us this year, we'd do something different next year."

The belly series was a forerunner of the triple option, the wishbone offense that would dominate college football in the late 1960s and 1970s. There was one fundamental difference. "We didn't want our quarterback running with the ball," said Dodd, who had run only when absolutely necessary while playing at Tennessee. "In the split-T and the triple option, the quarterback runs with the ball some. We didn't want our quarterback running the ball because our quarterbacks couldn't run, to start with. And we were afraid they'd get hurt.

"People like Broyles, he was not a runner, so we didn't believe much in the quarterback running the ball. Later, we had Bill Brigman and Pepper Rodgers, but Pepper couldn't run as fast as I could."

Dodd's revamped coaching staff of 1951 was critical to both his immediate and long-range success. It wasn't just the individuals he hired, but how many, and how he deployed them.

"He was the first coach to be chairman of the board," Frank Broyles said. "All other head coaches had been active in the on-field coaching and the assistant coaches just kinda helped out. But Coach Dodd was the first one who saw the advantages of being chairman of the board and delegating the responsibility. So he delegated to me the offensive part of the game, and to Ray Graves the defensive."

"I coached the coaches," Dodd said, "and then they coached the players."

Dodd's decision to become the chairman of the board was a shrewd, timely maneuver. The two-platoon system had gradually been accepted (1950 was the first year players chosen for the all-American team were separated into offensive and defensive categories). No longer did the 11 best athletes have to play both offense and defense. No longer did players have to perform all 60 minutes. The age of specialization had dawned in college football, and Dodd was wide awake well before dawn.

"We started playing a boy for what he could do, and nothing else," Dodd said. "If he could cover a punt, we'd let him cover a punt. If he could cover a kickoff, he'd cover a kickoff. If he could play defense, we'd play him on defense. We just played him on what he could do.

"And we carried 55 players, whatever was necessary. We'd keep 'em all, and we kept 'em all happy 'cause they were all getting in the game, and we were winning with it. We were very specialized, *very* specialized."

Naturally, the coaches had to be as specialized as the players. "One thing that helped us a great deal is that that was the year I organized my coaching staff into offense and defense," Dodd said. "Three offensive coaches, three defensive coaches. They had their group meetings. I had a B team coach and a freshmen coach. We had a good organization, real good. And we had more coaches than most people had at that time."

All of that is now standard coaching and organizational procedure in college football. It was an innovation in 1951, however, and Bobby Dodd was one of the original innovators. In addition to Broyles and Graves, Dodd brought in Whitey Urban and Lewis Woodruff to work with the offense, and Jack Griffin and Tonto Coleman to help Graves on defense.

Tonto Coleman—who would later become Dodd's assistant athletic director and then commissioner of the Southeastern Conference—became Dodd's defensive end coach. "Tonto loved 'em," Dodd said. "In coaches meetings, you couldn't criticize the defensive ends, or Tonto'd get mad. You couldn't say anything about 'em. Tonto was something. He loved 'em like each one was his own son and treated 'em just like that. And they all loved him."

Dodd wanted to keep all his players happy, not just Tonto Coleman's defensive ends, but he had special instructions for his assistants regarding the proper care of freshmen. "I wanted my coaches to be good to those freshmen. I didn't want them leaving 'cause they were unhappy. It's bad enough to come to Georgia Tech to be a football player and have to go to school and study as much as you had to, without being cussed out on that football field. I was afraid they'd get depressed and pack up their bags and leave. They did that a lot of places, you know. And I told my freshmen coaches, 'You keep 'em happy, we'll do the coaching next year.' "

If a boy got homesick, Dodd let him go home, stay for three or four days, and come back when he was all right. "We petted 'em and pampered 'em like they were prize bulls," Dodd said. "I made my coaches be interested in 'em, talk to 'em every day: 'Are you all right? Got any problems? Anybody unhappy at home?' If a boy was unhappy, we wanted to know why he was unhappy. We treated 'em better than anybody in the United States."

"That's why they still love Bobby so much now," Alice Dodd said. "They realize they had it pretty good. They were well treated, and he always loved them."

The feeling was mutual. "If you played football for Coach Dodd, you didn't like him, you loved him," Paul Duke said. "Anybody who's ever played regular for him would do anything for him. He made us think we could do anything. Same thing in academics. He had a way of motivating us and making us study. His talent to lead youngsters and his technical knowledge of football are his two touches of greatness."

A quarter-century after Frank Broyles returned to Georgia Tech, upon the occasion of Bobby Dodd's retirement as athletic director in 1975, he wrote his former coach and boss a letter of congratulations and thanks. "You taught me the true responsibility of a coach," wrote Broyles, "and that is to be most concerned with the welfare of the young men entrusted to you. If you do that, you can let the scoreboard take care of itself.

"That was a lesson to me in starting my career as a head coach," Broyles now says. "If every coach in America had coached under Coach Dodd, there would be a different attitude and philosophy now, and the image of college football would not have the black eye that it has today."

In 1951, everything came together for Bobby Dodd and Georgia Tech. Caught so short-handed the previous season ("We were playing B-teamers against the opposition," said Ray Graves), Tech suddenly had a surfeit of experienced players. The underclassmen from the 1949 and 1950 teams had played extensively because of the plague of injuries, and the rising sophomore class was exceptional. They all would benefit from several things: the two-platoon rule; the belly offense and monster defense; the energy and expertise of Dodd's new coaching staff; but mainly from Dodd himself. From his exuberant personality, unflappable sideline demeanor, uncanny strategies, and uncommonly courteous treatment of his players.

In the golden autumn of 1951, the golden age of Georgia Tech football had begun.

The chairman of the board
and the Rose Bowl Field tower.

Chapter 9
The Dawn of the Golden Era

FOR GEORGE MORRIS, THE GENESIS of the 1951 Georgia Tech football team actually began a year earlier, under circumstances that were anything but golden. Morris was a sophomore in 1950 on that awful November day when Alabama came to Grant Field and embarrassed Bobby Dodd and Georgia Tech as they had never before been embarrassed, 54-19.

"The last game we lost," Morris said, still cringing at the memory. "They had us 35-0 at the half. We tied 'em 19-19 in the second half. They killed us passing, and Bobby Marlow scored the first three times he touched the ball, one of them 92 yards.

"We went in at the half and Coach Dodd said, 'Well, it looks like we're gonna get beat,' " Morris laughed. "Then he said, 'But let's don't go out with our heads down.' And we went out and played 'em—head up—pretty good in the second half. We beat Davidson the next week, when it was seven degrees out here, and then we beat Georgia in Athens. But the second half of that Alabama game is when that team, that group of players, started maturing."

George Morris grew up the son of a military man and came to Tech from Vicksburg, Mississippi. Although his father was an Alabama graduate, he was delighted when Georgia Tech recruited George. Of all the schools courting his son, he felt that Tech had the best academic atmosphere, and told George, "The rest of them just want you to come play football."

One morning, while a high school senior, Morris took the train from Vicksburg with his father, who had some military business to attend to in Atlanta. While there, they also stopped by Georgia Tech to meet Bobby Dodd.

Despite the cold chill of a November rain, the father and son came away impressed with Atlanta, Tech, and especially Dodd. "He charmed me," Morris said, "and he explained to my father his philosophy about student-athletes. That wasn't the terminology they used in those days, but it was the student-athlete approach. Coach Dodd said, 'The boys get an education, and we treat them fair, and we treat them good. And one more thing: we play good football.' " All the basic ingredients of Bobby Dodd's recruiting pitch to prospects and parents.

Back home in Vicksburg, George Morris suddenly just knew. "I don't know whether you've experienced this or not, but I have a few times in my life," Morris said. "We always ate breakfast together as a family, and one morning I woke up and walked in and said, 'Dad, I've made up my mind. I want to go to Georgia Tech.' That pleased him immensely."

It also pleased Bobby Dodd. "That's the greatest day of my life as a coach, signing George," Dodd said. But it displeased most everyone else in Mississippi. "I caught hell for a few weeks in the newspapers," Morris said. "You know how they select all-state teams? Well, some of them didn't want me to make the all-state team because I had abandoned the state of Mississippi, and Ole Miss or Mississippi State."

"Those folks over there hated to lose a boy like that," Dodd said. "And to lose him to Georgia Tech. They hated me worse than anybody, 'cause I wouldn't play 'em.

"A lot of coaches don't want to say who's the best football player they ever had," Bobby Dodd said. "I don't ever say who's the best back I ever coached, because really, it's hard for me to say that. But George Morris is the best football player I ever coached. Not only because of his play on the football field, his physical play—his fierce tackling. But he was a great leader. George ran the football team when he was out there.

"And after I got him, I got his younger brother Jimmy. Both of 'em were captain of the football team when they came along [George, along with Hal Miller, in 1952 and Jimmy in 1955]. But I'll tell you, of all the people who ate, he and his brother could eat more than any three people at a damn training table. Miss Twiggs used to tell me that when she'd bring out a big bowl of mashed potatoes, instead of passing 'em around, George and Jimmy just took the bowl, and she had to go back for another."

As Morris and his teammates prepared for the 1951 season, Dodd was encouraged. "I could finally see some daylight after the gloom of the previous year," he said. But he could not foresee how his 1951 Jackets would fare.

"Not until we got into the season," Dodd said. "You don't really know when you've got a lot of new players coming in, and new coaches, but I knew we were doing a better job of coaching. The thing is, you don't ever know how good that other team is you're gonna play against."

For the next two-and-a-half seasons, none of those other teams were better than Bobby Dodd's. "That '51 season was a terrific season," Dodd said, "and the start of six great years of football."

Dodd had some fine players on offense—a pair of ferocious tackles,

Hal Miller and Lum Snyder, guard Ray Beck, center Pete Brown, end Buck Martin, quarterback Darrell Crawford, and the "Kid Backfield" which included senior George Maloof and two sophomores, Larry Ruffin and the undersized but untouchable Leon Hardeman. On defense, linebacker George Morris had ample support from players like tackle Lamar Wheat and a quiet, versatile kid named Larry Morris (no relation to George).

And not only did Georgia Tech have 22 talented starters, but Dodd had abundant depth as well. "We had good backups on both offense and defense," Dodd said. "If we had anybody hurt, we had pretty good talent in back of 'em. That team couldn't have been any better to coach, couldn't have had any better year."

Georgia Tech opened the 1951 season at home against Southern Methodist. The day before the game, Tech conducted its customary brief, light workout at Grant Field. Although his offensive and defensive starting lineups were set, Dodd still hadn't settled on a placekicker. His choices were two sophomores, running back Glenn Turner and backup quarterback Pepper Rodgers.

"Glenn Turner had the best form and could kick that ball high, had great range, and the ball came off the tee high," said Frank Broyles. "Pepper's ball didn't get very high and just barely got over the crossbar."

During the Friday practice, Dodd approached Broyles and said, "Frank, who do you think ought to do the placekicking?"

"No question about it—Glenn Turner," Broyles replied. "Look at the difference in the balls when they kick."

"Well, I'll tell you who's gonna be the placekicker in just a minute," Dodd said. "Follow me."

Dodd walked over to Turner and said, "Glenn, if I chose you to do the kicking tomorrow, do you think you can do it?"

"Coach, I'll give it my best effort," Turner said.

Then Dodd walked over to Rodgers and repeated the question.

"Coach, I'll never miss," Rodgers said.

"Well," Dodd told him, "you'll do the kicking."

Dodd not only instilled confidence in his players, he recognized and valued those players who arrived on the Flats already brimming with confidence. Players like Pepper Rodgers. Rodgers was perfect on all three of his placements against SMU, and Tech won 21-7. Pepper would go more than two seasons before missing an extra point, and he would later kick one of the most vital field goals in Georgia Tech history.

After shutting out Florida 27-0, the Yellow Jackets traveled to Lexington to meet Bear Bryant's Kentucky team. In 1950, the Wildcats had lost but once, 7-0 to Tennessee in the regular season finale, before stopping top-ranked Oklahoma's winning streak at 31 in the Sugar Bowl. But in 1951, despite having Babe Parilli at quarterback, Kentucky had lost two of its first three games.

Although Tech was greatly improved in 1951, Dodd felt Kentucky was still the superior team. By halftime, Dodd knew Kentucky was also the rougher team. The first half ended, and the Yellow Jackets went to their locker room, awaiting Bobby Dodd. "We waited, and we waited, and we waited," Crawford said. "He'd stopped to talk to the officials. Finally, the door bursts open and Coach Dodd strides in, as only he can. His hat's pulled down and his face is red. Frank Broyles was diagramming something on the blackboard, but when we saw Coach Dodd, everyone got so quiet you could hear a pin drop."

And then Dodd addressed his players. His men, as he always called them, or his "min," as Dodd pronounces the word.

"Min, I have been out there talking with the officials and I've complained to them and asked them to get this game under control. They have not given me any satisfaction. Min, I have never told this to any of my teams. But when you go out there in the second half, all I can tell you is, protect yourself."

The Jackets more than protected themselves. Johnny Hicks broke a 69-yard touchdown run. In the fourth quarter, on a fourth-and-one situation in his territory and leading 7-6, Bear Bryant ordered his team to go for the first down. The hole was there, a cavernous hole, but the running back slipped and Tech took over. On the first play, Crawford passed—a favorite Dodd ploy after a turnover or critical change of possession—for a touchdown and a 13-7 victory.

The following Monday morning, the telephone rang in Bobby Dodd's office. The Bear was calling.

"He said in that ol' gravelly voice of his, 'What in the hell is wrong with us?' " Dodd recalled. "And I said, 'Bear, you're getting penalized. You had 120 yards a game, you oughta been penalized 250. Your players are hitting out of bounds. They're not stopping on the whistle. You're clipping on every play. Your players are so damn scared of you that they don't pay attention to the whistle. It's hard to beat a good football team, Bear, when you're getting penalized that much.'

"And he said, 'Well, we won't be doing that anymore. What do you do?' "

For reasons both ethical and practical Bobby Dodd's teams were consistently among the least penalized in the South. Although Dodd was a fierce competitor, and was not above a little chicanery to get an advantage, he did not tolerate dirty football. He also remembered what General Neyland had preached before every game at Tennessee: The team with the fewest penalties wins. For years, that team was Georgia Tech.

Although it is now a common practice in college football, Dodd was one of the first coaches to have football officials work his intrasquad scrimmages. There was never a shortage of practice officials from which to choose. Many of Dodd's former Tech players, already out working in the business world, also went into officiating to stay involved with football in some capacity.

"Most people just scrimmaged and let them hit," Dodd said. "They didn't pay any attention to clipping or holding. We worked on our players, though, and we did it better than anybody else. We were one of the few teams in the United States that did that."

Coaches in those days, and especially in the South, were quite fraternal. They frequently, informally, shared views and information. "It wasn't uncommon for us to call if one of us had run into a tough team or something," Dodd said. "Coaches today usually aren't as close to each other. They don't trust each other. But Bear and I did that. That wasn't uncommon."

Theirs was an uncommon relationship that developed into an uncommon friendship. Highly competitive and eminently successful, Dodd and Bryant would become two of the most dominant collegiate coaches in the nation. Their methods, though, were drastically different, almost diametrically opposed. Yet there existed a mutual respect between the two men, and a deep friendship, which would only make their later difficulties even more painful.

"Bear and I kinda took a liking to each other," said Dodd, who had tried to hire Bryant as his first assistant when Dodd got the Tech head coaching job in 1945. "He felt real good about that. And then, when he got up to Kentucky, we got pretty close."

When Bryant took the Kentucky job, he called Dodd and asked him to come up to Lexington and help him install the T formation in spring practice. "When I did that with him," Dodd said, "then I got to know him real well."

Nearly a decade later, after Bryant had left Kentucky, left stories of brutality and the reality of probation at Texas A & M, and returned to his Alabama alma mater, the friendship was renewed and then strengthened. "Bear would come to Atlanta—he liked to come to the big city," Dodd said. "He'd go down to the Capital City Club and use my card. He liked to go to a nice place and have dinner."

After defeating Kentucky, Tech easily beat LSU 25-7. Next on the schedule was a tough Auburn team. Auburn had not defeated Georgia Tech since 1940, but Dodd was concerned, particularly with Auburn's defensive ability to stop the run.

On the Sunday before the game, assistant coaches Sam Lyle, Bo Hagan, and Bob Bossons watched scouting films with Frank Broyles.

"The more we looked at the film, the gloomier we got," Lyle said. "We couldn't see a thing we could run against Auburn's defense. They had everything stopped. Frank's head was just dragging between his legs and he said, 'I don't know what we'll do. What will we tell Coach Dodd?' "

In another room, watching films of the Auburn offense, defensive coordinator Ray Graves felt a similar sickness gnawing at his stomach. Graves thought this was the best Auburn offense he'd ever seen. "We went back home that night," Lyle said, "and the idea was for everybody to come up with something, *anything* that might work against them."

Each Monday morning, Bobby Dodd met with his staff in a conference room just off his office. Having watched the opposition's game films, the assistants—particularly Broyles and Graves—were to present to Dodd the basic game plan for that week. The Monday morning meetings were always held at nine o'clock. By eight-fifteen this morning, however, all the assistants were already in the conference room.

"On offense, nobody had come up with anything," Lyle said. "The defense had nothing, either."

Then the door at the far end of the meeting room flew open and in walked Bobby Dodd, smoking a cigar. "And then he threw his big ol' feet up on the corner of the table," Lyle said. Dodd always sat on the far left corner of the rectangular table, directly across the table from Graves and the other defensive coaches, and beside Broyles and his offensive aides. As usual, Dodd was chipper. On this somber morning, he seemed disgustingly chipper.

"All right, fellas," Dodd began cheerily enough, "what are we gonna do against Auburn?"

Silence. A prolonged, profound silence. Dodd looked at Graves and asked, "Do you think we can stop Auburn?"

"No," Graves replied. "This may be the toughest game we play all year."

"Frank?"

"I've tried everything, Coach," Broyles said. "I've gone back through the playbook and I can't think of a single thing we can do against them. That's the best defense I've ever seen."

"I can't believe you guys," scoffed Dodd. "Put the films on, let's take a look."

The lights were dimmed, and then the projector flashed the terrifying images of Auburn on the screen to Dodd's left. The first part of a scheduled double feature was Auburn's defense. Dodd had seen only the first quarter when he announced, "Turn it off."

The lights came back on shortly after the light had come on in Bobby Dodd's head. "Why, we'll run the Kingsport Play against these guys."

"Everybody wanted to know what in the hell the Kingsport Play was," Sam Lyle recalled. "We'd never run it, never even heard of it."

Frank Broyles was particularly dubious, as was his wont.

"When Dodd came up with something, Broyles would always look around like this," Lyle said, squinting, a look of concern on his face as he looked back and forth at the other assistants in the room. "Like Dodd is gonna give us something we're not sure of, or something we can't do."

"It's a simple little ol' play," Dodd assured them. "Paul Hug and I ran this at Kingsport High School. No one's ever stopped it."

Dodd was certain Auburn would not stop it, either. Like most teams back then, Auburn played a wide-tackle six defense, with two inside linebackers and a three-deep secondary. Like most defenses back then, Auburn concentrated on stopping the off-tackle play. "If you couldn't stop someone off tackle, you got beat," Lyle said.

In just the first quarter of film of the Auburn defense, Dodd realized how quickly Auburn reacted to offensive flow. Against an off-tackle play to the left, Dodd saw that the defensive halfback to that side fired up quickly to support against the run. The safety then rotated over to the defensive back's original area, and the weak side halfback moved to the middle. Dodd was certain the Kingsport Play would work, if quarterback Darrell Crawford made a good, prolonged fake to his left before boot-legging back to the right. Out of the straight T, right end Buck Martin would go down on all fours, as if throwing a block, seemingly out of the play, then suddenly rise and race for the flag in the right corner of the end zone.

That Monday afternoon, Dodd helped install the play from his tower, the wooden edifice on which the chairman of the board sat in a folding chair and oversaw practice. Dodd called down from the tower often that day, making certain that Martin ran his pattern correctly and that Crawford faked sufficiently before spinning back to the right. By the end of the day, Dodd was satisfied. By late Saturday afternoon, he was vindicated, on the scoreboard and in the wallet. Dodd and Graves had made a standing bet of ten dollars for every time the Kingsport Play was called. Dodd insisted Tech would score each time.

The safety on that 1951 Auburn team was a sophomore named Vince Dooley, who in 1964 would become the head coach at Georgia. That day, though, Dooley just became more frustrated as the game wore on. "I remember Buck Martin ran right over me," Dooley said.

Martin caught four touchdown passes on the Kingsport Play that day,

141

all thrown by Darrell Crawford, whose faking was as essential to its success as Auburn's aggressiveness.

"We set it up by running the off-tackle play two or three times," Crawford said. "We couldn't believe it would happen like Coach Dodd said it would, but it did."

It happened four times, exactly as Bobby Dodd had said it would. Crawford's touchdown passes to Martin, covering 14, 13, 73, and 31 yards, tied a Georgia Tech record shared by Eddie Prokop and Frank Broyles (Eddie McAshan broke it with five against Rice in 1972). Buck Martin still holds a share of the Tech single-game records for points scored and touchdown receptions. All because of the Kingsport Play.

"It's the only play we made any yardage on that day," Lyle said. "Ol' Dodd's Kingsport Play won the Auburn game, and I don't think anybody ever again questioned anything he did."

Tech was 6-0, but barely, after Glenn Turner's touchdown, a safety, and the mud in Nashville all combined to help the Jackets outlast Vanderbilt 8-7. Coming home for homecoming, Georgia Tech led Duke 14-7 on Crawford's quarterback sneak and a 50-yard return of a blocked punt by Ray Beck. Late in the game, however, Duke's Worth (a Million) Lutz enhanced his value with a two-yard touchdown run to tie Tech 14-14. That night would be the only Saturday evening all season that the Yellow Jackets had no cause to celebrate.

VMI fell easily 34-7, and then Dodd had the opportunity to avenge his worst defeat. Alabama. Dodd always respected and sometimes feared Alabama, but this time he was confident.

With good reason. Tech 27, Alabama 7. It could have been worse, much worse. "I called 'em off," Dodd said.

He did not call off the Jackets against the Dawgs, though.

Georgia had an exceptional quarterback in 1951 in Zeke Bratkowski. For Zeke, though, this day on Grant Field was the one exception to an otherwise outstanding season. "When you get behind us, and we know you've gotta throw," Dodd said, "we're a good pass defense team."

In all, Tech intercepted Bratkowski eight times, an SEC record. By halftime, Georgia Tech was already leading 34-0, the largest halftime margin in series history. By halftime, George Maloof had already scored four times from short yardage.

Leon Hardeman and Buck Martin would also score, and Larry Morris returned the eighth interception 55 yards for the seventh Tech touchdown in the 48-6 romp. It was Tech's third consecutive triumph over Georgia and is still the largest victory margin for Tech in the series. For Ed Danforth, it conjured up memories of the roaring '20s, of Tech's Golden Tornado, even its 1928 national champions. It gave Tech a share of the SEC title with Tennessee and a return to the bowl scene after a three-year absence. On New Year's Day in Miami, Georgia Tech would play Baylor in the Orange Bowl.

"This was very exciting to us because the Orange Bowl was very glamorous," Dodd said. "We didn't know much about Baylor, except we knew that anybody that won in that Southwest Conference was tough. I had great respect for the Southwest Conference, Texas, SMU, Baylor and those teams."

After this game, the nation would have great respect for Tech and, in subsequent years, even greater respect for the Yellow Jackets and their bowl prowess. But before the 1952 Orange Bowl, most people seemed more suspicious than respectful of Tech's bowl chances, primarily because of Dodd's bowl preparations.

"We went down there, and the newspapermen made big stuff of the fact that I didn't scrimmage my boys," Dodd said, "and the fact that I let them go out to events and parties. We'd go see the sights."

Unlike most of his coaching contemporaries—and even more coaches today—Bobby Dodd viewed bowl games as a reward for his players, for their good work during the regular season. Certainly, he wanted to win bowl games and expected his assistants and players to prepare properly and perform to their full capabilities. But he also expected them to enjoy themselves.

As right and proper as Dodd's attitude was, it may have been more appropriate for his time, when there was less pressure to win bowl games, both financially and in the polls. Bowls paid out far less money to college teams than they do now; indeed, that 1952 Orange Bowl was not even televised, and television rights are a major source of bowl revenue. Since there were far fewer bowls, fewer college athletic departments figured a bowl payoff into their annual operating budgets.

Also, the final wire service polls were conducted after the regular season and before the bowls were played. Numerous national champions were later beaten in a bowl game; in fact, Tennessee, the 1951 national champion, lost to Maryland in the Sugar Bowl.

Bobby Dodd's bowl philosophy was just part of his overall football philosophy, which he often recounted for Ray Graves. Said Graves, "He always said, 'In football, you're not supposed to go undefeated. Win about seven, lose three and tie one, go to a bowl game and play somebody you can beat.' He said, 'You can spoil 'em.' Not that Bobby liked to lose, though. He wanted to beat you in tennis, golf, gin rummy, fishing."

In everything. But for Georgia Tech, a bowl game was much more a scenic cruise than a crusade. "It wasn't like these coaches today," Dodd said, "the way they wrap their players up and won't let 'em get out and fussin' all the time, and having trouble with the other team and everything, like Penn State and Miami were having [in the 1987 Fiesta Bowl]. We didn't have those controversies. We had a good time. All my people had such a good time.

"We were a favorite of the bowl people because we brought a lot of people with us, a lot of fans, and they liked that. The hotels sure did. We acted the way they wanted us to act, and we attended all the functions. And my players were always dressed properly in coats and ties. We knew how to act."

And while his players often wore their Sunday best in Dallas or Jacksonville, they hardly felt confined.

"Nobody ever had as much fun on bowl trips as we did and still won," Dodd said. "That's one thing. If I'd lost, I would've had to quit doing it that way.

"I was so lenient with 'em, with the habits and rules and everything. But I got a big kick out of it, and I thought, 'They're not gonna let me down. They're gonna play for me when I'm good to 'em.' And they did."

After the regular season ended, after bowl bids had been extended, Tech would hold a couple of weeks of light workouts. There were final exams to be taken. And then, when Georgia Tech would let out for the holidays, Bobby Dodd would let his players go home for Christmas, just like the rest of the student body. After fattening up on home cooking, the Yellow Jackets returned to Tech on December 26. They would practice for a couple of days and then hit the bowl town two or three days before New Year's.

For many Tech players, bowl trips took on added significance. Dodd always took his coaches' wives to bowl games, as well as players' wives, so many Tech players would get married during Christmas and New Year's, and get an all-expenses paid honeymoon in Miami, or New Orleans, or Dallas.

In the closing days of 1951, the Florida press viewed the Tech "football as fun" attitude skeptically. It contrasted sharply with Baylor's more serious, conventional approach.

Furman Bisher, however, then a young sportswriter covering Tech for the *Journal*, saw it a bit differently. Bisher had been exposed daily to Dodd's team back in Atlanta. Where others saw Tech lolling in the Florida sun, Bisher saw a relatively feverish preparation.

Bisher described how very hard Dodd worked that day, especially for him. Indeed, it was "almost alarming," wrote Bisher, who, like everyone else, was accustomed to seeing Bobby Dodd in "a perfect state of relaxation." But this, Bisher knew, "was no pleasure trip for Tech."

"It was tough," Dodd said. "It was real tough."

It was also hot and humid in Miami that New Year's Day, the temperature in the 80s. To combat the heat, Dodd used even more players than he usually did. In the first half alone, 40 different Jackets played, including 22 on defense. Baylor coach George Sauer, meanwhile, used less than 30 players. The fatigue factor would play a critical role in the second half, particularly in the fourth quarter. With nine minutes to play, Tech trailed 14-7.

"We were having trouble scoring on them, making much ground," Dodd said. "They were just tough physically. I was sitting there by Graves—Broyles was up in the press box—and Graves said, 'How in the hell are we gonna make any ground? What can we score on?' I said, 'Let's try a screen pass. You got a chance on that, you got a chance.' "

Dodd called for a screen pass to George Maloof, who carried it 35 yards before being tackled inside the Baylor 20. On the next play, Dodd instructed Crawford to throw the pass he had completed against Kentucky for the winning touchdown. It worked again, to Buck Martin again, and when Pepper Rodgers kicked the point after, the game was tied at 14-all with less than six minutes to play.

Dodd decided against an onside kick. "I said, 'No, if we tie this game, Baylor's not gonna be satisfied with a tie, 'cause they were leading and thought they were a better team than we were,' " Dodd said. "And I thought maybe we'd get a chance to intercept a pass.

"So sure enough, we kick off to them, and they're back there around their 20, and they throw a pass and we intercept it."

Pete Ferris intercepted a pass in the flat thrown by Larry Isbell, Baylor's all-American quarterback, and Ferris returned it 36 yards to the Baylor nine-yard line. After three plays gained three yards, Dodd checked with sophomore Pepper Rodgers on the sideline.

"I kinda tried to get him loose," Dodd said. "I asked him, 'Pepper, you can make it, can't you?' " He said, 'Oh yeah, oh yeah, Coach, I can make it!' And he kicked it."

The ball had barely left Rodgers's foot when he threw his arms skyward, signaling to an Orange Bowl record crowd of 65,837 that the kick was indeed good. It was the first field goal ever to win an Orange Bowl, and it left Larry Isbell in tears in the locker room. It also gave Georgia Tech, already ranked fifth in both wire service polls, an 11-0-1 record. It was the first undefeated season for Tech in 33 years, since the national championship team of 1928.

This was painfully familiar to George Sauer, who had previously lost to Dodd in the 1948 Orange Bowl while coaching at Kansas. "Everybody has been wonderful here but that Dodd," Sauer said afterward. "Our team and all of our followers like Miami. But that Dodd . . . "

It was a feeling many of Bobby Dodd's bowl opponents would express. An aptly named Texas sportswriter, Jinx Tucker, expressed another popular sentiment about Dodd. In the *Waco News-Tribune,* Jinx wrote: "The fabulous Orange Bowl luck of Bobby Dodd, Georgia Tech coach, continued on this sunny afternoon. More than willing to settle for a tie with only nine minutes remaining to play and lagging behind 14-7, the Georgia Tech team scored a touchdown and a field goal to defeat the superior Baylor Bears."

Furman Bisher disagreed with the "luck" explanation. Dodd, Bisher insisted, should have been voted the college football coach of the year, and not Stanford's Chuck Taylor. Dodd, after all, had transformed a team with few expectations into an SEC and Orange Bowl champion. He had also begun a historic string of six bowl victories in consecutive years.

"There were two teams that we played during those six bowl games that might have been better than we were," Dodd admitted. "Baylor, and Pittsburgh, the first year we played them in the [1956] Sugar Bowl. Joe Paterno [then a young assistant to Rip Engel at Penn State] said Pittsburgh may have been the best college team he'd ever seen up to that time."

But then, Joe Paterno must not have seen Bobby Dodd's 1952 Georgia Tech team.

During spring practice in 1952, Woody Hayes flew down to Atlanta and climbed up on the tower at Rose Bowl Field to join Dodd and observe Georgia Tech's practices. "Woody looked down there at the offensive team on one side, and he's studying 'em—didn't say a word," Dodd said. "Looked over there at the defense, and he said, 'Bobby, I don't see how you're gonna win a game with those little ol' boys. They're the littlest bunch of boys I ever saw.' And I said, 'Woody, they're the best I got.' "

In Woody Hayes's defense, at least he saw Dodd's little ol' boys during spring practice, when they may have looked even smaller than usual. Bobby Dodd deplored spring practice, at least for experienced upper-classmen. In the 1950s, football was not the 12-month enterprise it has become. There were scant few off-season training programs; certainly Tech teams weren't required to lift weights all winter. Come spring, Dodd encouraged many of his older, more talented players to run track or play baseball. If they had to come out for spring football, just come out in sweats and help coach the younger players. Dodd didn't want his players to get an overdose of football and get stale; he wanted to keep the game fun.

As part of its 1952 college football preview, *Look* magazine ran a pictorial spread on Georgia Tech. "YEA, Georgia Tech!" proclaimed the headline, just to the right of a voluptuous blonde bursting out of a Tech block T letter sweater with the caption, "YEA, Marilyn Monroe."

Look ran numerous photos, including the Tech offense and defense practicing, and Dodd receiving a post-practice neck massage from a Georgia Tech football fixture, an old black masseuse and handyman named Porto Rico Whitehead.

"Charming old Atlanta is proud of Georgia Tech and treats football heroes royally," *Look* informed its readers. There was a photo of the Jackets eating at the training table, where they were especially well-treated.

Captain Hal Miller posed for *Look* with a girl named Barbara Bell. They talked under a canopy of dogwood blossoms on West Peachtree and relaxed in a convertible at the Varsity. They posed at Aunt Fanny's Cabin restaurant and picked tulips on campus, with the famed Tech tower as a backdrop. It all seemed so idyllic, the perfect picture of the big-man-on-campus football hero of the '50s. For Hal Miller and his teammates, what unfolded that season was true perfection.

"Everybody wrote us up, and I said, 'Yes, we oughta have a good football team,' " Bobby Dodd recalled. "I didn't moan. I knew we were a good football team. I had practically the same team back. Hell, we had to be a good team.

"And I told my players, 'We're a good team. We're better than that team. Don't you embarrass me by getting out there and getting beat, and getting knocked around.' Sometimes, they'd look kinda lackadaisical for a quarter and I'd jump on 'em, and then they'd start playing good football. They were capable. We looked at the schedule, and I knew we had a good chance to go undefeated."

Georgia Tech did more than merely go undefeated that season. It established a standard of excellence and an aura about itself that extended through the mid-1950s and that few football programs have ever equaled. "We were having a ball along about then," Dodd said. "We were winning and we were the only show in Atlanta. My players were making all-American and I wasn't overworking 'em. Everybody was getting to play. I'd use a lot of players, specialty teams. Give 55 letters, maybe. So we were having quite a ball then.

"The pro teams hadn't come to Atlanta yet. What are you gonna go to on Saturday afternoons? And they didn't have TV, you see. They didn't have Oklahoma-Nebraska coming into their living rooms. So you had to come watch Tech play. We had sellout crowds. Everybody wanted us to enlarge the stadium, and we did, all through those years.

"Some of those years there, we could have sold seventy-five to eighty thousand tickets, if we'd have had 'em," Dodd said. "See, we didn't have the big student body that everybody else had. We didn't have but over five thousand students, so we could sell almost all of our seats at full price."

Or above full price. At least that's what many Georgia Tech opponents and critics always contended. "Everybody was doing something wrong back then," said one man who coached against Dodd. "It was just a matter of degrees." The consensus among many schools was that Tech, which always drew huge capacity crowds playing in the largest city in the South, could recruit players and guarantee that their tickets could be sold for top dollar. Indeed, $25 a ticket for two, sometimes even four tickets, was big money back then.

"It was the clean way to cheat," said the coach.

Dodd doesn't deny his players were able to sell their tickets. It was a rare recruiting advantage for Georgia Tech, and there were no rules prohibiting it.

"Life couldn't have been any better then," Dodd said of the 1950s. "I had a good coaching staff, no morale problems. The coaches were all close. We had a real good time." In addition to Saturday night steak dinners at the Dodd house after games, Dodd's assistants regularly played in a lunchtime pickup basketball game. Dodd himself would often play tennis doubles with three assistants.

The day after ballgames, Dodd followed God's example. On the traditional day of worship and rest, that's usually what he, his staff, and his players did: worshiped and rested.

Dodd strongly encouraged his assistants and players to go to church on Sunday morning, a practice that gained him favor with many mothers of prospective Tech recruits. Indeed, because of attitudes such as this, a popular slogan evolved: "Send a good boy to Georgia Tech, and we'll send a good boy back home."

After church, some of the assistants and their families would go out to Harris Robinson's lakes, or down to Covington and go fishing, walk around the lake, have a late lunch, and just enjoy themselves.

Dodd would drive over to the WSB television studios, where he did his weekly live TV show with Ed Danforth of the *Journal*, and later Furman Bisher, as the host. It was an unabashedly corny and loving look—as all coaches TV shows are—at Tech football, and a chance for those unfortunates without tickets to see Tech game films. It was also enormously popular.

"We had a terrific following for that show," Dodd said. "People couldn't wait to get home from church. Many a wife told me her husband never sat at the table for Sunday dinner. He was in the den watching my TV show."

"The Bobby Dodd Show" aired every Sunday afternoon from twelve-thirty to one o'clock, in living black and white. After the show, Bobby

Dodd would go home, or go fishing, or go somewhere relaxing. Ray Graves remembers Dodd's admonitions about overworking. "During the week, if you stayed at the office till midnight, he said you'd go stale. We never stayed after ten, eleven o'clock. He always said, 'Any decision you make after midnight is a bad one.' "

During the off-season, of course, Dodd was invisible. "You never saw him," Frank Broyles said. "He fished, he had a good time and lived life. He was the new breed. Other coaches, Bear—and I know I was—were like this." Broyles cupped his hands around his eyes, as if he were a racehorse wearing blinders. "My wife could change the furniture, she could do anything—bought a new dress, changed her hair—and it'd be six months before I noticed.

"But Coach Dodd was different. The feeling that everybody had of him was that when the season was over and recruiting was over, he enjoyed himself. Thoroughly enjoyed himself. He was playing tennis, and fishing, and delegating. But he enjoyed himself. And I think that's one of the reasons he's healthy today."

Like his team, Dodd was in his prime in 1952. The audience was there, the money was there. And there was an abundance of football talent that was also regenerating. "Our players would sell other players on coming here," Dodd said. "The best selling in the world is to have your own players sell. We still had trouble getting that boy that could pass the work, 'cause we weren't gonna bring him in here if he wasn't gonna pass. If we did and he flunked out, that's all our opponents wanted to say: 'Look at ol' Jim Jones, he flunked outta Tech. Do you wanna do that?'

"If one of 'em missed class, we knew it immediately. Why he missed, was he sick? Not like at Auburn now, where [Brent] Fullwood missed the whole fall and they didn't know he wasn't going to class. I knew it immediately."

Bill Curry (a starting center for Dodd in 1964, who would later put into practice Dodd's lessons when he returned to Tech as head coach in 1980) cut an eight o'clock chemistry class one morning. By ten, he was in Dodd's office for a reprimand. By six-thirty the next morning, Curry was running the stadium steps in Grant Field until he threw up, then had to run some more. "That's when I decided I liked chemistry," Curry said.

"That's kinda the way we were," Dodd said. "We'd punish 'em like that, we'd run 'em. But we wanted to know why they weren't in class. We kinda had a deal with the professors up on the hill. I learned this early in my career. I had a boy my first year, in 1945, and he was having trouble in math class. I talked to the professor and I said, 'Isn't there any way we can tutor him? I don't want you to *give* him a grade. I want you to teach him enough to where he can pass.' And he said, 'Coach, would you let him play if he didn't come to practice? Well, I'm not passing him when he's not coming to my class'. "

Dodd could get help for any boy who attended class and showed an interest in learning. "Didn't make a difference how dumb he was—if he attended class, and didn't have any cuts, we could get him help," Dodd said. "Of course, I had faculty people tutor my athletes—I paid 'em to do it— long before other schools did, 'cause I had to. Tech was tougher.

"But no one could ever point out any boy of mine who ever flunked outta Georgia Tech. Because we wouldn't let him flunk out. If we got a boy who we knew was over his head, where they'd given him grades in high school—that's where it really hurt us, if they gave a boy a B instead of an F in math and he didn't know anything—and we had our tutors test him. They'd say, 'Coach, he can't make it here. He has no background at all. They gave him those grades in high school. Some of those grades were for courses he didn't even take'. "

And Dodd would have to call the boy in and explain, "Now look, you can't make it here. It's not our fault or yours. We took you and we thought you could. But I'll get you a scholarship. "

Usually, it was Wofford College in South Carolina or, for the better players, with Dodd's friend Andy Gustafson down at the University of Miami in Coral Gables.

"Kids didn't transfer too much back then," Dodd said. "If you lost 'em, it's mostly because they're unhappy and they're not playing. They were stars in high school."

But in 1952, nearly everyone on the Flats was happy. Deliriously happy.

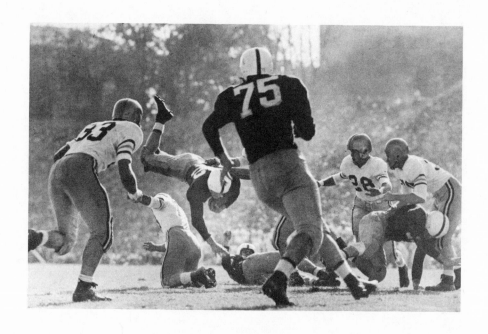

The $125,000 tackle. Jakie Rudolph
stops 'Bama's Bobby Marlow.

Chapter 10
The Greatest Season of All

AFTER OPENING THE 1952 SEASON with a 54-6 plundering of the Citadel, Tech barely survived Bob Woodruff's Florida team 17-14. Then a 20-7 win in Dallas over SMU preceded three consecutive shutouts.

The Yellow Jackets shut out Tulane 14-0, Auburn 33-0, and Vanderbilt 30-0. "I'd put that defense against anybody," Ray Graves still insists.

George Morris was joined at linebacker by Larry Morris, who along with left defensive end Sam Hensley and left guard Orville Vereen would all be chosen to the all-Southeastern Conference team. Of Tech's six all-Americans in 1952, two were on defense, George Morris and left halfback Bobby Moorehead.

The standard against which all defensive players were measured, though, was George Morris, who was as intense as he was intelligent. As with any dominating linebacker, of course, there were times when Morris might have been too intense. Occasionally, that extra effort resulted from Morris's desire to please his coach.

"Coach Dodd had an amazing way of talking to you one-on-one," Morris said. As a freshman, after Morris injured a knee, he was heading up to the press box before one game to spot for the radio announcers, for the princely sum of $5. On his way, he passed Ray Graves and Bobby Dodd. Dodd told the freshman, "Boy, I wish you were playing for me today."

"Hell, I floated upstairs to the radio booth," Morris recalled.

Two years later, however, Bobby Dodd addressed George Morris in a slightly different tone of voice.

"He was good at that when it became necessary," Morris said. One time, against Florida, Morris was called for 45 yards in penalties. "I even hate to say it now, but I was gonna throw Pappa Hall over the fence—they didn't have a chain-link fence then, they had a hogwire fence—and I was gonna throw him over that fence to the lettermen [Tech's varsity lettermen in other sports, who always sat in the same section during football games]. And we would have made it except I got tangled up.

"The next week, I'm coming off the hill with my books and equipment to go to school, and Coach Dodd is sitting in his office with the window open—this is before air-conditioning—and he's sitting there with his feet up in the window and smoking a cigar. He sees me and says, 'Come in here and see me.'

"God, I hated that. I didn't know whether I'd shaved or not, but I wished that I had when I walked in. He said, 'Put your books down,' and I said, 'Yes, sir.' And he said, 'You're a pretty good football player, but you're not worth 45 yards.' And I said, 'I won't get any more this year!' You know when you're gonna get fouls, and I held off. I had a couple of good opportunities. I mean, against Tulane, with that McGee, I had him dead to rights and I said, 'Uh-uh.' I made a commitment, I wasn't gonna get any more penalties.

"They talk about how nice and all Coach Dodd wanted his teams to play. But obviously, he knew what the game was all about. If you were fortunate enough, like I was on a time or two, to catch maybe a fullback on a draw play, and nail him—and nail him clean—the first man to meet you on the sidelines was Coach Dodd. And he'd say, 'That's the way to play football.' He understood it."

The 1952 season progressed nicely, relentlessly. Duke finally scored against Tech but succumbed 28-7. Dodd was as stunned as anyone when the Yellow Jackets thrashed Army 45-6. "That was a shock to me," Dodd said. "That was [Army coach] Earl Blaik, and I felt real bad about it. I had great respect for him. He had those great teams [in the late '40s, with Glenn Davis and Doc Blanchard] and I felt bad and kinda embarrassed that he got beat by that much. I said someting about that to him afterward."

What followed was, in Dodd's memory, one of the greatest games ever to be played on Grant Field. Alabama came to Atlanta for one of the earliest nationally televised college football games. "They had a terrific football team," Dodd said, "and so did we."

The Crimson Tide of Bobby Marlow, Bobby Luna, and Tommy Lewis scored first and took an early 3-0 lead on Luna's field goal. George Morris later recovered an Alabama fumble at the Tide 28. After an unnecessary roughness penalty advanced the ball to the nine, Dick Pretz scored to put Georgia Tech ahead 7-3.

In the fourth quarter, however, Alabama recovered a Tech fumble and moved to the Jackets' 14-yard line. On fourth down Bobby Marlow was stopped by little Jakie Rudolph. The five-foot, seven-inch, 155-pound Tech safety lowered his helmet and hit the leaping Alabama star. Marlow flipped over and came down short of the first down. It was one of the most memorable tackles in Georgia Tech history, and came to be known as a $125,000 tackle. With that victory, Tech clinched the SEC title and a bid to the Sugar Bowl, which was then paying each team $125,000.

"Alabama was the best team we were gonna face that year," said Dodd, whose team won its 10th straight of the season the following week, a 30-0 shutout of Florida State. With the FSU victory, Tech had won all eight of its 1952 home games, four by shutouts.

There was just one regular-season game left. "Now, Georgia was an underrated football team by a lot of people," Dodd said. "We knew they were good, and boy, they made it tough on us."

The Yellow Jackets carried considerable psychological baggage with them to Athens: the weight of a 24-game unbeaten streak. During a game film session the Monday night before the Georgia game, Frank Broyles heard Bobby Dodd say, "Boy, wouldn't we have it made if there was no Georgia." That made an everlasting impression on Broyles.

"That's the reason I went to Arkansas," Broyles said, "and stayed there and never left. Because I was at the only state university, rather than this situation at Tech. We could have lost that Georgia game and it would have been the whole season to us, that's what Coach Dodd was saying in just those few words."

That Saturday, Bobby Dodd said something to Frank Broyles that was at least as memorable, and infinitely more shocking. Georgia, with Zeke Bratkowski back at quarterback after throwing eight interceptions the previous year at Grant Field, took an early lead on Foots Clemens's three-yard touchdown run. Tech could only manage a Rodgers field goal and trailed 7-3.

"In the third quarter," Broyles said, "we came down to fourth down and four on their ten-yard line. We called time out and I was up in the booth. And Coach Dodd called and said, 'Frank, I'm gonna call the belly pass with Chappell Rhino throwing the ball.' I said, 'No! Coach! Chappell Rhino hasn't worked on that play in a year!'

"Now here we are in the biggest game of our life, fourth and four, and Coach Dodd wants us to use a young man who hadn't played more than 30 minutes all season. I'd never even worked Chappell on the running pass!

"So Coach Dodd got Chappell and said, 'Chappell, here's what's gonna happen. We're gonna set the flanker, Georgia will rotate, we'll fake the off-tackle belly play, the end will tackle the fullback, the quarterback will pitch it to you, and Buck Martin will be in the back of the end zone. If the halfback comes up, you lay it over to Buck for the touchdown. If the halfback stays back, you walk in for the touchdown.'

"It worked!" Broyles squeaked, his voice jumping two octaves, his eyes still wide in amazement at the memory of it. "I mean, it worked! I didn't watch. I thought we had blown the whole season."

Fortunately, Dodd didn't, and Tech had a 10-7 third-quarter lead it would never relinquish.

Pepper Rodgers later took an intentional safety, then scored after

Bobby Moorhead returned an interception to the Georgia one. Glenn Turner's 20-yard touchdown made the final score Tech 23, Georgia 9, but it was Dodd's decision-making that made the most lasting impression.

"We're down on the goal line and I know the only way we can score is on the running pass," he shrugged, "because their backs are supporting so fast. I took Chappell Rhino and asked him, 'Now Chappell, you can throw the running pass, can't you?' He said, 'Oh yeah, Coach!' I don't think he'd ever thrown one in a game. But he was a baseball player, he's a good competitor, had been a good high school player, and I had enough confidence in him. Although when you're sending a boy off the bench to pull one play in a big game like that, he can blow it.

"But I thought Chappell was enough of an athlete to where he could do it for me. And I didn't think he'd choke up on me, and he didn't."

"This One Belonged to Dodd" proclaimed the headline on Furman Bisher's column the next day. "Dodd's Finest Hour Came at Athens; He Took Responsibility for Daring Plays" heralded the headline above Ed Danforth's column.

Frank Broyles, for one, should have known Chappell Rhino would throw that belly pass as if he were George Mathews, simply because Bobby Dodd had conferred his blessing on both player and play.

"When I played for Coach Dodd," Broyles said, "I felt that his luck couldn't help but rub off. When I went on that field and Dodd patted me on the back, I thought I could do anything.

"I don't know how he did it, but some of the things Coach Dodd would pull would make the players understand that he was a person with a mystique that went beyond the average man."

Once during practice, Broyles was working with the kickers on how to punt the ball out of bounds. The punters were having problems with the proper steps and ball position needed to kick out of bounds near the goal line. Dodd, who was observing this from his folding chair in the tower, had seen enough. He climbed down and came on the field to give personal instruction.

Broyles: "He said, 'There's nothing to kicking a ball. Anybody can kick the ball for accuracy.' He was about 30 yards from his tower, and he said, 'See the chair on my tower?' Everybody looked. Well, he kicked the ball, hit right in the middle of his chair, so help me. About 30 yards. I could not believe it. How in the hell. . . . Any other coach in the world may have come close, but he wouldn't have hit right in the middle of the chair.

"I'd never seen Bobby kick, really. He used to kick with the players back in the '30s, but he didn't by the time I got to Tech and certainly not when I came back as a coach. I knew he'd been a great punter, but I don't think I ever saw him kick the ball before that time."

That was literally old hat to Dodd. Back at Tennessee Dodd heard Bob

Neyland tell his punters during one practice to kick as close as they could to Neyland's hat far downfield. On Dodd's first punt, the ball hit Neyland's hat squarely. "That about right, coach?" Dodd asked, grinning.

During another Tech practice, Broyles was working with his place-kicker on on-side kickoffs. "If you kick it on the upper third of the ball," Broyles knows, "it'll roll end-over-end and hit twice, and the second time it hits, it bounces in the air. There's something about a football so that some kickers can do this.

"But we could not get the kicker to kick it right so it would bounce twice and over the linemen's heads, and your man running down the other side could get the ball. It's a strategy you'd use from time to time. Well, Coach Dodd came down out of that tower, and I'd never seen him try a placekick in my life. But he came out of that tower, puts himself right on the spot, and says, 'There's nothing to it. You hit the ball right here. Line up!'

"I thought, 'This is not gonna work.' It'll take him five times before he could, before *anybody* could hit it to where it'll bounce right over the linemen's head. But he stepped up there, took two steps, kicked it, it rolled twice and bounced eight feet in the air and over the linemen's heads, and our man went down and fell on it. Well, you can imagine what that does to that aura, or that mystique, the team holds him in. He can do anything! He's above the man. I mean, he's got something about him that's above the normal human being.

"And that was all the time that I knew him. And anybody who competed against him—in golf, bridge, poker, gin rummy, tennis today—they think that he's gonna win. That somehow, the breaks are gonna go against you and he's gonna get every one.

"He did it constantly. Why he would put himself on the spot and come down out of the tower like that not having kicked the ball in 15 years? I doubt if he ever tried that before in his life. And the team just went wild."

"There's never been another coach like him," said Ray Graves. "He had a rapport with his players, with everybody, that was a rare gift of God. He instilled confidence in his players, and he believed he was lucky."

One of Dodd's axioms is "Think you're lucky and you will be." He believes it still in tennis, and he preached it while coaching football. Any kind of football. Graves recalls the early 1950s, when he accompanied Dodd to Texas. Dodd was lecturing at a high school all-star game. The opposing coach was Jess Neely of Rice who, naturally, as the local college coach, got the more talented team. Before the game Dodd told his players, "If you keep it even till the fourth quarter, I'm lucky, I'll pull you through."

With about six minutes left in the fourth quarter of a scoreless tie, Graves remembered, Dodd's team recovered a fumble, kicked a field goal and won 3-0.

"Whatever he told you, you believed in him," Graves said. "You believed he was right, and you went out and made it right. Everybody thought he was a gambler [in his coaching strategy], but he played percentages as far as what's right, as far as quick kicks, and if we had good defenses and could stop 'em.

"You could never put him in a computer, though, and know what he was gonna do. Bobby just always seemed a thought ahead of the competition. And when they played the 'Star Spangled Banner' and the game started, we felt we had the best coach on the sideline and felt we were gonna win the ballgame. And the players felt that way too."

"Anyone—Bear Bryant, General Neyland, anyone—who knew Bobby Dodd would tell you that he had the brightest football mind in the game," said Frank Broyles. "He was far, far ahead of his time in many areas, primarily offensive strategy."

That ability was primarily an innate gift and partially an outgrowth of the times. When Dodd played, and for most of his coaching career, quarterbacks had to call their own plays. On the sidelines, coaches could not use hand signals to call every play, as most do today.

In college, and when Dodd began coaching at Georgia Tech, there were few substitutions and thus no messenger system of substitutes carrying each play in from the sideline. Referees would lean into the huddle and enforce the gag rule: a substitute could not talk for at least one play.

So Dodd had to call his own plays, had to understand strategy at an early age. That requirement, coupled with his intuitive powers, made Bobby Dodd a master strategist. Dodd, in turn, made many of his quarterbacks superior strategists, and some even masters.

In 1952, the Southeastern Conference champion was not obliged to go to the Sugar Bowl, and the Cotton and Orange Bowls also wanted Tech. And if Bobby Dodd had had his way, the Yellow Jackets would have again celebrated New Year's in Miami. Instead, they wound up in the Sugar Bowl—against Ole Miss.

"I wanted to go to the Orange Bowl," Dodd said. "The Orange Bowl was gonna have Syracuse, which we knew was a patsy. Alabama wound up beating 'em 61-6. Hell, we could've just called the score against Syracuse and gone down to the Orange Bowl and had a good time. I let the players have a good time and everything, but hell, I was scared of that football game. I was mad the whole month, from the Georgia game to the Sugar Bowl."

Alternately mad and fearful of Ole Miss. "The Mississippis [Mississippi and Mississippi State] just hated my guts," Dodd said. "Particularly Ole Miss. They wanted their hands on me so bad, 'cause I wouldn't play 'em.

"I always had sense enough, schedule-wise, that if you're going to a bowl, you want to win the bowl game. You don't want to get beat in the bowl game, because people remember the last game that you played. As ol' Bear used to say, 'I won 44 straight regular-season games, but they talk about the damn bowl games I lost.'

"So I called my players in. Now I always let my players vote where they wanted to go, but I also did some brainwashing and selling as to where I wanted to go.

"I thought I'd already sold enough of 'em, about what a good time we'd had down at the Orange, what a big time we'd have, take the players' wives and everything. I thought I had it sold."

The team meeting was held in the old Tech gymnasium. His players, with co-captains Hal Miller and George Morris as spokesmen, told Dodd they had a few requests this time around.

"They started asking for all kinds of extras," Dodd said. "Every player wanted a U-Drive-It [rental car]. And I got mad and I said, 'I don't give a damn whether you want to go or not. I'll go fishing and you can stay home.' They changed their thoughts then."

They later changed their minds, to Dodd's chagrin. On the first ballot, Tech voted to return to the Orange Bowl. Immediately after the votes were in, Frank Broyles and Ray Graves rushed up to Dodd. Dodd recalls, "They said, 'Coach Dodd, they don't really want to go to the Orange Bowl, they're doing that because of you. They want to go to the Sugar Bowl!' "

"We thought it was more prestigious," Morris said.

Which, at that time, it was. Certainly, the Sugar Bowl would provide a more honorable opponent than Syracuse. For Ray Graves, that was part of the attraction of the Sugar Bowl. "Miami had a nice climate, too," Graves said, "but we wanted to play Ole Miss in the Sugar Bowl and be the real SEC champ [Ole Miss was also unbeaten in conference play, but had been tied by Kentucky and Vanderbilt]."

Dodd was upset by that prospect. Still is. "I said all right, I'll go out of the damn room and let 'em vote," Dodd said. "Well, that was a mistake. When I wasn't in the room, you know where they voted."

They voted to go to New Orleans, to play in the Sugar Bowl against Johnny Vaught's Mississippi Rebels, a team Georgia Tech had never deigned to play since it instituted football in 1892. "Ole Miss was tough as pig iron," Dodd said, "and I could just envision us going down there. Ole Miss, my Lord, they were so mad, they'd kill their own mothers to beat us. And they were a good football team. I thought we'd ruin the season by getting clobbered by Ole Miss.

"I knew those Ole Miss people, they'd bring everybody out of Mississippi and come in there to beat ol' Dodd, that ol' so-and-so. That was the only time I was ever put out with my assistant coaches. I was put out with Graves and Broyles, they were the leaders."

Immediately after the vote was taken, and until Tech left for New Orleans the day after Christmas, Broyles and Graves knew their boss was upset with them. They also realized that for the sake of their immediate professional futures, Tech had best beat Mississippi. "If we'd lost the game," Dodd said, "the two finest assistants in America would have been fired, because they got us into the game."

Back home in Mississippi, George Morris realized just how emotional his home state had become over the Sugar Bowl, and just how badly the Rebels wanted to beat Tech. The good people of Vicksburg threw a day in George Morris's honor. Bobby Dodd accompanied Morris for the festivities, which included a luncheon and a gift for the hometown hero: a sterling silver service.

"I was told that that's all the Ole Miss people were waiting for me to do, was accept that service," Morris said. "That would have made me ineligible for the Sugar Bowl. That's the reason I had to go back to Vicksburg after the Sugar Bowl and pick it up."

As usual, Dodd let his players go home for the holidays, taking their sweatsuits and football shoes to run in and stay in some semblance of shape. They reported back to Tech on a Sunday night, then had two days of light workouts outdoors in the December mist and rain of Atlanta, and also in the old gym where the ceiling was so low, passing the ball was virtually impossible.

"We really didn't get a whole lotta work in," Morris said. "And Ole Miss was over there in Biloxi, knocking each other's brains out practicing. Vaught wanted that game very badly."

"He'd have given his right arm to win that game," Dodd said. "Vaught didn't like me for two reasons. One, he thought he could beat me, and he was probably right. Two, he was jealous of the crowds we had and the money we made. At an SEC meeting once, Bernie Moore, the SEC commissioner, asked me, 'Coach, would you play Ole Miss?' And I said, 'No. I can make more money playing Girls High School on Grant Field than playing in Oxford, Mississippi. Johnny, it's nothing against you.' "

Vaught took it very personally, however, and honed his hatred, as well as his players, for Georgia Tech. "Weirdest game I ever saw," Dodd recalled. "The first five minutes, I thought we were gonna lose 50-0."

An enraged Ole Miss team ("They came out there with tears in their eyes," Dodd said) easily scored on the first possession of the game. Behind quarterback Jimmy "King" Lear, the Rebels took a 7-0 lead, forced a punt, then again drove down near the Tech goal line. Only Morris's fourth-down tackle at the one, on Wilson "Whiskey" Dillard's dive play, prevented Mississippi from bolting to a 14-0 lead. Georgia Tech regrouped, regained its composure, and tied the score at 7-7. Just before halftime, Pepper Rodgers kicked a characteristic field goal that barely cleared the crossbar to give the Jackets a 10-7 halftime lead.

George Morris was Tech's long snapper. "I looked up after snapping the ball, and after Pepper kicked it," Morris said. "And I see a nice-looking man with a gabardine topcoat—gabardine was a real nice fabric then— reaching over a barbed wire fence trying to catch that little ol' limp-legged ball that Pepper kicked. And he got hung up in that barbed wire, and tore that coat up! I said, 'Lookit the guy tearing the coat up!' "

After being mauled most of the first half, Tech jogged into its dressing room, grateful for its three-point halftime advantage. Bobby Dodd was sitting up on a wooden table, hat in place, legs crossed. "Well," Dodd confidently told his team, "looks like we got 'em on the run."

George Morris thought, "Man, you're watching a different game than I am."

The mood in the Mississippi locker room was quite different and more amplified. "Vaught's players later said he was just furious," Dodd said. "He was about to get beat by Georgia Tech."

Vaught was so mad, in fact, that he started his second team in the second half. One interception, one fumble, and one Georgia Tech touchdown later, Vaught reinserted his starters, trailing 17-7. Ole Miss never recovered, and Tech won 24-7.

"I never saw a team look as bad as we looked in the first five minutes of that game and still be a good football team," Dodd said. "They just ripped us to ribbons. Five, seven, six, five yards. Hell, we couldn't slow 'em down."

"Took a little while to get organized," said Morris.

With that, Tech completed its season 12-0, the finest in the history of the school, and its first perfect season since the 1928 national champions went 10-0. Tech now had a 26-game unbeaten streak, the longest in the nation. Six Yellow Jackets were picked as all-Americans: Morris and Bobby Moorhead on defense, and Hardeman, Miller, Martin, and center Pete Brown on offense. In addition, three more players were also named to the all-SEC team: defensive end Sam Hensley, defensive tackle Orville Vereen, and the multitalented Larry Morris.

Georgia Tech so dominated that it collectively outscored its 12 opponents 325-59. Ray Graves's defense shut out four teams and held six others to seven points or less. Only Florida managed to score in double figures. Tech was that overwhelming.

It was probably the greatest team in Georgia Tech history. To Dodd, George Morris, and many other members of that team, it was also the best in the nation in 1952. But if greatness touched those Yellow Jackets, melancholy tinges their memories.

Tech was number one only in the eyes of the International News Service, which voted the Yellow Jackets as the 1952 national champions. Both the AP and UPI wire service polls opted for Michigan State, the Big Ten champion, as number one and Tech as number two. In that era, the final wire service polls did not reflect bowl game results. Nevertheless, Tech had futilely hoped somehow to meet Michigan State in a bowl game, to determine the true national champion on the field.

"All the southern people voted us number one," Dodd said, "but they had so many votes up in the East and Midwest, they voted Michigan State number one." Even when all indicators seemed to favor Georgia Tech.

In 11 regular-season games, the Yellow Jackets had allowed fewer points than Michigan State had in its nine games. "And our offense was far better than theirs," Dodd maintains. With backs like Hardeman, Turner, and Teas, Tech rushed for a staggering 3,164 yards that season and passed for an additional 1,251.

"There wasn't any way we shouldn't have been number one," Dodd said. "But we just got outvoted. That was one of my two biggest disappointments in football. But it didn't hurt me as bad as changing that rule in '53."

Halftime tribute to the Bowlmaster.

Chapter 11
One Platoon . . . and Two More Bowl Trips

A MONTH AFTER HIS SUGAR BOWL triumph, Bobby Dodd was vacationing in the Florida Everglades, fishing in Lake Okeechobee. That's where the frantic long-distance phone call from the Georgia Tech athletic department reached him.

"They called me 'cause boy, they knew I'd be upset," Dodd said. "It'd come out on the wire, and they knew I wouldn't see it down there."

And they knew Bobby Dodd would be furious about the controversial decision of the rules committee of the American Football Coaches Association. The decision to reverse the free-substitution rule, scrap two-platoon football, and return to those Neanderthal days of one-platoon football. And the people at Georgia Tech were exactly right.

"Golly, I was furious," Dodd said. "I was so mad, I wanted to kill 'em."

His hit list consisted of General Robert Neyland, former Michigan coach and then athletic director Fritz Crisler, and Delaware's Davey Nelson. "They just took it upon themselves to change the damn game of football," Dodd said, still spitting out the words in disgust nearly 35 years later. "They were the leaders. There were about 12 people on the rules committee, but hell, you put Crisler and Neyland up there with some weak people, they dominated. Davey Nelson fell right in line with 'em.

"What it did was, it took away a lot of the coaching and put the emphasis on who can get the greatest athlete."

This effectively ruined Dodd's system of specialization, of using his best players strictly on offense or defense, and deploying his marginal players on specialty teams. "Hardeman, Teas, Turner, Brigman, the whole '52 backfield—none of 'em could play defense," Dodd said. "Pepper couldn't play a lick of defense. Hell, he was worse than I was.

"I didn't have many athletes. People like Larry and George Morris, now, they could play both ways. No problem there. And there's a few players like that, but hardly any off that '52 team. Even a guy like Hal Miller, a great offensive tackle, he wasn't a good defensive tackle at all. Maybe I had six out of the 22 that could play both ways. So we had to start over."

What further infuriated Dodd was that the rules committee made its decision despite the consensus among college coaches that two-platoon football was a good and worthy idea.

The entire coaches association had convened just a couple of weeks prior to the rules committee meeting. Before the convention, each coach received a questionnaire concerning any possible rule changes. Dodd clearly remembers attending that coaches convention early in 1953, as well as an overwhelming vote in favor of free substitution.

"I thought about 75 to 80 percent wanted the free-substitution rules left as they were," Dodd said. "Normally, the rules committee takes into consideration the coaches' suggestions."

But not this time. Neyland and Crisler, Dodd thought, were simply trying to return to the good old days, when men were 60-minute men and their teams—Tennessee and Michigan—dominated college football.

"We had to start all over again in '53," Dodd said. "That rule change hurt me worse than anything. I would have had another great team in '53. I'd a had another great team in '54 if they hadn't changed that rule. That just broke my heart.

"Now Notre Dame, of course, that was just like throwing a rabbit in a briar patch. They had all those great athletes."

The following fall, the Yellow Jackets were thrown stinger-first into an Irish briar patch.

"In '53, that was a big disappointment because of the rule," Dodd said. "But we sucked it up, and we played pretty good ball, even against Notre Dame."

By the time Georgia Tech traveled to Notre Dame, the Yellow Jackets had extended their unbeaten streak to 31 games. After opening with a 53-0 destruction of Davidson, Tech and Florida played to a scoreless tie in Gainesville. "We had a better team than they did," Dodd said. "That game was played in a hurricane. There was so much water on the field, the ball would float away if you didn't hold it down. The referee had to hold it until the center took the ball. We were all over their goal line, but we never could get it across."

In a classic Bobby Dodd game, Georgia Tech sent Southern Methodist back to Dallas a 6-4 loser. Leading 6-0, Dodd ordered two intentional late safeties, to enable Tech on the subsequent free kicks to punt out of danger and keep SMU out of the end zone.

After a 27-13 victory at Tulane, Tech annihilated Auburn 36-6. "It looked like we had a good day against Auburn all the time," Dodd said. "Didn't seem to matter how good they were, like in '51. Back then, Auburn and Clemson couldn't beat us."

The Yellow Jackets were 4-0-1 and unbeaten in 31 consecutive games. Next up was undefeated Notre Dame.

Neil Worden scored quickly to give the Irish a 7-0 lead, but before the first half ended, coach Frank Leahy became ill and was carried from the field on a stretcher. At halftime, Notre Dame still led 7-0.

"The thing I remember the most up there is that it's almost like playing in a gymnasium," said Wade Mitchell, a freshman quarterback who played the entire game after Pepper Rodgers was injured on the opening kickoff. "I was aware of how close the fans were to the field, and how both teams shared the same tunnel [leading from the locker rooms]."

Before the second-half kickoff, Tech was in the tunnel, waiting for the signal to return to the field. "I don't know whether it was protocol or what," Mitchell said, "but the decision was made that Notre Dame needed to go out first. We were standing there, and I had my back to them when I heard the clatter of their cleats. And above the cleats I could hear all this, 'Sniff, sniff, sniff.' "

"I turned around and looked at these guys," Mitchell said. "And they were monsters—weighed 240 pounds. And every one of 'em had tears just running down their faces like that. I was talking to Frank Broyles, and I said, 'Frank, it's gonna be a long second half. I don't know what those guys said in there, but somebody gave 'em one of those Get this one for the Gipper speeches.' I don't think any of us knew at that point that Leahy had had a breakdown. They were all upset."

The Irish had much more talent, but Georgia Tech played them tough, and close. In the third quarter, Mitchell intercepted a Ralph Guglielmi pass, drove the Jackets to the Irish one, and then scored to tie it at 7-all. Notre Dame regained the lead on Guglielmi's nine-yard touchdown pass to Joe Heap, the first scoring pass Tech had allowed in 22 games. The Fighting Irish clinched it when Jimmy Morris's high snap sailed over punter Jim Carlen's head, and Art Hunter recovered in the end zone to make it 21-7.

Notre Dame eventually won 27-14 and went 9-0-1, with only a tie with Iowa preventing a national championship. "The rule change couldn't have been more beneficial for Notre Dame," Dodd said. "They had the finest bunch of athletes, who could play both ways. They were athletes. It didn't make any difference to them whether they were on offense or defense.

"They were better than we were in every way. I'll bet we had two players that could've made their team. Now, if we'd had offensive and defensive personnel like I had in two-platoon, we could've given them trouble. But not where you played both ways."

By 1953, fresh substitutes were no longer forbidden to speak, and the liberalized substitution rules made it possible for coaches to use subs as messengers, shuttling in plays from the sidelines. When the experienced Pepper Rodgers was injured on the opening kickoff against Notre Dame,

Dodd decided to call the plays for the freshman Mitchell.

But Dodd wanted to make sure an overly excited player wouldn't give a garbled message to his young quarterback. So he would tear off a little piece of paper from his ever-present yellow legal pad, write his play selection on it, and hand the scrap of paper to a substitute to take into the huddle.

But Wade Mitchell had a problem. Each time a substitute would carry in a play on a piece of paper and hand it to Mitchell, the freshman would take it, then worriedly look about.

Said Mitchell, "I kept thinking to myself, 'I think this is a violation. What am I gonna do with these things? If I drop it, the official's gonna find these things lying all around here.' "

So Wade Mitchell stumbled on a solution. After reading each play, he took each piece of yellow paper and stuffed it into his gold football pants.

"I just had it in my head that that little yellow slip I had, I wasn't supposed to have," Mitchell said. "About the fourth quarter, I was rustling like a full bag of leaves."

For Bobby Dodd, the yellow legal pad served another purpose. "Coach Dodd had a reputation for being so cool and so much in control, and nerves of steel and all that kind of stuff," Mitchell said. "You never know what's going on inside of somebody. But I had some clues, because he would start with one single sheet of paper, holding it in his hand, on game day. And he'd tear those pieces off, and chew on that thing, and I don't know how many of those he'd eat in the course of the game."

"That's the truth," Dodd said. "Many times, I was just boiling inside, but you couldn't tell it. I didn't show it. I always felt that if the coach panics, the players will panic. Any why in the hell should I panic? I've been playing football since I was 12 years old. I'm not supposed to panic.

"And I didn't. Ol' Bowden Wyatt of Tennessee—great guy, I loved him—he'd meet me out there before Tech-Tennessee games, we'd go out there and shake hands and he'd say, 'God, coach, I'm about to die, about to die! You look so calm. How do you do it? I'm about to die!' And I'd say, 'Bowden, it's just another game, you know, just another football game between Tech and Tennessee.' Now I was boiling inside, just like he was. But they never knew it."

After the Notre Dame loss, Georgia Tech righted itself with a resounding 43-0 win at Vanderbilt and then, as usual, beat Clemson at Grant Field 20-7. The Yellow Jackets, however, lost any chance for their third consecutive SEC title by losing to a tough Alabama team 13-6 at Legion Field in Birmingham. After struggling to a 13-10 decision over Duke, Tech sustained the Drought for a fifth year with a 28-12 victory over Georgia. Pepper Rodgers ran for one touchdown and threw for another.

"Wallace Butts was a fine football coach," Dodd said, "but I had better material in the early '50s than he did."

With an 8-2-1 record and a unanimous all-American center-linebacker in junior Larry Morris, Georgia Tech was more than welcome to return to the Sugar Bowl. West Virginia, however, did not receive much hospitality in New Orleans. "The New Orleans newspapers rode the Sugar Bowl people for inviting West Virginia," Dodd said. "They said they didn't have any business coming in here and playing against Georgia Tech, that they weren't in our class. But I was delighted to have 'em, 'cause I thought we could outrun 'em and throw against 'em. Outside of St. Mary's, they were the weakest bowl team we ever played. But I knew those big West Virginia boys would be tough, 'cause I'd grown up in the mountains."

A fierce linebacker named Sam Huff—who would go on to play for the New York Giants, become Jim Brown's nemesis and make the NFL Hall of Fame—played for West Virginia, as did Joe Marconi, later a fullback with the Chicago Bears. Despite the media ridicule in New Orleans, West Virginia came to town confident, particularly after its coaching staff had scouted the Tech-Georgia game and came away visibly unimpressed with the Jackets' passing game.

Naturally, Dodd capitalized on that. Howard Ector remembers Dodd's locker room speech before the West Virginia game: "Now min, they don't think we can throw the ball. Pepper, I want you to come out throwing."

And Pepper did. On the first possession of the game, Rodgers hit Sam Hensley with a bomb for a 7-0 lead. He never let up. Rodgers completed 16 of 26 passes for 195 yards and three touchdowns, and also kicked a field goal and two extra points. Tech set Sugar Bowl records for pass attempts (35), completions (20), and passing yardage (268), and amassed 438 yards total offense.

"We were gonna screen pass and screen pass, we were not gonna run toward those big West Virginia linemen," Dodd recalled. "'Cause they'd whip our linemen. But we went out here, and out here, and we outran 'em. We threw short passes, screen passes and we just wore 'em out. I finally called 'em off. I didn't want to embarrass the Sugar Bowl people 'cause they were already catching hell about having 'em in there."

Final score: Georgia Tech 42, West Virginia 19. This was Bobby Dodd's fifth bowl victory without a loss, his third in three years. As usual, the Yellow Jackets were as relaxed as they were victorious.

While West Virginia had established a rigorous training camp in Biloxi, Mississippi, two weeks prior to the Sugar Bowl, the Jackets had spent Christmas at home. This time, they weren't required to return to campus until December 28, two days later than usual. That day, they leisurely ran around in tennis shoes. For the next two days, it rained, so Tech worked out lightly indoors, in sneakers. On the thirty-first, West Virginia arrived in New Orleans tense, determined. Tech strolled in and casually posed for photos during its last pre-game workout.

And then Georgia Tech implemented another Bobby Dodd game plan to perfection, and won yet another bowl game.

By the fall of 1954, Bobby Dodd was at the top of his profession. That year, *Bobby Dodd on Football* was published, and became a bible of sorts to young coaches, particularly those coaching in high school. The book was dedicated, of course, to the late Bill Alexander, Dodd's former boss and mentor who had died in 1950. On Alexander's death, Dodd had also become Tech's athletic director.

Although *Bobby Dodd on Football* was primarily a technical and instructional football primer, it also dealt with many other aspects of coaching. Chapter 2 was entitled, "Football Is a Game." In it, Dodd said two articles written during the 1952 season best summarized the football philosophy at Georgia Tech. Before the 1952 Duke game, Benny Marshall wrote in the *Birmingham News*, "Football is a game at Georgia Tech and the men who play it enjoy it. They're glad they came." Later that year, *Time* magazine decided, "At Georgia Tech, they come as close as any big-league squad can to playing football for fun."

Dodd believed in coaching football players as he would have wanted himself, or his son, to be coached. Toward that end, he offered tips on preventing practice from becoming drudgery.

"Do not have extremely long practice periods." [Indeed, Tech seldom practiced more than an hour-and-a-half, total. Said Darrell Crawford, "Coach Dodd always said, 'If you can't get it in an hour-and-a-half, and you keep drilling them on it and stay out there for three hours, you're not gonna get it.' "]

"Do not keep a player doing the same thing over and over again until it becomes monotonous to him."

"Make every practice, and every segment of practice, as competitive as possible since competition appeals to most every boy."

"Have certain periods of practice that are definitely outlined as relaxing and fun."

"Sometimes break up practice with touch football games, volleyball with a football over the crossbar, foot races, punting games, touch pass scrimmages, etc."

"Get linemen in on the fun. Design a play that ends up with a lineman receiving a lateral; even if you never end up using it in a game, it's good for morale."

"Encourage the natural comedian on the squad."

"Urge church attendance."

"Don't have a great number of training rules." [Bobby Dodd basically had just three training rules at Georgia Tech: An eleven o'clock, in-your-room curfew during the season. No drinking. Attend church on Sunday.]

Dodd also dealt with "Quarterback Generalship" and "Preparation and Game Organization." Preparation included everything from selecting a staff to game day. "Preparation," he wrote, "is as necessary to successful coaching as weather is to the weatherman—i.e., there must be some of it every day."

There was even a chapter on "The Spectator," advising how fans could best watch games and enjoy them more. And, of course, there was chapter 12: "The Coach and Public Relations," written by the master.

Of all the coaches in all the games of sport, Bobby Dodd was surely one of the most accommodating, friendly, honest, and helpful to the media. It was his way, his nature to befriend people, but it was also one of his many gifts. Good public relations with anyone—the public, players, school administrators and faculty, alumni, boosters, other coaches, and especially the media—was an absolute must.

"Be sincerely friendly with the press," Dodd advised. "If the coach deals frankly and fairly with newsmen, he will find they will be just as frank and fair with him." Dodd always wanted his sports information directors—first Chuck Hosch and then his long-time aide, Ned West—to assist the media in covering Tech games. Make sure they have a good seat, spotters, statistics, post-game quotes from the locker room, and plenty of food.

"The newsman working in sports is usually doing so because he loves it just as the coach does," Dodd said. "Give him cooperation and he will repay in kind."

Bobby Dodd was repaid tenfold for his cooperation and kindness to the media. Reporters could not help but sing his praises. Dodd was humble in victory, gracious in defeat, and never alibied. "He gave us assistants credit for any success we might enjoy," Ray Graves said. "And he took the blame for everything that went wrong."

Dodd was as country and quotable ("Old syrup-mouth," Dan Jenkins once called him in *Sports Illustrated*) as he was accessible and helpful. Writers flocked to the tower on Rose Bowl Field, where the "Gray Fox"—one of Dodd's nicknames—often granted them audiences. He would sit up there in his folding chair, wearing a Tech windbreaker, his whistle around his neck, and football cleats on his feet, which were propped up on the tower railing. Some 30 feet above the ground, Dodd was down to earth, patiently answering reporters' questions, in effect helping them write their stories. And always, he was honest. Well, almost always.

Once, when a writer was stuck for a story angle, Dodd moved one of his tiniest backs, a 135-pound scrub, to fullback. The story ran on the national wire the next day—the same day Dodd moved the little sub back to halfback.

In the 1950s, in the prime of the Dodd era that was as glistening as Tech's gold helmets, newspapers in Birmingham, Nashville, Chattanooga, and Jacksonville all regularly wrote up Tech practices, in addition to covering all Tech games. Dodd received overwhelmingly positive press in Atlanta, of course. How could it not be? He was friendly and helpful, wildly successful, and always went first-class. So, too, did the sportswriters, who enjoyed ringing in each New Year in Miami or New Orleans or Dallas nearly as much as the Tech players did.

Not all sportswriters were so enthralled, however, particularly those in some other SEC cities. One Tennessee writer called Dodd's Atlanta press coverage "the greatest propaganda machine since Goebbels." And while most people repeated the phrases "In Dodd We Trust," "Dodd Almighty," and "Dodd's Luck," sportswriter Tom Anderson of the *Knoxville Journal* chose to christen his boat the "Dodd Damn."

Regarding a coach's relations with his players, Bobby Dodd wrote in his book no personal likes, or dislikes, should sway his judgment of any player. Play no favorites and avoid promises—they must be kept. Don't criticize players in front of their teammates. ("If I had to say anything to them, I'd wait till after practice and talk to them inside," Dodd said. "On the field, about the only thing I ever had to do was say softly, 'You're loafing, and if I catch you again, you're gonna lose your job.' That's all I had to say.")

And finally, a coach should listen to all of his players' problems, even the most trivial. "The coach who genuinely loves boys and loves working with boys will usually be loved by them in return," Dodd wrote. "The coach who does not love working with boys should not be coaching."

After flying to Honolulu in late July to lecture at a high school coaching clinic and attend an all-star football game, Dodd returned for the 1954 season. Despite the constrictions of one-platoon football, Dodd had another successful year. Georgia Tech lost three games, by a combined total of nine points.

After a successful 28-0 debut against Tulane, Tech was beaten at Grant Field by Florida 13-12. It was the first time since 1941 that the Gators had beaten Tech. And it was the first home defeat for the Yellow Jackets in 23 games, since that 54-19 loss to Alabama in November 1950. Tech regrouped for a narrow 10-7 win at Southern Methodist and then returned to Atlanta and beat Louisiana State 30-20.

"They were a pretty good football team," Dodd said. "But if you could get 'em out of Baton Rouge, we figured we could beat 'em. In Baton Rouge, it was tough." At least as tough as playing Georgia Tech in Atlanta. "Get us off Grant Field, that's what most people tried to do," Dodd said. "They didn't want to play us here."

Most people didn't have any choice. Georgia Tech consistently sold out Grant Field, and the gate receipts were very lucrative. Bobby Dodd could schedule so many home games (at least six a season, sometimes seven, and occasionally even eight) because so many schools were willing to come to Atlanta and lose in exchange for a big payday. Indeed, their athletic budgets often depended on the six-figure checks they could bring home from Atlanta.

Among those willing victims, Auburn and Clemson were the most prominent. From 1913 through 1959, Georgia Tech and Auburn played every year but 1943. And they played every one of those 46 games on Grant Field. Not until 1960 would Dodd, as athletic director, finally break down and permit Tech to travel to Auburn.

Vince Dooley, who played at Auburn from 1951 to 1953 and returned to his alma mater as an assistant coach in 1956 before taking the Georgia head coaching job in 1964, recalls, "At that time, Georgia Tech was a bigger rival than Alabama for Auburn. The Auburn people just hated every time they had to go to Grant Field. But that was the only thing that made Auburn's budget. The Georgia Tech game was always figured into Auburn's budget. That was a big thing, to be able to bring people into Grant Field and give them a fat check and send them home losers."

Clemson had to wait even longer to pry Tech away from Atlanta. That series was initiated in 1898, and Georgia Tech would not play in Death Valley until 1974. Before Dodd became Tech's head coach, the Jackets had beaten Clemson in 18 of the previous 19 games. After that 21-7 defeat in 1945, Bobby Dodd never again lost to Frank Howard and Clemson, winning eight straight. Howard had some curious memories of Grant Field and those colorful meetings of remarkable men.

"Dodd didn't play us except when he knew he could beat us," Howard said. "He was a smart schedule-maker. But I always wanted to play 'em. We could get big gate receipts out of 'em. It was better than a bowl game back then.

"So we always liked to play 'em; we'd play 'em any time they'd play us. But we always had to go to Atlanta. Our fans liked that 'cause all the women liked to go and shop. Then they'd beat our ass, and we'd take home a hundred thousand dollars.

"I remember one game we's playing down there, and Teas returned a punt and ran behind Dodd on the sideline. 'Course, I thought they's gonna call it back, but they let him go to the two-yard line. Dodd was on the sideline and Teas ran right behind him. The picture was in the paper the next day and it said, 'Wonder what Coach Howard'll say about this?'

"I remember another time we was playing 'em down there and they punted, and the ball hit right on the sideline, knocked up the dust and everything, you know, the chalk. And it's right in front of my bench, and it bounced on down to about the 20-yard line. But I didn't say nothin'. I said, 'Well, the official, he'll bring it back here to around the 50 and it'll be our ball.' So I didn't get up and say nothin'. Georgia Tech was always nice to you, they had a cop on the sideline all the time. That cop came over to me and says, 'Coach, you sit there on your butt and take that kinda stuff, you oughta get the hell beat outta you.'

"So, Dodd had a lot of good breaks down there."

Vince Dooley remembers those "breaks" too. "Back in the '50s, there was a real mystique about Tech," he said. "You knew some way, somehow Tech was gonna win. Some called it 'Dodd's Luck' and others called it Tech officials.

"Tech had the advantage of playing most of its games in Grant Field. A lot of Dodd's players became officials, and many Auburn people were sure that because of the officials, you couldn't beat Tech. Many, many calls went Tech's way. They said, 'It couldn't just happen to be the intangibles and mystique for so many things to happen.' But I think that's what it was."

In 1954, Tech sent Auburn home a loser for the 13th consecutive time, 14-7. The following Saturday, however, Blanton Collier's Kentucky team produced a rare 13-6 upset at Grant Field. By the middle of the following week, Bobby Dodd was even more upset. With Billy Teas.

In the 1940s and '50s, Tech was famous as a foundry of backs as swift and elusive as they were diminutive. Backs like Leon Hardeman, one of dozens of Jackets who prepped at Baylor Prep in Chattanooga. In high school, Hardeman played in the same backfield with Glenn Turner, Billy Teas, and Dave Bristol (who would later manage the Cincinnati Reds and Atlanta Braves).

Hardeman, Turner, and Teas all made a pact together in high school—similar to the one Bobby Dodd and Paul Hug made in Kingsport—that they would attend college together. Turner wanted to go to Alabama and Teas preferred Vanderbilt. Neither of those schools, however, wanted little Leon. To Bobby Dodd and Georgia Tech, though, what was another 5-foot-6 running back? Only Tech would take the trio intact. So Turner and Hardeman enrolled at the Flats in 1950, Teas the following year.

By the time Leon Hardeman played his final game in the 1954 Sugar Bowl, he had rushed for a school-record 1,794 yards and set another Tech mark with 22 touchdowns. Many contend Hardeman was the best back of the Dodd era and perhaps the greatest in the history of the school. Turner, meanwhile, was a powerful fullback. He was particularly effective in short-yardage situations but managed to rush for 1,329 yards, still the 12th-highest total in Tech history.

And then there was Billy Teas, possessed of the gift of the game-breaker, both as a running back and punt returner. Teas's 48-yard punt return for a fourth-quarter touchdown beat Duke in 1953, 13-10. Teas led the Yellow Jackets in rushing in 1952, again in 1953, and was pacing Tech midway through the 1954 season.

At that time, Teas had rushed for 1,689 yards in his two-and-a-half seasons on the Flats, leaving him just 105 yards shy of Hardeman. With four regular-season games left and a bowl bid a certainty, Teas seemed destined to surpass his old prep school teammate as Tech's all-time leading rusher.

The Wednesday before the Duke game, however, Billy Teas ran afoul of one of Bobby Dodd's few training rules. "Actually," Howard Ector recalled, "they were looking for another boy, Jake Shoemaker." Shoemaker was another Chattanooga boy, the starting right guard, who had not been too mindful of Dodd's eleven o'clock curfew. So this night, Dodd—who periodically held unannounced bed checks—sent his trainer, Buck Andel, to Shoemaker's dormitory and instructed him to wait and catch the boy coming in after hours.

Buck Andel never saw Shoemaker come in that night. Just before 2 a.m. though, a car pulled up. Billy Teas was driving. Teas, who was married, dropped off teammate Larry Ruffin, a running back. Then Teas drove home to his apartment.

Andel reported back to Dodd on Thursday morning. The coach called in those three players, plus a fourth who'd also broken curfew. "I just couldn't put up with that—Wednesday before a big game, homecoming up at Duke," recalled Dodd, who had once been benched in high school by LeRoy Sprankle for breaking curfew the night before a game.

"I couldn't suspend any of 'em unless I suspended 'em all, my star as well," Dodd said. "So I called in Teas and I told him I was gonna have to let him go."

Not just suspend him for the Duke game. But for the rest of the season. In effect, for the rest of his collegiate career. Billy Teas, an all-American candidate on the verge of breaking a school record, was finished playing football for Georgia Tech.

"Maybe I was a little harsh on him, but I felt like I had to do it," Dodd said. "I kept him on scholarship, though. I was very fond of the boy. But I just didn't feel I could let him play. Maybe I should have just suspended him for the one game, but then what am I gonna do if the next guy gets drunk and stays out? Am I gonna suspend him one game?"

Nothing could dissuade Dodd. Not even the telegram he received on December 1, from Mayor Percy Ferebee and 249 other citizens of Teas's home town of Andrews, North Carolina, pleading for Dodd to reinstate Billy Teas for the Cotton Bowl and give him the chance to break Leon Hardeman's career rushing record. Dodd refused to even comment on the telegram.

At first, Billy Teas was understandably distraught and visibly upset with Dodd. Several years later, however, having reconciled their differences, Teas said Bobby Dodd's suspension was "the best thing to ever happen to me."

The suspensions also had some positive fallout, on the team. "It straightened 'em all up," Dodd said. "I didn't have any trouble for quite a spell, I can tell you."

Except for the second-half trouble that Saturday at Duke. With Georgia Tech leading 20-0, Duke rallied around quarterback Jerry Barger and shocked the Yellow Jackets 21-20. Regaining its composure, Tech manhandled Tennessee 28-7, with George Humphreys scoring twice and George Volkert returning a punt 65 yards. The Yellow Jackets then shut out Alabama 20-0. Jimmy Thompson, yet another little halfback, scored two touchdowns, Paul Rotenberry ran 45 yards for the third, and for the first time since 1941, the Crimson Tide failed to score against Georgia Tech.

And then, in the rain and mud in Athens, it seemed the Drought might finally end for Georgia. "That game hurt Butts, and I don't blame him," Dodd said. "That game would've killed me if I'd been on the other sideline. Butts later told me, 'I still wake up at night in a cold sweat thinking about that game.'

"We went over to Athens and the mud was this deep," Dodd held his hands six inches apart. "Just a quagmire. *Quagmire.* And I, of course, told my kickers, 'We're gonna kick on third, second, even first down. We're not gonna kick on fourth down the whole game.' "

Dodd was a staunch advocate of the quick-kick. ("The only reason I got to play quarterback was that I'm bowlegged," Darrell Crawford said. "I didn't have to move from side to side. The center could snap the ball through my legs for a quick-kick. Didn't matter if I could throw a lick.") Dodd also would often punt on third down, much to the chagrin of what George Mathews called "the circus maximus," the Grant Field crowd, which howled in protest, even in victory, when Dodd punted early.

Against Georgia in 1954, however, Dodd punted early and often, with no explanation necessary. "The first half, every time we got the ball, we kicked on first or second down," Dodd said. "Georgia would make ground on us but they couldn't score. Finally, they got close enough to where Joe Graff kicked a field goal in that damn mud. I don't know how in the world he ever did it."

At halftime, Georgia led 3-0. "We hadn't even made one first down," Dodd said. He conferred with Frank Broyles. "We couldn't drive on 'em," Dodd said. "Their line was bigger than ours, stronger than ours. We couldn't knock 'em outta there in that mud. We said the only way that we can score is on a pass, and we'd better throw it early before the ball gets muddy and soggy. Back then, they only gave you a new ball at the first of the game and at the half. You used that ball the whole time. They didn't take it off and wipe it off like they do today. So we said we're gonna throw the first time we got the ball in the third quarter.

"As fate would have it, we kicked off to them and they fumbled it around their 20." Tech guard Franklin Brooks recovered the fumble at the Georgia 19. On the first play, Wade Mitchell dropped back and hit Henry Hair for a touchdown and a 7-3 lead. "For the rest of the game," Dodd said, "we just kicked the ball and let Georgia fight it through the mud. They had a big ol' fullback named Foots Clemens and he made a lot of three yards, four yards, five yards, but nobody could make a long run on that field."

Georgia Tech could make only two more first downs all day. That 7-3 victory gave Tech six straight over Georgia and gave Wally Butts a recurring nightmare.

"That's the toughest game for a coach to lose. I know how Butts must have felt. He must have wanted to shoot himself. They go up and down the field and can't score; we have three first downs, one on that touchdown. Of all the games I coached in my entire career, I know we were outplayed more in this one than any other."

With that, Dodd's Luck was now a certified unnatural phenomenon. "That was along when Butts was calling me lucky and everybody said I was lucky with everything I did," Dodd said. "We just did the best we could with what we had. Kick the ball, let them have it, hope they make a mistake, fumble. They did fumble, and we scored the only way we could score. But you still have to be lucky to win a game where you get outplayed like that."

Understandably, Wally Butts would later say, "If Bobby Dodd were trapped at the center of an H-bomb explosion, he'd walk away with his pockets full of marketable uranium."

Georgia Tech was invited to its fifth consecutive major bowl game, the first time Bobby Dodd had taken a team to the Cotton Bowl. In Dallas awaited Arkansas, coached by Bowden Wyatt.

"Coach Dodd talks about how smart he was and how he could pick and choose his bowl opponents," Wade Mitchell said. "Well, he didn't do a very good job of picking Arkansas. That was the meanest bunch of guys I ever saw. I don't know who else was available, but I remember we'd all gone home for Christmas, came back to Tech and played three days of volleyball, went out to Dallas and had been to several parties.

"We waddled out from the dressing room to the bench to warm up before the game. Everybody was 10 pounds overweight, and we were out of breath by the time we got out there. Then Arkansas came out there, and the whole team lined up and they ran three one-hundred-yard wind sprints. And we're standing there, looking at them with our mouths open and looking at Coach Dodd like, 'This guy did this to us.' "

Arkansas scored first, taking a 6-0 lead. Four times in the first half, Georgia Tech drove inside the Arkansas 10 but couldn't score. Just before halftime, the Yellow Jackets were threatening again. Mitchell found himself faced with a fourth-and-three situation. Dodd signaled for a timeout.

"I said, 'Whew, pressure's off,' " Mitchell recalled. "He's gonna come up with some grand plan to get this damn ball in the end zone. I'm not gonna have to worry about it. So we were lying around there, looking at that blue Texas sky and not thinking anything except 'The Man', the great man who's gonna send us a play in here and get us outta this mess.

"And the next thing I knew, the official says, 'Play ball!' And there hadn't been any word at all from 'The Man'. Nothing has happened. He and Broyles are standing over there in a great debate, and I look over there and they're still in a great debate, but it's time to play, and I don't have anything.

"Well, we ran a play and Paul Rotenberry scored a touchdown. Going in at the half, I caught up to him and I said, 'Coach, I thought you were gonna send me a play.' And Mr. Cool, he says, 'I just wanted to give you time to think about it.' "

("Many times I asked my quarterbacks what they thought," Dodd said. "'Cause they had a feel for the game out there that we didn't have.")

Arkansas had won the Southwest Conference title in 1954. "They played the kicking game and good defense, and we knew they were gonna be tough to score on," Dodd said. "Their athletes were probably as good as our athletes. We didn't get that great athlete during many of those years. They were fast, and they were intelligent, and they were light, and we coached 'em well."

They also didn't overwork 'em, unlike Bowden Wyatt and his staff. "It seemed to some non-subscribers to bowl-training rigors that Wyatt might have been conditioning his Hogs for a trip across the desert," Furman Bisher wrote in his game story the next day. "The day before the game, he worked them for two-and-a-half hours. When they hit the field Saturday, they went into wind sprints. By the second half, their feet were anvils and the burning enthusiasm was gone. They weren't dangerous any longer."

Arkansas, a second-half team all season long, was shut out in the second half of the Cotton Bowl. Mitchell, meanwhile, scored for Tech and the Jackets won 14-6. Georgia Tech was 8-3, and a bowl victor for the fourth straight year. The 1954 football season had been another success.

"Any time you beat Georgia and win a bowl game, you had a great season," Dodd said. "Don't make a difference what you did against Florida or Kentucky or Duke, they forget those things. They remember that Georgia game and that bowl game. That was big stuff."

Tech had had another successful year, despite the confusing substitution rules at that time. "They started letting you substitute one guy, then two guys," Dodd said. "Just ridiculous rules. I had to keep a man on the sideline, and the other teams were always getting penalized for illegal substitutions. Sending the guy back in the game, you know. I had my man keeping track of substitutions—a mathematician, Roy Mundorff [a manager on the '51 and '52 teams]—and if one of my coaches started to send in number 67 and he was illegal, Roy wouldn't let them send him in. No telling how many times in those years he saved us a penalty by telling us, 'This guy can't go in, he's ineligible.' Coaches forget about it in the heat of the battle. But we always had good organization on the sidelines. And we had Roy keeping track of those substitutions."

The 1956 team and coaching staff
travel to another victory.

Chapter 12
The Mid-Fifties—Tribulations and Triumphs

TO OPEN THE 1955 SEASON, Georgia Tech beat Bobby Dodd's buddy, Andy Gustafson, and his Miami Hurricanes 14-6. It was only fitting that Tech should play in the first nationally televised football game shown in color. It was also the afternoon portion of a day-night doubleheader at Grant Field. That evening, Georgia met Ole Miss.

Dodd's Luck, of course, had returned for another season of eligibility. Paul Rotenberry scored the first Tech touchdown when he picked up a bouncing punt and ran 60 yards to score. There were two keys to the play: Bill Fulcher's block and Miami's claim that Tech had signaled for a fair catch. The officials ruled otherwise.

Jimmy Morris later returned an interception 25 yards for Tech's second touchdown and first win of the season. That evening, Johnny Vaught brought his Rebels onto Grant Field. If Vaught could never play Dodd there, at least he could play somebody from the state of Georgia on Grant Field.

Georgia Tech won its first four games, including a 7-0 shutout of LSU in Baton Rouge. But then Auburn finally ended 15 years of frustration with a 14-12 victory, its first win over Bobby Dodd in 11 tries and the end of a 14-game losing streak to Tech.

Early in the second half, George Volkert sped 59 yards for a touchdown and a 12-7 Georgia Tech lead. Wade Mitchell had scored the first touchdown but missed both crucial extra points. Against an outstanding Georgia Tech defense, Shug Jordan had his quarterback, Howell Tubbs, respond by throwing the ball. Tubbs directed a breaktakingly suspenseful drive and eventually sneaked in himself for the winning touchdown.

Auburn was the only team all season to score more than once against Georgia Tech. The Yellow Jackets held three regular-season opponents scoreless (plus a fourth, Pittsburgh, in the Sugar Bowl) and two others without a touchdown. In 11 games, they surrendered just 46 points, Tech's lowest total since 1927. After losing to Auburn, Tech then shut out Florida State 34-0 and Duke 27-0 before settling for a 7-7 tie with Bowden Wyatt's first Tennessee team. There followed a resounding 26-2 win over Alabama and then a seventh straight conquest of Georgia 21-3, which left the water table in Athens dangerously low.

In 1955, Dodd had one of his best and deepest backfields. His starters were Mitchell at quarterback, Dickie Mattison at fullback, and Volkert and Rotenberry the halfbacks. Their backups, respectively, were Toppy Vann, Ken Owen, Jimmy Thompson, and Stan Flowers. All eight of those backs would return for the 1956 season, along with such outstanding linemen as Carl Vereen, Allen Ecker, Ormand Anderson, and Don Ellis.

"We had a lot of good football players on both the first and second teams," Dodd said. "If I could have picked out the 11 best offensive and 11 best defensive players, they would have been terrific. That's what killed me all through those years, when we had to play 'em both ways."

Georgia Tech still managed to finish 9-1-1 and ranked seventh in the nation. But not before becoming inadvertently involved in one of the ugliest and most controversial incidents in college football history.

Before the New Year's Day bowl selections were made, Harry Mehre, the former Georgia and Mississippi coach, wrote an article for the *Atlanta Journal,* as he often did. Commenting on Bobby Dodd's success—his teams had won four major bowl games in the previous four years and six-of-six overall under Dodd—Mehre wrote that such an achievement was "comparable to Bobby Jones's Grand Slam in golf."

Dodd and Georgia Tech, Mehre noted, accomplished all that with fine teams, good teams, and just fair teams. But always, Tech won, and won despite good weather, bad weather, and terrible weather in which to prepare for those bowls.

"Dodd may be lucky," Mehre decided, "but Lady Luck is so fickle that she doesn't hover over the same coach for six years."

She would hover again come January 1 in New Orleans, but there was nothing lucky or fortunate about the incidents that followed the Sugar Bowl selection of Georgia Tech and Pittsburgh.

Pitt was a powerful team. As Joe Paterno, then a young assistant to Rip Engle of Penn State, would tell Bobby Dodd years later, Pittsburgh was the best college team Paterno had ever seen. The Panthers had an abundance of talent. They also had a fullback named Bob Grier, who was black. Or, as civil southerners then called blacks, a Negro. In the segregationist South of 1955, an integrated opponent was considered even more despicable than having to play at Notre Dame against all those Catholics.

Georgia Tech, remember, had held out Hoot Gibson in 1934 in exchange for Michigan withholding Willis Ward, a black player. Bill Alexander feared the segregationist reaction back in Atlanta if Tech returned home having played an integrated team. There had been no such incident in 1953, however, when the Yellow Jackets played an integrated Notre Dame team in South Bend. Back in Atlanta, the populace was more concerned about the end of Tech's 31-game unbeaten streak than about Notre Dame's complexion. Georgia, too, had played against integrated football teams, but always on the road.

When Tech agreed to play Bob Grier and Pitt in the 1956 Sugar Bowl, however, Atlanta became hell on earth.

"Ban Interracial Sports—Griffin" screamed the front-page headline in the Friday, December 2, edition of the *Atlanta Journal*. Georgia Governor Marvin Griffin called for an emergency meeting of the state Board of Regents to prohibit Georgia football teams from competing against integrated teams. When asked if he wanted to cancel the Tech-Pitt game, Griffin would only say that a telegram he sent that day to Robert O. Arnold, chairman of the Board of Regents, "speaks for itself."

The telegram:

> It is my request that athletic teams of units of the University System of Georgia not be permitted to engage in contests with other teams where the races are mixed on such teams or where segregation is not required among spectators at such events. The South stands at Armageddon. The battle is joined. We cannot make the slightest concession to the enemy in this dark and lamentable hour of struggle. There is no more difference in compromising integrity of race on the playing field than in doing so in the classrooms. One break in the dike and the relentless seas will rush in and destroy us. We are in this fight 100 percent, not 98 percent, not 75 percent, not 64 percent—but a full 100 percent. An immediate called meeting of the state Board of Regents to act on my request is vitally necessary at this time.

Bobby Dodd had earlier received a telegram from one Hugh G. Grant, an official of the States' Rights Council, a militant pro-segregation organization whose founders included several Georgia political leaders—including Governor Griffin, former Governor Herman Talmadge, and Regent Roy Harris, a vehement segregationist from Augusta. Grant's telegram sought Dodd's "cooperation" in preventing any "mixing of the races" in the Sugar Bowl. Grant wanted Dodd to pull out of the bowl game. Dodd would not even dignify the telegram with a comment. He was determined to play the game. Dodd recalls:

"Really, that took a lot of guts on my part. There was so much fussin' about the blacks in those days by the rednecks, and with all the trouble over in Alabama, and with ol' Roy Harris over there in Augusta. He was rabid. And here we are, we're gonna break the racial barrier in the South. We're gonna play against a black boy for the first time in the South.

"I got permission first from the players. They said it didn't make any difference to them, which I knew to be true. Then I went to the president of the school [Blake Van Leer] and he said he'd back me. I went to the governor, and Marvin Griffin said, 'I'll back you, but not publicly.' "

Howard Ector, then the business manager for athletics at Tech, remembers a phone conversation with Griffin that Friday, December 2. A half-hour later, Ector got a phone call from WSB, asking for a comment on the governor's announcement moments earlier that said, in essence, he would seek to stop Tech from playing Pitt in the Sugar Bowl. It was not Ector's place to comment for Tech, but he had an inkling of Griffin's true intent.

"He was ranting and raving out of one side of his mouth and winking at you on the other," Ector said. "He knew this was all because of the political situation, with the black and white situation. But Marvin wasn't about to cancel that football game."

Griffin's telegram to the regents, however, resulted in an emergency meeting as well as a police emergency. The regents wouldn't convene until eleven-thirty Monday morning, but, by Friday night, an angry crowd of two thousand people—mostly Tech students—was demonstrating around Atlanta.

"That was my first experience with a civil rights march that had absolutely nothing to do with civil rights," said Wade Mitchell.

Indeed, those who supported Georgia Tech's right to compete in the Sugar Bowl based their argument on football, not civil rights, considerations. They wanted to see their Yellow Jackets play in another big bowl game.

"Tech Students Jeer at Capitol, Mansion" read the page one headline in the *Atlanta Journal* on Saturday, December 3. "Burn Griffin in Effigy in Protest of Bowl Ban." Early the previous evening, Wade Mitchell was looking out his dorm room window as hundreds upon hundreds of Tech students—after burning an effigy of Griffin on campus—began marching downtown toward the gold dome of the state capitol. "To lobby the governor," Mitchell said. "I don't know why they expected to find him down there at night."

En route, the crowd burned another effigy at Five Points and then arrived at the capitol. The students carried signs that read, "Griffin sits on his brain," "We want to go to the Sugar Bowl," "We play anybody," and "Talmadge puppet does it again."

Some demonstrators tore up historical markers on the capitol lawn.

Others burned yet another effigy of Griffin. Many marchers then stormed past Georgia Bureau of Investigation agents and smashed two ground-floor doors to get into the capitol building.

They emptied garbage cans and scattered sand from cuspidors on the first floor. They shattered the glass paneling around the information desk. From the capitol, the crowd—now described as a mob by the *Journal*—marched back through downtown, overturning more trash cans, tearing out parking meters, and breaking the taillight on a police car.

By the time the students arrived at the Prado, police had cordoned off the governor's mansion. Atlanta police were supported by police from DeKalb, Cobb, and Clayton counties. Twenty-five State Patrol cars had arrived, too.

The crowd drew to within 50 feet of Griffin's home but got no closer. Police, most armed and also carrying nightsticks, held them back, and Muggsy Smith, a former Tech player, a state representative, and a neighbor on the Prado, finally convinced the crowd to disperse.

By then, it was three-thirty in the morning. Earlier, Marvin Griffin had been pacing the floor inside the mansion, but the governor never came out to address the demonstrators. Later Saturday morning, before leaving Atlanta to hunt quail in south Georgia, Griffin told the *Journal*, "It was an orderly demonstration. They hooted and sang and hanged me to a sour apple tree, but it was just a bunch of college boys having a good time, and I never get excited about that."

Even as the governor was saying that, however, an unnamed spokesman for the Griffin administration had told the *Journal*, "Georgia Tech will be allowed to play in the Sugar Bowl." The spokesman said that in wiring the Board of Regents and seeking a meeting, Griffin was hoping to prevent teams from the University System of Georgia from playing against integrated opponents or before mixed crowds.

As for the Sugar Bowl, Georgia Tech had already entered into an agreement to play the game. Although Dr. Blake Van Leer declined comment to the Atlanta media on Saturday, the Tech president told an NBC reporter in Chicago, "I have never broken a contract, and I'm not going to break one now."

Bobby Dodd said, "We still have a contract to play, and until I'm told otherwise, I intend to fulfill it."

Like Dodd, *Atlanta Journal* sports editor Ed Danforth realized the future implications raised by Griffin's stance. Danforth wrote:

"If Tech and Georgia must refuse to play any team on which a Negro plays or in a stadium in which segregation is not maintained, then the intersectional athletic program of both schools will be wrecked. No team in the Big Ten or on the West Coast would sign to play either Tech or Georgia. Nor would Notre Dame, the Army, or the Navy set up games with two state schools because they could not guarantee segregation would be observed on the team or in the stadiums.

"Tech and Georgia would be promptly dropped from all bowl game calculations. Lack of intersectional games would hurt them at the gate and the whole athletic program supported by football would suffer."

"We wanted to go to the Sugar Bowl," Dodd said, "and we knew that if we accepted, we were gonna have to play against a black boy. And I wanted to break the racial barrier, 'cause if we're gonna play any eastern teams, they're all gonna have blacks. A lot of coaches told me, 'If anybody can break the racial thing, y'all can. Tech's the best team to break it.' We were recognized nationally, we're in a big city. It'd be harder to do it in a little town like Auburn or Tuscaloosa.

"And I just wanted to break it. Hell, I knew we had to get rid of that damn racial thing."

His players just wanted to play ball. "I remember the meeting where Coach Dodd talked to the team about it," Wade Mitchell said, "and I remember thinking at that time that this was no big deal. Two years before when we went up to Notre Dame, they had two or three black kids playing for them up there. Of course, we were out of our region.

"But I was shocked at all of the turmoil this created. I was getting telephone calls from *Time* magazine wanting to know what I thought about going down there and playing against this black kid. It surprised me. If I'd stopped to think, maybe it was more historic than I realized. But we just wanted to play, and it didn't make a difference who we played."

"Tech Students Stir Up Storm, Apologize to Pitt" was the lead headline in the combined *Atlanta Journal-Constitution* of Sunday, December 4. George Harris, president of the Georgia Tech student body, sent a telegram to Pitt that said: "The student body of Georgia Tech sincerely apologizes for the unwarranted action of Georgia's governor. We are looking forward to seeing your entire team and student body at the Sugar Bowl."

Other Georgians had other views. Another front page story that Sunday was headlined "Drinkard Out to Stop Funds If Tech Plays." State representative John P. Drinkard of Lincoln County advocated cutting off state funds to Georgia Tech if the school permitted the Yellow Jackets to play Pitt. At the time, Drinkard was the chairman of the State of the Republic Committee, which handled administration legislation. Drinkard also proposed that "any person making application to any unit of our University System for admittance should state, plainly and unequivocally, whether (he or she) favors mixing of the races in our schools and colleges. If the applicant so states, there should be a law denying him or her entrance."

The telegrams that began arriving at Tech over the weekend

expressed concern, outrage, and opposition to Drinkard and Griffin. Many were from Georgia Tech alumni clubs and individual alumni around the country. "Please do not allow one demagogue to ruin Georgia Tech's good name, national reputation, and entire sports program," read one telegram. Another called Griffin's position "asinine, absurd, and ridiculous." A College Park man implored Blake Van Leer not to allow "racial bigots to dictate action that will embarrass your great institution." And an Atlantan wired: "As an American born in Georgia, I hope we never return to the days of the 1920s when the Ku Klux Klan ruled our state and spread its poison against Negro, Jew, and Catholic alike."

The Citizens Council of New Orleans, however, commended Griffin in a telegram: "A great majority of the people of New Orleans were disappointed at the Sugar Bowl committee's decision to invite Pittsburgh to play in the annual football game. New Orleanians have always wholeheartedly supported the annual classic but if the Sugar Bowlers persist in agitating the segregation issue by permitting a game where the races are mixed and the seats sold on a nonsegregated basis, the Sugar Bowl will soon lose the support of the people."

In a front-page Sunday editorial on "Griffin's Teapot Tempest," the *Journal-Constitution* ridiculed the governor's actions and criticized the demonstrators. "An incalculable disservice has been done the state and its University System by the nationwide notoriety resulting from the ill-considered actions of both Governor Griffin and the indignant Tech students who burned him in effigy. Particularly incongruous is the Governor's precipitating such a controversy so close on the heels of his recent jaunts to New York, Chicago, and Cleveland for the laudable purpose of inviting new industry to Georgia. How can he expect this state to attract anything except ridicule when its chief executive so constantly seizes upon the slightest excuse to make political capital?

"It is our hope that reason will reassert itself—both at the Flats and in the Governor's office—and that Georgians will be spared any further unnecessary humiliation. It is a time to consider our major problems in a calm and reasonable way and not to incite fiascoes over the piddling ones."

In that same issue ran a brief, two-paragraph wire story out of Pittsburgh, under the heading, "Sorry About Dispute, Negro to Play to Win." "All this trouble will not affect my play," Bob Grier was quoted as saying. "I'll be there to win. But I'm awfully sorry all this trouble has come about."

On Monday, December 5, representatives from Tech, including Dr. Van Leer, Coach Dodd, and Howard Ector, met with the state Board of Regents committee on education. Ector recalled that at one point during the heated meeting Dr. Van Leer told the board, "Either we're going to the Sugar Bowl, or you can find yourself another damn president of Georgia Tech."

The regents backed down and permitted Tech to participate in the game. That afternoon, the headline of the final edition of the *Atlanta Journal* declared, "Regents Give Full Okay to Tech-Pitt Bowl Game." The regents, however, also resolved by a vote of 14-1 to continue its standing policy of segregation in athletic contests played within the state of Georgia. Athletic teams of the University System would be allowed to compete against integrated teams, but only outside the state.

"I commend the members for their thoughtful and courageous action relative to future athletic contests," Governor Griffin said afterward at a press conference. "Let me reemphasize that I am unalterably opposed to the unsegregated conditions which the Sugar Bowl committee is permitting this year for the first time.

"I can't regulate the customs of that state," Griffin said regarding the regents' decision to permit out-of-state games against integrated teams in accordance with laws and customs of the host state. Griffin had been asked specifically about the impending Georgia game at Michigan scheduled for 1957.

"I will not give one word of comfort to white folks and Negroes playing on the same field," Griffin said, "but I make no protest."

As usual, Tech's opposition arrived first at the bowl site. Pittsburgh flew into New Orleans on Monday, December 26, the day Tech was just reporting back to campus. Shortly after arriving, Pitt held a workout—a workout that dramatically altered the outcome of the game.

While hitting a blocking sled, starting fullback Tom Jenkins severely injured cartilage in his knee. That left Jenkins on crutches and highly doubtful for the game. And that left Bob Grier, a 196-pound senior and the first black player invited to the Sugar Bowl, as the probable starting fullback and linebacker.

"I think everything will be all right if my knee stands up in practice and during the game," Grier said Tuesday. "Everybody down here has been real nice. And I don't believe any of us are too nervous about the way we'll play."

"Grier is a good boy," said Pitt coach John Michelosen. "In fact, he's a better runner than Jenkins. The running game may be stronger and the defense not quite as sharp with the switch. He's not quite the linebacker and blocker that Jenkins is, but he's improving there."

Like Atlanta and the rest of the South, New Orleans was a "closed," or segregated, city in 1955. Bob Grier, however, practiced, ate, and roomed with the rest of his teammates at a Tulane dormitory. There were no off-field incidents involving the first black player to participate in the Sugar Bowl.

"Everything was great," Grier would later reflect. "I felt no pressure."

On Thursday, Georgia Tech boarded three Delta planes in Atlanta and finally flew into New Orleans. The Yellow Jackets held a workout that afternoon. So, of course, did Pitt, practicing in the shadow of the Sugar Bowl. Tom Jenkins watched from the sidelines, still on crutches. Fluid had been drained from his knee earlier in the day, and Jenkins said he was in less pain. But he was still very doubtful for the game; at practice, Jenkin's only physical activity was a short game of catch with a spectator.

By Friday, John Michelosen resigned himself to the fact Jenkins would be unable to play. By practice Saturday afternoon, Bob Grier was definitely Pitt's starting fullback. Georgia Tech practiced Saturday morning, at the request of Dodd's players, who wanted to watch the Auburn-Vanderbilt Gator Bowl on television that afternoon. That the Yellow Jackets were in condition to practice Saturday morning seemed remarkable to some people, especially the Pitt team.

Dodd and his team had enjoyed a customary pre-bowl evening of dining, dancing, and a floor show at the Blue Room of the Hotel Roosevelt, while the Pitt players took in an early movie after being sequestered all week.

"The Panther expedition is deadly serious," Ed Danforth wrote, "and they are wondering how the Yellow Jackets get away with it."

By game day, smaller, swifter Tech was a solid seven and one-half-point favorite over slower, more powerful Pitt. With 80,175 spectators looking on, Tech received the opening kickoff but was forced to punt. After managing one first down, Pitt quarterback Pete Neft fumbled the snap on the tenth play of the game. Allen Ecker recovered for Tech at the Pitt 32. Hoping to capitalize quickly, Dodd, characteristically, instructed Wade Mitchell to pass.

It was the Kingsport Play. As Mitchell faked to Paul Rotenberry off left tackle and then bootlegged to the right, Joe Walton—then a Pitt end, now head coach of the New York Jets—wasn't fooled. Hoping to elude Walton, Mitchell kept scrambling to his right, stopped, and threw downfield just before Walton hit him. Mitchell threw for Tech end Don Ellis, who, ironically, was guarded closely by Bob Grier.

As Grier fell at the goal line, Ellis leaped for Mitchell's pass, but the ball sailed over his fingers. "As they crossed the line near the flag, Grier pushed Ellis and fell down," wrote Ed Danforth, who, like his sports-writing contemporaries, did not have the benefit of instant replay in the press box. "Ellis was knocked off balance and missed the ball."

But as the ball bounced harmlessly in the end zone, a penalty flag fluttered to the ground.

Pass interference on Grier.

"You ask Don Ellis today if he got interfered with," Mitchell said, "and he won't answer you."

Grier protested the call to the officials. The Pitt fans booed vociferously. The call stood. Georgia Tech had a first-and-goal at the two. After a Pitt offsides penalty, Mitchell sneaked in for the touchdown and a 7-0 lead. It was the only score of the game.

Pitt dominated play that day. The Panthers rushed for 217 yards to Tech's 142 (Grier led all rushers with 51 yards on six carries). Pitt passed for 94 yards to none for Georgia Tech. The Jackets attempted only three passes, all incomplete. Just before halftime, Pitt had driven to the Tech one, but on fourth down, Mitchell and left tackle Carl Vereen stopped Pitt quarterback Corny Salvaterra.

Afterward, sitting on an equipment trunk in the Tech dressing room, Bobby Dodd admitted, "I guess we do win a lot of games when the other team does most of the moving."

In the Pittsburgh locker room, meanwhile, Bob Grier was in tears. After composing himself, Grier denied pushing Ellis and told reporters that Ellis had pushed him. "I couldn't say if it was intentional," Grier said, "but he pushed me from behind. That's why I fell forward."

Despite the controversy, Grier also said of his role as the first black player in the Sugar Bowl, "I would be happy to have any son of mine go through the same experience. The publicity didn't bother me. I have no regrets."

The crowd, according to Grier, had been "real nice" to him. When Grier injured his knee in the fourth quarter, a couple of Tech players helped him off the field.

Later, Grier attended the annual post-game party for players and coaches at the traditionally segregated St. Charles Hotel. He did not, however, attend the ball, buffet supper, and dance that followed the private dinner. Instead, Grier left with a Pitt coach for a party at Dillard University, a black college in New Orleans. Most of his white teammates and most Tech players stayed at the St. Charles for the dance.

On Tuesday, Georgia Tech returned home to a warm Atlanta embrace. With its 7-0 victory over Pitt, Tech had finished its season 9-1-1 and ranked seventh in the nation. The Jackets had won their fifth major bowl game in five years, and a record fourth Sugar Bowl in just four attempts.

"It was a great year," Dodd said. "We lost by two points to Auburn and tied Tennessee. We were three points away from an undefeated season."

The Atlanta newspapers chronicled the Jackets' homecoming and ran photos of George Volkert posing with assistant coach Jack Griffin and Griffin's young daughter, Leigh, waving a Tech pennant, also, fullback

Ken Owen escorting Dodd's daughter, Linda, to her car. Front-page articles that day included the reopening of a suit filed in 1950 by a black Atlanta man named Horace Ward, seeking admission to the law school at the University of Georgia; and in Tennessee, a federal judge ordered Anderson County—adjacent to Knoxville—to integrate its public schools that fall.

The following day, in his State of the Union message, President Dwight Eisenhower recommended to Congress the establishment of a bipartisan commission to investigate alleged civil rights violations in the South. "It is disturbing," Eisenhower said, "that in some localities allegations persist that Negro citizens are being deprived of their rights to vote and are likewise being subjected to unwarranted economic pressures."

Of the Sugar Bowl controversy that was finally resolved when he spoke before the Board of Regents, Tech President Blake Van Leer later said, "These were the toughest four days of my life." Six weeks after the controversy, Blake Van Leer died of a cerebral hemorrhage at the age of 60.

The 1956 Georgia Tech Yellow Jackets. "There was probably more talent on that team," Bobby Dodd said, "than on any other team I coached.

"We had a real good football team here," Dodd said, pointing to his first team on a 1956 depth chart. "And one right here behind it just as good." He pointed to the second team. "And we even had boys over here [pointing to the third team] that were good football players.

"We were strong.

"Of all the teams I coached in 22 years at Georgia Tech, the 1956 team had by far the best material," Dodd said, "particularly in the backfield."

All the players from the first- and second-string backfields returned. Ken Owen had moved ahead of Dickie Mattison as the starting fullback, joining Wade Mitchell, Paul Rotenberry, and George Volkert. But Mattison played a considerable amount, as did backup quarterback Toppy Vann and halfbacks Jimmy Thompson and Stan Flowers. The entire right side of the starting offensive line returned: guard Allen Ecker, tackle Ormand Anderson, and Don Ellis. Carl Vereen was back at left tackle; the 1955 captain, center Jimmy Morris, had been replaced by Don Stephenson, who would make all-American teams in 1956 and '57.

"There was a lot of good skilled talent on that team," Mitchell said. "But I'll tell you this: they were as talented as they were because of Coach Dodd. He's a great philosopher in a lot of ways. I never realized it until after I left what he was doing to us. I saw somewhere after I got out of Tech that 'If you give a dog a good name he'll live up to it.' And that's exactly what he was doing.

"When I was a freshman, Dave Davis was the punter. And Dave Davis, hell, he was six feet, five inches tall, weighed 220 pounds, and could kick the ball 80 yards, just perfect stuff. The next year, we were trying to find a punter out there. Everybody's kicking knuckleballs and shanking 'em, and *nobody* can kick the ball. And then I pick up the paper one day and Coach Dodd says, 'We got two of the finest punters in the SEC: Johnny Menger and Ken Owen.' Menger didn't weigh but 150 pounds, but damn, the next day he starts kicking the ball 70 yards, and Owens starts doing the same thing. And Coach Dodd did the same thing to me that year."

Dodd was desperate. He had Bill Brigman and Pepper Rodgers and Joe Hall as quarterbacks, all fine offensive quarterbacks, but none were skilled defenders.

"Couldn't tackle *me*," Dodd said.

"And I knew a little bit about defense from high school, but not a helluva lot," Mitchell said. "But I picked up the paper before I'd played a game at Tech that year, and he says I'm the finest defensive safety in the SEC. I said, 'Oh my God, what is he talking about?' But he told us how good we were, and then we were afraid not to be."

As talented and deep as those 1956 Yellow Jackets were, though, only 11 could play at a time. The one-platoon rule imposed by Neyland and Crisler prevented the 1956 team from fulfilling its potential, perhaps more than any other Bobby Dodd team of the 1950s.

Georgia Tech opened the 1956 season with six straight victories to extend its unbeaten streak to 12 games. After narrowly winning at Kentucky 14-6 and SMU 9-7, the Jackets returned home to thrash LSU 39-7, and, with Johnny Menger running 60 yards for one touchdown and returning a punt 87 yards for another, Tech avenged its loss to Auburn the previous year 28-7. The Jacket defense then recorded consecutive shutouts, pummeling Tulane 40-0 and winning at Duke 7-0.

With that 6-0 record, Georgia Tech was ranked second in the nation. Tennessee, with Bowden Wyatt in his second season as head coach and the versatile Johnny Majors at tailback, was also 6-0 and ranked third. On game day, November 10, scalpers were getting up to two hundred dollars a ticket.

"That was probably the greatest old-time defensive football game that's ever been played in the South, before or since," Bobby Dodd said. "They don't play defense now like they used to. They have greater athletes today, but nobody plays defense like we played it back in those days."

Especially on that day, November 10, 1956. "See, Bowden and I were both of the Tennessee philosophy," Dodd said. "We both learned under Neyland. Both knew the value of the kicking game and the value of field position. We want the other team to have the ball on their 20. We don't want it on our 20. What's the use of having it on our 20? We know we're not gonna drive 80 yards for a touchdown. And we don't want a mistake down there.

"So, field position was important."

So, in the glow of an autumn sun, Georgia Tech and Tennessee reflected each other. They played a mirror-image football game, stressing defense, the kicking game—especially the quick-kick—and field position.

Several times Tennessee reversed unfavorable field position with remarkable kicks, as Johnny Majors quick-kicked and Bobby Gordon punted the Volunteers out of trouble. The two teams played to a standoff—except for one play.

A fluke won the game for Tennessee. Flukes are appealing to old fishermen like Bobby Dodd, but flukes are anathema to old football coaches like Bobby Dodd. They are particularly painful when they ruin a perfect season and a possible national championship.

The first half was scoreless, but in the third quarter Tennessee crossed into Tech territory. Volunteer end Buddy Cruze ran a down-and-out pattern and Johnny Majors hit him for a 10-yard gain. On the next play, Cruze faked the down-and-out and ran a break pattern, down-and-in, slanting and splitting Mitchell, the safety, and Paul Rotenberry, the left defensive halfback.

"Paul is absolutely innocent in all of that," Mitchell said. "I just took the wrong angle. I was the safety in a three-deep and it was about a 10 or 12-yard break route. Instead of hitting the man, Paul and I ran together, and Cruze caught it and ran down to the one-yard line."

Mitchell's sore shoulder complicated the situation. He played in spite of the injury, and on that play he twisted himself to hit Cruze with his healthy shoulder. Instead, Mitchell and Rotenberry collided, Cruze held onto the ball, bounced away, and was finally caught at the one. Fullback Tommy Bronson dived in for the touchdown. The conversion failed, but Tennessee led 6-0.

In the fourth quarter, Georgia Tech posed its last serious threat. Naturally, it was a serious defensive threat. "Through the kicking game and playing good football," Dodd recalled, "we got Tennessee backed up to their 20-yard line."

But the Tennessee kicking game came through again. Bobby Gordon got off a tremendous 72-yard punt that George Volkert fielded at the Tech eight. Volkert lateraled to Stan Flowers, who was tackled back at the two. "And that was the game," Dodd said. "We never got another opportunity to score."

"If I have had one person remind me of that game and that pass play in 30 years now, I must have had a million," Mitchell said. "Vernon Crawford got me as good as I've ever been gotten about eight years ago. I was over at Tech to speak at a student-faculty industry dinner and Vernon Crawford was introducing me. So he started off and said a couple of nice things you normally expect the fellow introducing the speaker to say.

"And then he proceeded for about seven minutes, in living color and gory detail, to tell four hundred people out there how I had screwed this thing up and I had cost us the national championship and all this kind of stuff. And I'm sitting there listening. He finally got through and said, 'Wade, I guess you're wondering why I take this opportunity to tell all these people this.' And I said, 'Well, Vernon, yes.' And he said, 'Well, I'll tell you. Because I've never forgiven you.' "

Tech took out its frustration the next three weekends, both offensively and defensively. The Yellow Jackets fashioned three consecutive shutout routs, giving them five shutouts in their last six games. Alabama fell 27-0, Alabama's worst loss to Georgia Tech since 1910. The Jackets dominated Florida 28-0 and then humiliated Georgia 35-0.

"We," Dodd said, "were a great football team."

Stan Flowers scored twice against Georgia, on a two-yard plunge and 12-yard pass from Toppy Vann. Rotenberry, Mitchell, and Mattison each ran for a touchdown, and Georgia Tech had reached several milestones. This was Bobby Dodd's one-hundredth coaching victory, against only 28 losses and three ties. For Georgia, this was the eighth straight loss to those insufferable Yellow Jackets and that damn Dodd. For Georgia Tech, this guaranteed its sixth consecutive major bowl invitation.

This time, however, Tech did not select one of the three New Year's Day bowls—Sugar, Orange, or Cotton—for which it was eligible. "The Gator Bowl people were my friends down there, some of 'em real close friends of mine—Tech people," Dodd said. "They'd been courtin' us all year, of course. They were up here every year trying to get us to come to the Gator Bowl. They wanted a team of stature coming to Jacksonville to make the Gator Bowl a major bowl."

At the time, the Gator Bowl was the fifth-ranking bowl—in terms of prestige and money—behind the four major New Year's Day bowls. But the Gator Bowl had a unique offer for Dodd and Tech, something the Sugar, Cotton, or Orange couldn't match: a rematch.

For Dodd, this became a real dilemma. "I wanted to help the Gator Bowl become a major bowl, because I knew we were gonna have a chance to play there some," he said. "But I hated to play Pittsburgh again, not only because how tough they were, but because they wanted revenge. I knew we were a better team this year than we were the year before. Not necessarily because of the record, but all those juniors from the year before were seniors now. I knew it would take a good football team to beat us."

Dodd talked to his team to see if his players had a preference, to see how they felt about playing Pittsburgh again. "They said it didn't matter to them who we played," Dodd said. "But our people all wanted us to go there, because Jacksonville's the closest of all the bowl games to Atlanta. They all wanted to follow us and watch us play. We had a big bowl following back then, they'd find the money to go.

"So we agreed to play 'em. And we went down there, and we didn't have any problems. They didn't have any blacks that year. Grier had graduated. But they were still a great football team. But so was my '56 team."

Ken Owen scored Tech's first touchdown on a two-yard dive for a 7-0 first-quarter lead. With 2:02 left in the half, George Volkert threw an option pass to junior left end Jerry Nabors for a 14-7 Tech lead at halftime. Pitt fumbled the second-half kickoff, and Wesley Gobbs recovered at the Panther 37. Paul Rotenberry punctuated the drive with the winning touchdown, a five-yarder for a 21-7 advantage. Pitt came back and scored after a long drive, but Tech held on through a scoreless fourth quarter to win 21-14.

"It made the Gator Bowl," Dodd said. "We gave 'em national prestige."

Tech finished 10-1 and ranked fourth nationally. Bobby Dodd's Yellow Jackets won an unprecedented six consecutive bowl games in as many years, and his overall postseason record was 8-0. There was no doubt now. Bobby Dodd was the bowlmaster.

While preparing for the Gator Bowl, Dodd was agonizing over a major career decision. Through the years many colleges had unsuccessfully tried to lure Bobby Dodd away from Atlanta and Georgia Tech. But this time was different. This wasn't Rice or TCU, Baylor or Vanderbilt. This was Texas. The Longhorns were looking for a new head coach.

And Bobby Dodd had always maintained, "There's only one school I'll ever leave Tech for: the University of Texas."

"The reason my name probably came up," said Dodd, "was that I had these four major bowls, and one of 'em was in Texas [the Cotton Bowl victory over Arkansas]."

When the chairman of the Texas selection committee—a multi-millionaire from Midland—invited him to interview, Dodd asked for a day or two to think. "I'd had good years at Tech, been to bowl games, my players were good and I hated to leave them," Dodd explained. "He called me every night, as well as I remember for about a week. And I remember at the end of it, he said, 'I'll make you a millionaire in five years, put you in the oil business, if you'll come out here and coach.'

"Boy, for a guy who's never had any money, that was more temptation than I could hardly stand."

But Dodd hesitated, and then declined. Even though the offer was more appealing and more lucrative, he stayed at Tech for essentially the same reasons as before. He was established and popular. His family loved living in Atlanta. And he loved Georgia Tech.

"And I knew if I left here and went to Texas, I'd have to start all over again and prove myself. In Texas, I'd have to go all over the state and make speeches in every town in Texas, and sell those Texas people on Bobby Dodd. And I hated to travel. To go from Austin to El Paso is like going from here to Pennsylvania. I didn't like that part, knowing I'd have to recruit and travel all over the state and be gone a lot.

"But I love Texas people. They're like Georgia people but with more money. I just *loved* 'em. When I'd go out there to those bowl games or go out there to play, they'd give me that big Texas hat. I'm even bowlegged like those Texans. And they'd say, 'Boy, you oughta be a Texan, you look like a Texan!'

"I was rawboned, bowlegged. They said, 'You'd make a great Texan!' I said, 'I sure would.' I'd a made a great Texan. I'd love to be one of those Texans with a million dollars. Hell, I wasn't making more than thirty or thirty-five thousand dollars at Tech.

"But I still loved Atlanta. I'd gotten to know so many people in Atlanta. You know, Atlanta before World War II was just a big country town. You knew nearly everybody. I knew everybody on the north side of town. I could tell you whose house that was, whose house this was, they're Georgia people, they're Tech people.

"And we're still the only show in town. Our games are terrific, I've got great press. The sportswriters here just treated me royally.

"So I just had everything going for me here. It was just tough to leave it and start all over. So I turned it down. The last night when the chairman called me, he said, 'Coach, I don't believe you're gonna come. If you were in my place, who would you go get?' And I recommended one man. I knew a little bit about him from people, from coaches, and I said, 'There's a young boy named Darrell Royal. I believe I'd go get him. I think you could go get one of the older coaches, like Duffy Daugherty or one of the other established coaches. But I'd get this young person; he'd stay with you a long time, and he's a good coach.' "

As Dodd was trying to make up his mind, Darrell Royal waited anxiously in Texas. Each night, he called his close friend, Tonto Coleman, Dodd's assistant, to see if Dodd had accepted.

When Bobby Dodd finally decided not to leave Tech, Royal was named the new Texas head coach, a job which he held for 20 years. Like Dodd, Royal became a hero, a legend in his own time. His teams won 164 games, lost 47 and tied 5. He won 11 Southwest Conference championships, 3 national championships, and, on the strength of the wishbone offense, the Longhorns won 30 straight games from 1968 to 1970.

Bobby Dodd, meanwhile, remained at Georgia Tech. Almost immediately, Dodd regretted the decision. "If Texas," he said, "had offered me that job about a year or two later—which they probably wouldn't have because of my record—I'd a probably gone to Texas or any other real well-known football school."

The best sideline strategist ever.

Chapter 13
The Drought Ends—More Clouds in the Forecast

ON JANUARY 8, 1957, *Look* magazine celebrated its 20th anniversary with a special commemorative issue. There, among the political leaders, actors, entertainers, and the other most recognizable figures in the world, was an article about, and written by, the Gray Fox. Such was Bobby Dodd's status in society, much less the closed fraternity of college football, by the end of the 1956 season.

"The Head Coach Doesn't Coach Anymore" was the title of the *Look* article, written by Dodd in collaboration with Furman Bisher. It detailed the chairman-of-the-board existence that all major-college coaches live today and that most (at least the successful ones) were living by that time. An existence whose founding father was Bobby Dodd.

Several photographs accompanied the article. One captured Dodd at work, which was really Dodd at play. Taken during the 1956 LSU game, the photo showed Dodd—luxuriating on the sideline and spiffy in his snap-brim hat—leaning back in his folding chair, looking to his left, and, with his hand, casually summoning a substitute in that 39-7 Tech romp.

The text and photos—and the fact that *Look* ran an article about Dodd at all in such a prestigious issue—spoke eloquently of the station in life to which Bobby Dodd had risen.

Some people said that he was more popular than the governor. One thing is certain, the governor called Dodd for favors. "I'd have ol' Herman Talmadge, the governor of the state, calling me for tickets the morning of the Alabama game," Dodd said. "The *morning of the game*."

From 1951 through 1956, Bobby Dodd compiled the most enviable of records. His Tech teams won 59 games, lost just 7, and tied 3. That's 59-7-3. That's a winning percentage of .894. Consider also that most of those triumphs took place at Grant Field, where Dodd wanted to—and usually did—play as often as possible. For the opposition, Grant Field became Grant's Tomb. And who was buried in Grant's Tomb? Everybody.

After that awful Alabama loss in November 1950, Georgia Tech went 23 games in Grant Field without losing. The Jackets were unbeaten at home in 1950, '52, and '53, tying Duke in '51, and losing finally to Florida in the second game of the 1954 season. Overall, Georgia Tech was 34-3-2 at home from 1951 through 1956, an astonishing winning percentage of .919.

Little wonder, then, that Georgia Tech football became the pre-eminent event—athletically and socially—on the Saturday calendar in the 1950s.

"It was by far the big thing in town, the only game in town," Dodd said. "If you didn't have a ticket to Tech football, you didn't rate socially. That west stand? That's where Atlanta society was on Saturday afternoons.

"A lot of people had brunches at their homes before games, and we had our games at one-thirty or two o'clock, because we found out that was the best time. People could drive up from Macon, Augusta, come to the games, and then drive back that same night. And drinking was at a minimum. We kept an eye on that."

And all of Atlanta kept an eye on Georgia Tech. "Football season was Georgia Tech football," Dodd said. "We had terrific crowds. And my football players, they had a ball. I'd give 'em four tickets on the 50-yard line for every game, and then they'd take those tickets and sell 'em.

"Then, when their mothers or their girlfriends came, I let them sit on the sideline—not use up their good ticket on their family. I had three hundred on the sideline. That's how many tickets I printed for the sideline. Those were freebies."

Tech tickets were at such a premium that before the west stands were double-decked in 1967, Dodd had temporary bleachers installed atop the press box. "I checked out the press box to see if it would hold," Dodd said, "and I put about 10 rows of bleachers up there. I got about four hundred tickets up there. Boy, that was great."

Those tickets went to high school football coaches who wanted to watch Tech, and whose players were essential to Dodd's continued success. Even members of the Georgia football team, if the schedule called for a bye or Friday night game, drove over to Atlanta and sat up in those press box bleachers.

"I was always hunting seats," Dodd said. "Shoot, we could've sold another twenty to twenty-five thousand tickets if we'd a had 'em during the glory years. We had to keep some tickets available for the visitors, but otherwise, we could've sold out just about the whole stadium with season tickets."

For Bobby Dodd, Saturday—game day—was usually enjoyable, often joyous, and seldom cause for an anxiety attack. "It wasn't that tough," Dodd said. "We got up at a reasonable hour. I wasn't any six o'clocker be in the office."

Dodd usually slept soundly the Friday before games. His teams and preparation were that good. The sleeping pill he always took the night before each game didn't hurt, either. "I've always been a sleeping pill man," Dodd said. "Our team physician would give any of the coaches who wanted 'em a sleeping pill."

After awakening at seven-thirty or eight o'clock, at a most reasonable hour, Dodd dressed, put on his suit and tie—he always wore a suit that was in style—and hopped in his car. He didn't eat breakfast the morning of a game. His stomach was unsettled enough without some sausage and biscuits bouncing around in there. Then Dodd would drive the ten minutes to the athletic office building at the northwest corner of Grant Field. He arrived at nine.

"My job on Saturday mornings was meeting prospects and their mothers and fathers," Dodd said. "I'd talk right up until almost game time, until the time I was gonna meet my players."

Dodd sat in his office and his assistants ushered in recruit after recruit, parent after parent, for an audience of almost papal proportions. Dodd was one of the first college coaches to have a full-time recruiter, an assistant who did nothing but recruit—and not just on Friday nights at high school football games but at practices during the week. Thus, by Saturday mornings at nine, Dodd knew the necessary information about the boy and his family.

"What type of people are they," Dodd said. "Are they working people, what's their financial situation? Are they Christian people? Is the boy dumb? How good a football player is he? If he's a great one, you know, we pay more attention to him."

Just prior to game time, Dodd would meet for the final time with his players in a cramped room under the east stands, at the northeast corner of Grant Field.

Dodd delivered his pre-game and halftime speeches there. Particularly in his pre-game oratory, he was seldom one for fire and brimstone. He sounded more like a corporate chief executive officer than a Sunday morning TV evangelist. He was calm (at least outwardly so), collected, absolutely prepared, and as honest as he was inspiring.

"I didn't rant and rave," Dodd said. "I didn't want my players going out there with tears in their eyes. That wears off in a couple of minutes."

After finishing his brief, to-the-point pre-game speech, Dodd led his players out of the tiny meeting room. Impeccably dressed, he stood at an open gate leading onto Grant Field. The Georgia Tech band played the famous school fight song, "Ramblin' Wreck." (The Rambling Wreck car, the 1930 Ford Cabriolet Sport Coupe that now escorts the Jackets onto Grant Field, wasn't introduced until 1961.) Hundreds of Tech freshmen formed a human gauntlet for the football team. The freshmen wore their Rat Caps, gold beanies that all Tech freshmen were expected to wear at the start of the school year. They could remove them if Tech defeated Georgia (there were an inordinate number of Tech freshmen walking around campus with cold heads during the winters of the Drought); if Georgia won, the Rat Caps had to be worn until the spring.

And as the freshmen applauded, and the band played on, and another capacity crowd sang and cheered, the Georgia Tech Yellow Jackets swarmed onto the lush carpet of green grass in Grant Field. They did so confidently. Whenever John Hunsinger, the backup fullback in 1953 and starter in '54, ran past Dodd at the gate and onto the field, he knew his coach was "completely relaxed, poised, and mentally ready to finesse the game." Like most everyone who has ever played for Dodd, Hunsinger "always felt regardless of the score that he could figure out a way to win the game. The few times we lost, I was not only down but surprised."

The Yellow Jackets then headed toward the west sideline, where Bobby Dodd assumed his customary pose: sitting at a table in a folding chair precisely on the 50-yard line, with several sheets of paper from his yellow legal pad rolled up in his hand. That was the throne from which Dodd orchestrated the action that unfolded before him.

Like any good director, Dodd had his cast deployed perfectly and always at his disposal. His sideline was the picture of organization, as if it were a movie set or theater stage marked with adhesive tape to position actors to deliver their lines.

Dodd sat at midfield, a couple of yards from the sideline, with a phone on the table in front of him. He used the phone to call upstairs to his offensive coordinator in the press box, but usually Dodd merely had to look to his right or left for assistance. To Dodd's right was his offensive team, with an assistant coach and the starting quarterback nearby, and the rest of the offensive players stretched up the right sideline: backs first, then the linemen, then the receivers.

To Dodd's left sat his defensive coordinator, for years Ray Graves. The punter sat beside Graves, and then the rest of the defenders.

The sideline organization benefited the assistants and players as much as Dodd. "I didn't think they could think good running up and down the sidelines," Dodd said. "They couldn't find the players. So we had everybody lined up. We didn't have to scream. The players knew what they were gonna do. And I felt like if we stayed calm on the sidelines, they'd stay calm and play better football.

"You want your people where you can get to 'em. Not like Bear's sideline. Bear's hunting guys, 'Where in the hell's so-and-so? Where's so-and-so?' And they'd say, 'Uh, coach, he graduated last year.' That's what they tell on ol' Bear."

Dodd charged his assistants with the job of preparing the Tech players to be able to think during the heat of a game. "My quarterbacks knew exactly what to call against the defenses," Dodd said. "We did the best job of that, probably, of anybody at that time. We were the best organized. While other teams were out having a knock-down scrimmage, we were over there checking things: What do we expect? What's the favorite play they're liable to run on first and 10 at their 20?"

Bobby Dodd didn't bait officials. He rarely yelled at them, rarely criticized them from the sidelines. He would, however, talk to an official whose call he disagreed with, while leaving the field at halftime.

"You'd think coaches would catch on," Dodd said. "Ironically, when they screamed at an official, when you saw the films, the official was in the right. But it's too late then; you've already made a fool out of yourself."

Dodd's sideline wardrobe seldom varied: always a coat and tie, always a snap-brim hat, usually the brown one he wore most every day but sometimes a gray hat. "People still ask him, 'Where is that hat?' " Alice Dodd said. "They always think of Bobby with a brown snap-brim hat." Dodd wore that familiar hat during more than one Georgia Tech victory. "I didn't think it was absolutely luck, but I just got in the habit of doing it," Dodd said. "Certainly didn't hurt us."

On extremely cold or rainy days, Dodd opted for boots, sweatsuits, raincoats, anything to keep out the chill and the moisture. Sometimes, Dodd wore three layers of clothing, complete layers, plus a parka. But those times were seldom. "We had beautiful days here—October and November are so pretty in Atlanta," Dodd said. "We'd go out there and a lot of people came to the game in their shirtsleeves. The sun's shining."

"And their furs shining in the sun," Alice Dodd said. "Burned up. Had to get dressed up. People really got dressed up for Tech games."

Afterward, as the various assistants finished their post-game duties—some taking recruits back out to the airport—Dodd's staff would all eventually assemble at his house for the Saturday night steak dinner ritual.

Alice Dodd always had the choicest cut of steak. "And they all loved that," Dodd said. "Lord, to get a big steak on a Saturday night. We enjoyed it. We talked about the game, talked about next week, talked about everything. Soon as we got through dinner, I sent 'em home. Everybody was gone by about eight-thirty. They'd all go do something else, and I went on to bed. I was dead. Mimi and I were tired. We'd had a busy day."

Georgia Tech inaugurated the 1957 football season with a 13-0 shutout of Kentucky. But the next three games exposed the most pressing problem facing Bobby Dodd: a lack of talent and experience, particularly in the backfield.

Tech had lost its entire starting backfield from the 1956 team and seven of the top eight backs. Along the line, only left end Jerry Nabors and all-American center Don Stephenson, now the captain, returned. One-platoon magnified and contributed to the deficiencies.

With one-platoon football, there were only 11 potential openings each year. And there were scant few openings in the glorious mid-50s. Consequently, some recruits who worried about how much playing time they'd get at Tech attended school elsewhere.

"I didn't have the players coming up to replace this great backfield," Dodd said. "The great players were going to other places because they thought they had a better chance of playing."

After the Kentucky victory, Tech sputtered to a scoreless tie with Southern Methodist. The Yellow Jackets managed to score twice in Baton Rouge but surrendered 20 points and lost to LSU 20-13. Back at Grant Field, Tech was shut out for the second time in three Saturdays, losing 3-0 to an Auburn team that would eventually win the national championship before being placed on NCAA probation.

That defeat left the Jackets at 1-2-1, but they responded with victories over Tulane 20-13 and Duke 13-0. Tennessee won convincingly in Knoxville 21-6, but Georgia Tech rallied for 10 points in the fourth quarter in Birmingham to edge Alabama 10-7.

Prowling the Alabama sideline that day was another reason why Tech went into a decline in the late '50s: the Bear. Bear Bryant returned to his alma mater in 1957. Alabama football would never be the same again. The Bear made a splash in the talent pool of Alabama that sent ripples throughout the South. Recruiting was about to get even tougher for Bobby Dodd and Georgia Tech.

By the end of the 1957 season, there were already rumors that Bobby Dodd, about to turn 49, might retire. Ray Graves was the logical successor, Broyles having left Tech after the 1956 season to become the head coach at Missouri for a year before moving to Arkansas. Although the 1957 season didn't hasten Dodd's retirement, it certainly didn't make life any more bearable for him, either.

The Drought finally ended for Georgia in the 1957 finale. The scoring came in a brief, but deliciously satisfying shower. After eight straight losses to Georgia Tech, Georgia finally won one, 7-0.

"Theron Sapp, the Drought Breaker," Dodd said, recalling the name of the Georgia fullback who scored the Bulldog touchdown, and the nickname by which he became known and later immortalized. "We just didn't have enough football players."

Georgia had barely enough. No matter. Georgia finally had a victory over Tech. "They were just elated," Dodd said. "You can imagine the state university getting beat by the other school in the state eight straight years. It was more than embarrassing, it was just humiliating. People like Lewis Grizzard, I'll betcha they could've killed me if they could get their hands on me. They just hated me.

"But I was very humble. Oh, Lord. I'd brag on Coach Butts and tell 'em that they had bad luck, and I was lucky to do this. Listen, I was as humble as a man could be, 'cause I knew the time would come when they're gonna clobber me."

But Georgia fans didn't need to clobber Tech. They just needed to win. After eight tears, *any* margin of victory would be wonderful.

Georgia had great cause for celebration. Of all the expressed emotions—written, oral, and physical—what best describes Georgia's joy and relief at finally beating Tech can be found in the new Butts-Mehre athletic building on the Georgia campus. On display are mementoes of the Bulldogs' greatest athletic heroes. And right there along with Herschel Walker's retired jersey, number 34, is Theron Sapp's retired jersey, number 40. All Herschel Walker did was win the 1980 national championship for Georgia and win the 1982 Heisman Trophy for himself. To older Bulldogs who suffered through the 1950s, however, Theron Sapp's singular accomplishment was greater. He ended the Drought and finally silenced those arrogant slide rules from the North Avenue Trade School.

That's why an epic poem was composed in Sapp's honor: "The Drought Breaker." That's why his number was retired. And never mind that had he not scored that touchdown against Tech, Theron Sapp would be just another face in just another Georgia team picture in the Butts-Mehre building.

"Theron was just a good ol' plugging fullback," Dodd said. "Nothing great about Theron. But he was great that day, because he broke that drought. And when you're hurting as bad as they were, it was a great relief."

To ardent Bulldog fans, those eight years seemed never-ending. To Bobby Dodd, though, the Drought was a remarkable achievement. Tech had not only beaten a good football program eight consecutive years. Rather, Tech had beaten the football program of the major state university in its own state. A university that boasted more alumni, more facilities, and more academic courses of study, as well as the prestige and power inherent in every major state university in the country.

(As early as his second season as head coach at Tech, Dodd acknowledged the superior position he knew Georgia enjoyed. One day that fall, Dodd stood outside the Tech athletic offices, talking to George Mathews and Bob Davis about Georgia. Mathews: "I remember he said, 'If I can beat Georgia one out of three years, I'd consider that doing pretty good.'")

After the Georgia game, Tech's season was over. Bobby Dodd's bowl streak had ended. Georgia Tech had won its six consecutive major bowl games, but for the first time since the 1950 season, the Yellow Jackets were not invited to a bowl game, primarily because they had not reached another destination—the end zone—frequently enough. Although Tech allowed only 71 points and shut out four opponents in 1957, the Jackets scored but 75 points and were shut out four times themselves.

The 1957 season is an important landmark in the history of Georgia Tech football. It marked the end of the golden era of Bobby Dodd, and it was the start of four seasons of relative mediocrity on the Flats. "In 1957, '58, and those years, I just did not have a good football team," Dodd said. "I just could not recruit players."

Dodd saw several reasons for the recruiting troubles of the late '50s. Some were new, while some were all too familiar.

In the past, a young man with a Georgia Tech degree could make much more after graduation in the business world than by playing pro football. With the growing popularity of the pro game, however, salaries increased, and life as a professional athlete began to look more and more glamorous.

In addition, football programs throughout the South began to improve and new coaches brought fresh enthusiasm and energy to the recruiting battle. Dodd found it harder to get boys from Mississippi, Alabama, Florida, and Tennessee.

But his primary handicap, as Dodd saw it, was still academic. He was at a terrible disadvantage where it counted most—in Tech's home state.

"Our school system is poor in Georgia, as long as you can remember," Dodd said. "And here we are sitting over at Georgia Tech at what I call an Ivy League school. We were out of our class, really. If we'd had Georgia Tech sitting in the middle of Pennsylvania, where Penn State is, hell, I could have recruited players just like Penn State with no problem. There are lots of kids up there qualified to come to Tech. But we can't find 'em here. And I was getting out-recruited. They could go to Auburn and Georgia and Tennessee and play against me, but they couldn't come to

Tech. I remember one boy came in and cried and said, 'I wanted to play for you since I was 12 years old and I can't get into school.' "

Even some boys who could have qualified for admission to Georgia Tech didn't enroll. Not after a rival recruiter had stopped by the boy's house to make his pitch and, before leaving, left some light reading: a calculus textbook. Calculus was a required course for every Tech student. Recruiters—Georgia in particular practiced the ploy—would drop off the calculus text and the question, "Do you think you can pass this?"

"Whenever I'd come into a boy's house," Dodd said, "and see that damn calculus book, I'd say, 'Hell, Georgia's been here.' "

Meanwhile, some schools tried to improve their chances in other ways—and some got caught. After the 1957 season, Auburn was declared the national champion. The War Eagles were absolutely euphoric, at least until the NCAA probation hit. Auburn was caught improperly recruiting athletes and later illegally paying football players. The most prominent finger pointed at Auburn came from the right hand of Dodd.

"He was a stickler for the rules," Frank Broyles said, "and was the first person to turn other schools in and publicly say, 'Turn me in if we do anything wrong, because I'm gonna turn you in. We're destroying the game, we're abdicating our responsibilities to the game if we ignore recruiting violations.' He was unpopular at that time with certain schools because he was the only coach publicly to do that.

"He did that with Auburn, in particular, and he didn't make any bones about it. He said publicly, 'I turned Auburn in,' and Auburn people hated him. But he had the courage to do that, and I don't think anybody else in his time did. He was the first, absolutely the first."

The NCAA probation hit Auburn hard, and a full-blown storm came rushing through the loveliest village of the plain. "Auburn was penalized for three or four violations," Dodd said, "and, as I remember, I turned them in for one. They were openly violating recruiting rules, but the worst thing was they thought everybody was doing it. All their people thought that. Their president even said that."

By that time, Vince Dooley had returned to Auburn as an assistant on Shug Jordan's staff. "The feeling was that Dodd and Tech were sanctimonious and that they were hypocritical," Dooley said. "That they did those things, too, but they were so smooth, they got away with it. That was the feeling at Auburn and at a lot of places."

Dooley recalled one statement Dodd made during the late 1950s. "He said that coaches should lose their jobs for cheating," Dooley said. "At the time, Auburn was on probation and there was great sensitivity. Coach Jordan was very angry and said Dodd should just stick to his coaching."

Unlike many Auburn people, however, Vince Dooley found much in Bobby Dodd to appreciate, and emulate. "You just naturally want to study anyone who's successful," Dooley said. "I liked Dodd's style, so I always read everything he had to say, whenever he was quoted."

By 1958, Dooley became Auburn's head scout. From 1958 to 1963, Dooley assigned various members of Jordan's coaching staff to scout various opponents. But Dooley, already planning for the day he would become a head coach, always personally scouted two teams: Georgia Tech and Alabama. More precisely, he scouted two coaches: Bobby Dodd and Bear Bryant.

"I just wanted to study their teams," Dooley said, "and I wanted to watch them on the sidelines. There was quite a contrast between them, but the success ratio is the primary thing. Naturally, I preferred the way Coach Dodd did things, but I appreciated Bear's success, too."

In 1958, Georgia Tech began the season with a 13-0 loss at Kentucky but then won three straight. A 74-yard punt return by Frank Nix helped beat Tennessee 21-7, and then Tech managed an emotional 7-7 tie with Auburn's defending national champions. Following a 20-0 defeat at SMU, the Jackets edged Duke 10-8 on a Tommy Wells field goal and then shut out Clemson 13-0. But season-ending losses to Alabama—Dodd's first to Bryant since the Bear had returned to the Tide—and to Georgia left Tech 5-4-1 and left Dodd despondent.

"I was very depressed during this period, during the late '50s," Dodd said. So depressed that had the Texas job, or another prominent coaching situation, been offered, Dodd would have been sorely tempted to accept. "I had established myself as a coach here then, and was popular," he said. "I could probably stay here forever with 6-5 seasons.

"But for my own personal satisfaction, I wasn't winning enough football games to satisfy me. But I put up with it and went through those four years. And in the early '60s, we ended up with a pretty decent football team."

Dodd's dissatisfaction grew after Bear Bryant spoke to his good friend about the perks any self-respecting major-college football coach should have. One was a suitable house that was provided, if not paid for, by the university and/or boosters. Howard Ector, then athletic business manager, remembers a meeting of the Georgia Tech athletic board at which Dodd remarked that every football coach and athletic director in the South-eastern Conference lived in a nice house. As both coach and AD at Tech, Dodd wanted such a house, too. Initially, the athletic board denied his request.

"He was really blue, really down about the house," Ector said. "He said, 'I just can't believe they turned me down about a home.' " When Ector realized how sincerely upset Dodd was, he spoke to a prominent member of the athletic board, who introduced a motion at the next board meeting regarding a new house for Bobby Dodd. The motion passed unanimously, the Dodds found a fifty thousand dollar house in Sherwood Forest, the board agreed to buy it, and the Dodds moved in, having agreed to pay rent.

The board deeded the house to the state Board of Regents for use by the athletic director at Georgia Tech. After Dodd retired, an agreement was reached allowing Bobby and Alice Dodd to rent the house for the rest of their lives.

Through the years Georgia Tech alumni and boosters have shown their appreciation in many other ways, but Dodd never had the long-term, multimillion-dollar contracts so many coaches now enjoy.

In 1959, Georgia Tech improved slightly. With a fierce linebacker named Maxie Baughan—who became Tech's eighth all-American center—the Yellow Jackets went 6-4 in the regular season. Those six victories included a 14-7 triumph over Tennessee and a thoroughly satisfying 14-10 win at Notre Dame.

"The Notre Dame fans gave us a lot of crap about our tearaway jerseys," said Taz Anderson, the fullback on the 1959 squad. They also hit the Jackets with snowballs, more often and much harder than the Irish hit Tech.

The Tennessee games were always meaningful for Dodd, of course— ring games, watch games, *Tennessee* games. In 1959, in Knoxville, before the Tech players had even exchanged their jackets and ties for helmets and shoulder pads, they were ritually walking around the field in Neyland Stadium. That's when Dodd put his arm around Taz Anderson's shoulder and whispered, "You know, I helped make this place what it is today. I really want to win."

"I literally went inside the locker room and started throwing up," Anderson said. "I was so excited. I knew how much he wanted to win."

Duly inspired, Taz Anderson went out, made several key tackles, and scored both touchdowns in Georgia Tech's 14-7 victory.

The regular schedule ended with a loss to SEC champion Georgia— the third consecutive refreshing victory for the Bulldogs after the Drought. Still, the Gator Bowl was delighted to welcome Bobby Dodd back to Jacksonville and post-season play after a three-year absence.

Awaiting Dodd was his former protégé, Frank Broyles, and an Arkansas team featuring Lance Alworth.

In 80-degree heat and humidity, the Yellow Jackets spent themselves early in establishing a 7-0 lead and lost 14-7. It was Bobby Dodd's first bowl defeat as a head coach after eight straight successes, and it took a Dodd disciple to defeat him.

After flying home to Atlanta, and anticipating criticism, Dodd called Al Thomy at the airport. He told the *Atlanta Constitution* sportswriter, "Al, I want it understood by the public that a bowl game is a reward for our players. We're not going to work them so hard they won't enjoy the trip. That's not what football is about."

For Bobby Dodd, the 1960 season was not what football is about, either.

Alice and Linda Dodd watch as
Bobby Jr. helps Florida upset Tech
in 1960.

Chapter 14
Dodd vs. Dodd—
How Sharper than a Gator's Tooth!

THE YEAR 1960 MARKED Bobby Dodd's 30th year at Georgia Tech and his 16th season as head football coach. It also marked what some regarded as one of the major crises in Dodd's professional life.

Dodd's coaching staff had had nearly a 90 percent turnover in the previous four years. Besides Broyles, Ray Graves was also gone, leaving after the 1959 season to succeed Bob Woodruff at Florida.

The 1960 season began with promise. After opening with a 23-13 victory over Kentucky at Grant Field, Georgia Tech traveled to Rice and won 16-13. The Jackets were on the road the following weekend for a game in Gainesville, Florida. A game Bobby Dodd had fervently hoped he'd never have to play.

A game against his son.

Throughout their childhood Bobby Jr. and Linda enjoyed the expected advantages of being the children of Bobby Dodd, accompanying the team on trips and sitting on the Tech sidelines during games. Linda sat with the players' wives and girlfriends, and Bobby Jr. had a special seat at the far right end of the team bench.

"I was in heaven," Bobby Jr. said.

The blessing was at times mixed, however, as Bobby Jr. remembers. "Daddy had a higher profile than the governor, so I was the target of a lot of abuse, particularly from people in the stands when I was playing sports. People assumed we were rich and conceited because of Daddy. Well, we sure weren't rich, and we had no reason to be conceited—Daddy was the one who was famous. But I took a lot of harassment, and as a defense, I got pretty introverted. I figured they couldn't say too much about someone who was quiet all the time."

Also, because of the heightened expectations that naturally followed his son's athletic career, Bobby Dodd was much more comfortable taking Bobby Jr. fishing than watching him play sports. "I didn't watch him play much when he was in high school," Dodd said. "It made me nervous to watch him play, made me very nervous. I was afraid he was gonna make a mistake, or look bad, or something. You've got to be tight whenever you watch somebody you care about playing. And I cared so much about Bobby.

"Mimi [Alice's nickname] was the one that went with him, all the way from grammar school through high school. I didn't see him play but just a few games. I wish now I'd watched him play more."

In his senior year, Bobby Dodd, Jr., a quarterback, naturally, was chosen to play in a high school all-American game. "And that was inappropriate," he said. "I think writers assumed people were more interested in hearing about Coach Dodd's son than Joe Smith's boy. I know I got a lot of my press for that, and I know I was selected as a high school all-American because of Daddy."

Bobby Dodd's son, an all-American quarterback, an honor student. No high school senior had ever had better reason to think he would soon be playing on Grant Field wearing the white and gold. But it was not to be.

"I had to tell him for the first time that I didn't think it was fair to him or me if he came to Georgia Tech," Dodd said. "If he was a guard or tackle or linebacker, it might have been different. But being a quarterback, we'd both be second-guessed to high heaven if I played him."

Dodd knew about other coaches and their sons, who'd played for their fathers and prompted more heartache than heroics. "If he was head and shoulders above everybody else, you might get away with it," Dodd said. "Bobby was a good, solid quarterback, the kind I liked. He didn't make mistakes, didn't beat you, and I might have been inclined to play him."

"Daddy would have been the ideal coach for me to play for," said Bobby Jr.

Instead, the father told the son to play for someone else. "I *had* to tell him," Dodd said, "and I'm sure it disappointed him."

After turning down a scholarship to Yale, Bobby Jr. finally settled on attending the University of Florida. His freshman year at Gainesville was delightful. As always, he did well in class. His freshman football team was talented and undefeated. There were numerous lakes near campus that were choice fishing holes. And the following fall he found a constant fishing companion, a coed named Margie Brown, who would later become his wife.

By his sophomore year, though, there'd been some changes made. Bob Woodruff, Bobby Dodd's former assistant, was replaced by an old family friend: Ray Graves, a defensive mastermind who turned most of his offense over to a young backfield coach named Pepper Rodgers.

"When Ray Graves came to Florida, that actually hurt me," Dodd said. "I went there to get away from people I knew."

As a sophomore at Florida, Dodd alternated at quarterback with Larry Libertore, as dynamic as he was diminutive. "A very colorful runner," Dodd called him. "We ran the option and Larry was just unbelievable. He'd sometimes get a standing ovation for losing five yards. He'd double back and double back.

Just 138 pounds, Libertore wasn't much of a passer, however. So Dodd, who also played safety on defense, usually replaced Libertore in obvious passing situations. On October 1, 1960, he would do so against his father.

"I didn't want to play against him," Bobby Dodd said of his son. "Truthfully, he wanted to play, but he didn't care about beating his daddy. We're too close for that. But he's playing on the University of Florida, and he's got to try to beat us. The same thing applies to me. So, there were big doings all week about the game."

The pre-game, father-son media coverage was overwhelming. "I had not been exposed too bad, I suppose," Bobby Jr. said. "You're going to class, they can't find you. But it was horrible for Mother. I think she had the worst role of all."

During the week, Alice Dodd was asked for whom she would be rooting. "I hope Bobby Jr. has a fine day," she replied, "and I hope Tech beats the devil out of them."

But for Alice Dodd, the most agonizing experience was the game itself, and later the post-game family reunion. *Look* magazine was so intrigued with the father-son showdown, it decided to cover the game, and more. A photographer was assigned to do nothing during the game but shoot pictures of Alice and Linda Dodd, sitting in the stands watching the two men of the family fight it out on the football field.

"I must have seen six hundred photographs they took of Mother," Bobby Jr. said. "It was just miserable. They never saw the game, just watched her facial expressions. She suffered the most. Daddy had a job to do, I had a job to do. I consciously, I guess, didn't think about it a whole lot or try to give it any in-depth evaluation. I had friends on the team. You have that esprit de corps, you play well for them.

"But that game was truly remarkable . . . it's like when you see a Super Bowl and it really is close. This was a game that they built up, and the dang thing really did turn on something right at the end."

Like Georgia Tech, Florida was also 2-0, the Gators having beaten George Washington and Florida State. Still, Tech was a 10-point favorite, even playing in Gainesville. For most of the afternoon, Tech played as such.

The Yellow Jackets took early leads of 7-0 and 10-7, on Stan Gann's 15-yard touchdown pass to Taz Anderson and Tommy Wells's 40-yard field goal, only to see Florida tie the score each time at 7-all and 10-all. Late in the third quarter, though, Gann hit Billy Williamson in the flat, and the halfback went 40 yards to the Florida eight. Chick Graning struggled for three yards and then Williamson took a pitchout for the final five yards and a 17-10 lead.

For much of the game, Larry Libertore quarterbacked Florida while Bobby Dodd, Jr., played safety. Midway through the final period, though, Dodd and Libertore combined to move the Gators one last time when Florida took possession at its 12-yard line with 8:35 to play.

Bobby Dodd, Jr., made the most critical play in the decisive drive. On the sideline, young Dodd was talking with his defensive backfield coach, John Donaldson, and watching Billy Williamson, now playing left defensive halfback for Tech.

"Whenever you rolled away [from Williamson's side of the field], Billy was just firing out and rotating too fast and too far [toward the flow of the play]," Dodd said. The moment to capitalize on Williamson's aggressiveness came with Florida facing fourth down and 23 yards to go, and the knowledge that, if Tech took over, the Jackets would likely run out the clock.

"You know how it gets sort of hectic on the sidelines," Dodd said, "and nobody knows what to call. Graves and Rodgers are up there mumbling around, trying to decide what to call, and I went up to them and said, 'I can hit the throwback on them.' I volunteered the play and they put me in to run it. At that stage, they were glad to pass the buck to somebody and let him make the decision.

"I was sure it would be there. And sure enough. . . . "

Dodd dropped back, rolling to his left, stopped, turned, and threw back up the right sideline. Said Dodd, "I fanned left and when I pulled up, it looked like Don Deal was out for a walk. He had flared back the other way, and he was wide open. Williamson was a good athlete and fast. He got back over there and made the tackle before Don scored.

"But I purposely floated it. I didn't throw it hard. When you got the guy wide open, just get it to him. You don't try to make a beautiful throw when a guy's wide open. So I threw it softly, slowed him down, hit him, and he took it down."

Took it down the right sideline 33 yards to the Tech 25. With Dodd and Libertore alternating, the Gators advanced to the four, where Dodd sneaked for a crucial first down. On third-and-goal at the one, there was a fumble on the exchange, but Dodd managed to recover at the three. From there, Libertore faked a handoff to fullback Don Goodman, then rolled to the right. Just before being hit, Libertore pitched back to the trailing halfback, Lindy Infante, who barely—and disputedly—made it inside the red flag and into the corner of the end zone before being knocked down on the sideline.

"Lindy doesn't even know whether he stepped out or not," said Bobby Dodd, Jr. "People that watched down the sidelines said that he did, that he was out. But you don't know whether that's his last step or not, so nobody knows."

With 32 seconds remaining, Florida was within 17-16 and Florida Field was in an uproar. For an instant, placekicker Billy Cash appeared on the field and the cheering turned to booing. Florida called timeout. A famous photograph shows Ray Graves holding up two fingers on his right hand, instructing the Gators to go for the two-point conversion and victory.

"No question," Graves said. "I couldn't have faced the players."

"Of course he's got to go for two points," Dodd said. "Because the fans, well, you just don't go for the tie when the game's almost over. The fans'd give him too much hell. But I don't mean I would have done it."

Graves elected to go for two, and victory or defeat. "Graves was brought up on the conservative side," Dodd said. "He was brought up under Neyland and me, and we would have normally gone for the tie. If there'd been two or three minutes left, he'd have gone for the extra point. But those Florida people, the student body and everybody, they're all, 'Oh go for it! Go for it!' "

Libertore rolled right again on a run-pass option play, but this time he threw to fullback Jon MacBeth, who was wide open in the back of the end zone, for the two-point conversion and the 18-17 upset. The upset was certified after Tech received the kickoff and Stan Gann's last pass was intercepted.

"And you never saw such a commotion," wrote Furman Bisher. Florida Field was in tumult over one of the greatest victories in Florida history.

In the Tech locker room following the game, Dodd told reporters, "That dadburned Graves has come down here to Florida and forgotten all his training. He knows I've told him never to try for two points when one will get you a tie."

The sportswriters surrounding Dodd all laughed. Dodd didn't. He was absolutely serious. "I'll bet Ray has told me a thousand times that a tie never hurts anyone. Remembering all this, I honestly thought he'd kick an extra point." Dodd reiterated that he would have played the percentages and kicked the extra point for the tie.

When informed of Dodd's comments that day, Graves laughed and said, "I had to change a lot of things when I came down here. When I was with Coach Dodd, I thought like Coach Dodd. Now I think a little differently.

"There was never any doubt whatsoever that we'd try for two. The boys wanted two, the fans wanted two, and the coaches wanted two. We had made up our minds when we were on the 15-yard line."

Asked about his son's performance, Bobby Dodd said, "I'm happy for Bobby, but very sad for myself."

"Libertore's the fellow who beat 'em," Bobby Jr. said afterward. "Wasn't he wonderful?

"I hate to see Daddy lose such a tough one, but I've been saying all week I thought we'd win."

Alice Dodd, meanwhile, paced in a runway beneath the stadium. Fittingly, she was halfway between the Florida and Georgia Tech locker rooms. "I'm happy . . . and I'm sad," Mrs. Dodd said softly to herself as reporters listened. "No woman should have to endure what I had to endure out there today. I wanted Bobby Sr. to win very much, but I wanted Bobby Jr. to play a good game. I guess it was asking too much that both wishes should come true. There is one consolation: It was a great game."

The winner appeared first. Bobby Jr. walked slowly up to his mother and sister. They hugged him, and Alice said, "You were great. I'm real proud of you."

When her husband finally arrived, Alice hugged him, kissed him once, twice, then gripped his hand tightly. They didn't speak at first, just looked into each other's eyes. "The trim little lady was the real champion of the day," Jack Williams wrote in the *Journal-Constitution*. "She met a winner and a loser, and conquered them both with smiles."

That afternoon and the events leading up to it were emotionally wrenching for the entire family. Reflecting on that crucial fourth-down pass completion and its effects, Bobby Dodd, Jr., says this: "There was no real way for me to win. Daddy is such a great competitor. He wouldn't have been proud of me if I had done less than my best, and when you're in the game, you want to do everything you can to win and help your teammates win. But in absolute terms, if I had to weigh my loyalty to the University of Florida, or some abstract concept like that, against my loyalty and love for Daddy, I'd have thrown that pass six rows into the stands."

"I was very proud of Bobby, the way he played," said Bobby Dodd, "but it was a tough loss. Whenever you lead the whole game and lose in the last minute, well, it's about as tough a loss as you can have.

"But we got even with 'em."

Georgia Tech shut out Florida the next three years. In 1961, Tech dominated Florida at Grant Field 20-0. In '62, it was 17-0 back in Gainesville, then a season-opening 9-0 shutout in '63. After that, Georgia Tech and Florida didn't schedule each other and did not play each other again until Bobby Dodd's final game as a head coach. The series was suspended for a number of reasons, but primarily because Dodd wanted to play the games in Jacksonville instead of Gainesville.

The 1960 football season immediately became better for Bobby Dodd and Georgia Tech, but only briefly. The week following the Florida game, back home at Grant Field, Tech led Louisiana State 3-0 late in the second quarter. LSU mounted a drive, however, and reached the Tech one with 25 seconds left in the first half. But on fourth down, safety Walter Howard stopped LSU fullback Donnie Daye inches from the goal line. Georgia Tech kicked a second field goal in the second half, Dodd ordered a safety, and the Yellow Jackets had a memorable 6-2 victory.

It was one of the few pleasant memories of the 1960 season. There followed a 9-7 loss at Auburn, the first time Dodd ever deigned to play at Auburn. After a 14-6 win over Tulane, Tech lost 6-0 at Duke. A 14-7 triumph over Tennessee preceded two heartbreaking, one-point defeats, 16-15 to Alabama and 7-6 at Georgia.

The Alabama loss was particularly galling. Georgia Tech led 15-0 at halftime. Alabama starting quarterback Pat Trammell was injured, however, and backup Bobby Skelton came on in the second half to lead the Crimson Tide to a 16-15 comeback victory, Bear Bryant's third straight over Dodd.

Against Georgia, Pat Dye blocked the conversion attempt after the only Tech touchdown and the Bulldogs prevailed for the fourth straight year, 7-6. Georgia Tech finished the season with a deceiving 5-5 record, having lost five games by a total of 11 points.

There would be ample improvement the next season, but also more controversy and heartache for Bobby Dodd and Georgia Tech.

Meeting with the "Bear" after the
1963 Alabama game at Legion Field
in Birmingham.

Chapter 15
Unbearable Situations Force a Break with 'Bama and the SEC

TO OPEN THE 1961 SEASON, Georgia Tech flew to Los Angeles to meet the University of Southern California. Before playing, the Yellow Jackets toured Paramount Studios. A Georgia Tech alumnus, Frank Freeman, was then president of Paramount Pictures. Surprisingly, the game was nearly as enjoyable as the Paramount tour, when all the Tech wives were thrilled to meet one of Bobby Dodd's idols: John Wayne.

Dodd had expected a difficult day against an opponent such as USC. The Jackets won easily, however, 27-7, which pleased Dodd immensely.

Through the first seven games of the season, only LSU was able to handle Georgia Tech. Another feverish Saturday night in Baton Rouge ended in a 10-0 Tech defeat, but after avenging the 1960 Florida loss with a 20-0 shutout, the Yellow Jackets were 6-1.

The next week Tech lost a close game at Tennessee 10-6. And then came the Alabama game.

Bear Bryant already had his dynasty in place at Alabama. The Crimson Tide would go undefeated in 1961, win the Southeastern Conference, win the Sugar Bowl, and win the national championship. But for many people, particularly Georgia Tech people, the 1961 'Bama team is best—or worst—remembered for what a linebacker named Darwin Holt did to Tech's starting left halfback, Chick Graning.

During the fourth quarter of that 10-0 Alabama victory at Legion Field in Birmingham, the Tide's Billy Richardson was downfield, awaiting a Tech punt and waving, signaling for a fair catch. Graning, covering the sideline against a runback, was away from the ball. Richardson made the catch—the play was over—and Graning relaxed. Holt then slammed his elbow under Graning's face mask and trotted off the field before looking back.

Graning lay unconscious on the field. His playing career was over.

By Friday of the following week, Tech physician Dr. Lamont Henry had made a full diagnosis: fracture of the alveolar process (facial bones); five missing front upper teeth and the majority of the remaining front teeth broken; fracture of the nasal bone; fracture of the right maxillary sinus and sinus filled with blood; fracture of the right zygomatic process (bone beneath the right eye); cerebral concussion; and possible fracture of the base of the skull.

"The worst facial injury I have ever seen in my 20 years of association with athletics," said Dr. Henry.

Looking back, Bobby Dodd is still hesitant to reopen an old, and painful wound, but he remembers it vividly.

"It was on an open field," Dodd said. "Everybody saw it because it was a punt return. Everybody screamed bloody murder, all the Tech people who saw it. We saw it. And it even looked worse when you saw it in the film."

Amazingly, no official saw the blow. Holt was not even penalized 15 yards, much less ejected from the game. Even worse, though, was the attitude of Holt's coach, Bear Bryant.

Immediately after the game, Dodd issued a "No comment" about the Holt incident, although Dodd was livid. Instead, after reviewing the game films the next day, Dodd called his good friend Bryant.

"My feeling was, and still is, that this kind of thing needed to be settled in private, not in the newspapers," Dodd said. "I told Bear that I felt Holt ought to be punished. That our people were really just furious over what had happened. They'd seen the films. And Bear said, 'Coach, I just don't think it's anything you can punish a boy for.' That was his attitude. I said, 'Take him out, keep him out a game or two.' But Bear didn't want to punish him."

Dodd first decided not to show the play on his weekly Sunday TV show, but he later relented. Although he never mentioned Holt by name and afterward again declined comment, the film prompted a vast public outrage in Atlanta and throughout Georgia. The Atlanta media was outraged as well.

"Stop It Now!" was the headline on Jesse Outlar's impassioned *Constitution* column on growing violence in college football. Outlar called for Holt's dismissal from the Alabama squad and suggested that future incidents of this nature result in the coach's suspension by the SEC—although Outlar knew only too well, too regrettably, that the SEC, an impotent organization, had no such power.

"The New Darwin Theory" was the headline on Furman Bisher's scathing attack on Holt, Bryant, and Alabama, the first of several columns Bisher would write on the controversy. "Bisher was just incensed over the whole thing," Dodd said, "and he just let Bear have it. And the Alabama people, and the Tech people, and all the newspaper people got stirred up against each other. It got completely out of hand, and I regretted that."

Years later, in *Bear*, his autobiography, Bryant recalled, "I did a small thing I wish I hadn't done. I had one of my assistants go down with the game film and show it to the Alabama writers, had him point out all the violations Tech had committed. They made more than we did by a bushel.

"Dodd resented this, and I don't blame him. It was a small thing and showed no class. If I had it to do over I wouldn't, but our people thought the Atlanta writers were trying to destroy me."

Bryant said that shortly after the game had ended, he told Tonto Coleman, Tech's assistant athletic director, that Holt wanted to apologize to Graning. "But we decided it might not be the thing for him to do so close to the heat of the battle," Bryant told reporters. "Holt plans to write a letter apologizing."

Holt insisted he did not know Richardson had signaled for a fair catch. "I never look at the ball carrier on a punt," Holt said. "I hit Graning with my forearm in an attempt to block him. It definitely wasn't intentional because I like Graning and I was talking to him all during the game."

Holt later came to see Graning to apologize personally, and Graning offered forgiveness. Bryant forgave Holt a lot sooner, though. He said he would not take any disciplinary action against him.

"It's never happened before and it'll never happen again," Bryant insisted, "because Darwin Holt is not that kind of a young man. Nobody carries on that kind of stuff and plays on this team."

Others disagreed, including Bobby Dodd.

It seems that someone remembered seeing Holt deliver a similar blow the previous week against a Virginia Tech player. Dodd looked at the game film and confirmed the story. And then, when the team doctor told Dodd that Holt had bitten Tech's Billy Williamson on the leg in a pileup, Dodd knew more action was necessary. "These things mounted up on Holt," Dodd said. "That he was doing this, that he was a wild man on the field. They say they called him Tarzan."

Dodd filed an official protest to the University of Alabama, and wrote confidential letters to Bryant and university president Dr. Frank Rose. Dodd and Tech's president, Dr. Edwin Harrison, then met with Bryant and Rose.

"They didn't feel that it warranted punishing the boy," Dodd said. "Dr. Rose, I remember well, he said, 'This Holt boy is just as nice as can be. He babysits for us.' I said, 'Well, I don't question he is off the football field. But on the football field, he's a wild man.' He's just one of these football players that goes wild when he gets on the field.

"There are some players like that. Hell, I've had boys get carried away with emotion during the heat of the game, too." In fact, two years later, Tech's Ted Davis, a fine end and a potential all-star, kicked an Auburn player in the head and was ejected from the game. Afterward, Dodd said it

223

was "certainly a flagrant foul" and that he "deplored it" and "regretted it."

The following Monday morning, before talking to any of his coaches, Ted Davis issued a statement. "I know that what I have done was not only wrong on the football field," he said, "but also it violated every standard that Coach Dodd sets for his football players." He then resigned from the team.

Dodd commented, "Although, of course, I do not condone what Ted did in the football game Saturday, and like all of us at Georgia Tech I am most sorry it happened, I am proud of Ted this morning, because he had the courage to face his mistake publicly."

It would be several years after the Graning incident before Dodd and Bryant reconciled. Dodd never could, however, reconcile Bryant's way of coaching, as exemplified by the Holt incident and Bryant's handling of it. "Bear liked 'em to play rough," Dodd said. "He probably thought that was great.

"Bear Bryant was probably the toughest man that ever coached college football. That was his style. But it wasn't my style, at all."

"That was one of the most traumatic times in Bobby's life," Ray Graves said. "Here was one of his best friends, Bear, approving or condoning Holt. We'd seen this before. And for Bear to condone Holt was a deep wound. For years."

It was widely assumed, particularly in Alabama, that the Graning-Holt incident ultimately led to the discontinuation of the Tech-Alabama series after the 1964 season. Dodd emphatically denies that.

"In fact," Dodd said, "what they didn't know was I had already told Bear, 'I'm not gonna play you when this contract runs out.' I said, 'Bear, I'm getting tired of getting beat by you, in the ninth game of the season. Here we are, getting ready to have a good bowl bid and we lose to you and it hurts my record. A lot of other people are getting beat by you, but they don't have sense enough to drop you from the schedule. I'm the athletic director, and I can drop you.'

"I knew he was getting good football players at Alabama, better than I was getting. He was a better defensive coach than I was. I don't think he was any better coach than I was the day of the game. He always said I was the best. And offensively, I could out-coach him, but I couldn't out-coach him defensively.

"And he got good football players, real good football players. They could get players I couldn't get in school. I could see the handwriting on the wall. It was very obvious that Bear was gonna set up a dynasty over there like Coach Wade had way back.

"But when Bear got there, everybody got behind him recruiting-wise. You couldn't get anybody out of Alabama. I was getting good players out of Alabama every year and when Bear got there, I couldn't get a damn boy out of Alabama.

"In fact, it was hard for 'em to go to Auburn. You can imagine how much more influence Bear had throughout the state than Shug Jordan had, or anybody else. Hell, Bear just controlled the whole state.

"Beside that, he'd go out and get Joe Namath and get him in school. So Bear got the poor student and he got some good students: Pat Trammell was a good student and fine high-type boy. So were Lee Roy Jordan and Bill Battle.

"So I just quit playing him, and I was glad I did. I have never had any regrets. I dropped two schools, Alabama and LSU. It was not fair to play LSU in Baton Rouge on Saturday night. It was not fair to any football team, those Cajuns screaming. And it's the same today, you can't hear the damn signals. I wasn't gonna play them and I wasn't gonna play Bear.

"I still had a strong schedule. I'm playing Tennessee, Duke, Auburn, Georgia, I'm playing a lot of good schools in our area. But of course, I didn't have to worry about the schedule as far as selling tickets.

"Every once in awhile, I'd schedule a game like Southern Cal for a trip. And we were getting good trips on bowl games, which helped us. But my kids didn't care that much about traveling, unless it was a good trip. Going up to Durham and spending the night didn't mean much to an Atlanta kid. Going to Birmingham, that's nothing to 'em. They'd much rather play here. They can be with their girlfriends right after the game."

After the Graning-Holt incident, Georgia Tech finally beat Georgia. With Billy Williamson scoring twice, the Yellow Jackets ended a four-game losing streak to Georgia with a decisive 22-7 victory. In the Gator Bowl, though, an exceptional Penn State team—with a near-sighted quarterback named Galen Hall, now head coach at Florida, throwing three touchdowns and a ferocious end named Dave Robinson—manhandled Georgia Tech 30-15. Still, Tech finished 7-4, its best record since 1956.

On June 9, 1962, Linda Dodd married one Joe Thompson. That climaxed a courtship that began several years earlier. Thompson had come to Georgia Tech on a football scholarship, but never played. He was chronically injured and endured a couple of knee operations. Thompson was only a sophomore then, but, clearly, his football career was over. Bobby Dodd's concern for him, however, was not.

"He said, 'I sure am sorry for your sake, not Georgia Tech's,' " Thompson recalled. "He put me on what was called a work scholarship."

Since he was unable to play any longer, Thompson would work for his scholarship. He was assigned to work the entrance gate to Tech practices at Rose Bowl Field, screening those affiliated with the football team, those who had received special practice passes from Dodd, and the curious who had no business being there. It was at that practice gate that Joe Thompson met Linda Dodd. She had been involved in a car accident near campus. Linda was fine but her car was totaled, and police had driven her to Tech's practice, which she often attended anyway.

As usual, Linda was introduced as Coach Dodd's daughter. While that often brought many privileges, it was not always advantageous. "Everybody knew Daddy, everybody liked him," Linda said. "It was not a burden, but the only thing that bothered me was always being introduced as his daughter. I got real self-conscious about it.

"I didn't think people really wanted to get to know *me*. I would be introduced, and they'd say, 'You're Coach Dodd's daughter!' So I thought they wanted to write down my phone number just to ask me for football tickets.

"I had a real complex about it, about being his daughter, but as I got older, I got over it. Now, I'm so proud of him, I'll tell people who I am. Daddy has been an even better daddy than he was a football coach."

Joe Thompson didn't need tickets, and he didn't need a second introduction. A few years after meeting Coach Dodd's daughter, Joe Thompson put on the only suit he owned, went to Bobby Dodd's office and summoned the courage to tell the coach he was about to propose to his only daughter. Dodd slowly stood up, reached across his desk to shake Thompson's hand, and said but one thing: "Well, she'll make you a good wife."

"He knew Joe didn't have a job, didn't have any money," Linda said. "There's a lot of things he could have said, like, 'Joe, well, you don't have a job.' But he didn't. That takes something. I hope I can do that well with my kids."

In the succeeding 25 years, Bobby Dodd has told the story of Joe Thompson hundreds of times, always in connection with his passion for graduating football players. He tells it after dinner, before lunch, whenever he's called on to speak publicly. He tells it as follows:

"After my experiences in high school and college, when I became head coach at Georgia Tech, I became obsessed with the idea of graduating every boy who comes under me. And I damn near did. I graduated some dumb ones, too. I want to tell you about one special case that paid off. I had this big ol' boy come to me from here in Atlanta. He's 6-5, weighs 220—that was big back in those days. He's all-state in football, all-state in basketball. But when he got over to Tech, he had a bad knee and we had to operate. When that got well, we put him in a scrimmage, we tear up his shoulder. We had to operate. When that got well, we put him in scrimmage, we tear up the other knee. He's been here five years, he's had three operations, and he hasn't had on a varsity uniform yet.

"And my faculty advisor came down to me and he said, 'Coach Dodd, this lad will never graduate. He's dumber than you were.' And I said, 'Gosh, he needs a degree so bad, I've got to get him a degree.' He said, 'You're wasting your money.' I said, 'I'll waste it.' Well sir, after six years and 380 hours of private tutoring, we graduated that boy. You know where he is today? He's my son-in-law. Ol' Joe married Linda, gave me four of the finest grandchildren ever. And ol' Joe was a state senator for 12 years. You know what I say? If I'd a had ol' Joe one more year, he'd be governor today."

By 1962, Bobby Dodd had another exceptional starting quarterback in junior Billy Lothridge, whom Dodd had described as so reminiscent of himself. Not only did Lothridge pass, kick, and think like Dodd—and run nearly as slowly—but he could also shoot a little pool. Indeed, the night before high school prospects could sign letters of intent in 1960, Dodd invited Lothridge and his Gainesville High School teammate, end Billy Martin, over to the Dodd home.

Wally Butts and Georgia were also recruiting Lothridge and Martin but could not find them to present any last-minute recruiting pitch. Bobby Dodd had the two boys down in his basement, shooting pool. Lothridge, like the young Bobby Dodd, loved to shoot pool. The boys played for hours, until precisely one minute past midnight, when they legally signed to play football for Georgia Tech and then resumed playing pool.

As a sophomore, Lothridge was the backup quarterback to Stan Gann but did all of Tech's placekicking and punting. As the starter in 1962, Lothridge led the Yellow Jackets to a fine season. After opening with decisive victories over Clemson and Florida, Georgia Tech lost to LSU 10-7, when Jerry Stovall returned the second-half kickoff 97 yards for a touchdown. Tech shut out Tennessee 17-0 but stumbled at Auburn 17-14. The Jackets easily defeated Tulane and Duke, tied FSU, and then came Alabama.

On the morning of the Georgia Tech-Alabama game, Kim King was granted an audience with Alabama's answer to the Pope. A senior then at Brown High School in Atlanta, King was a highly recruited left-handed quarterback. He would later sign with Tech and become one of Bobby

227

Dodd's favorite and most productive players. But that morning, King, his parents, and his girlfriend were invited to the Georgian Terrace Hotel, where the Alabama team was staying. King was escorted upstairs and into Bear Bryant's suite to meet the coach of the defending national champions—who were undefeated again in 1962, who hadn't lost in 26 previous games. Yet that morning, Bear still had the fear of Dodd in him.

"He was sitting by the window, with a pack of Benson and Hedges and a pack of Chesterfield's," King recalled. "And he was chain-smoking, one from one pack, one from the other. And he kept looking out the window at the rain and saying, 'This is Dodd's kind of weather, this is Dodd's kind of weather. He'll figure out how to play in this kind of weather. He knows how to win in this kind of weather.' He was obsessed with it."

Bryant's forecast was prescient. Dodd perfectly combined all the elements—the rain, the mud, a resolute defense, and a strategic kicking game—and orchestrated his greatest victory, 7-6.

That afternoon, Georgia Tech, after blowing an early opportunity, scored first. Mike McNames, a senior fullback from Vidalia, Georgia, who had walked on at Tech, leaped to intercept a Joe Namath pass and returned it 26 yards to the Alabama 14. Two plays later, McNames started to his left, abruptly changed direction, and scored from the five. Lothridge kicked the extra point to make it 7-0.

For Tech the second half evolved into desperate defense, strategic kicking, and a struggle for survival. 'Bama finally scored after Lothridge, having fumbled the snap on a punt, touched his knee at his nine while picking up the ball. Following a five-yard Alabama penalty, Namath hit Bill Battle at the two, then Cotton Clark barely scored on fourth down. It was a controversial call, and Tech end Ted Davis objected so vehemently that he was ejected from the game.

Bryant ordered Jack Hurlbut, Namath's alternate at quarterback, to go for two points. Rolling out, Hurlbut seemed destined to score until McNames shed a blocker and tackled Hurlbut at the one.

Twice more Alabama would threaten. Twice more Georgia Tech would stand fast, finally prevailing in the final minute when Don Toner intercepted for Tech at the Jacket 14. Tech won 7-6, touching off a glorious celebration in Grant Field and later in the Tech locker room. There, with his players swarming around him, a joyous, beaming Dodd threw his left arm around Don Toner, who still clutched the ball he'd intercepted. With his right hand held high, Dodd made a triumphant clenched fist. Behind him, Billy Lothridge gave the winner's gesture of that era, the index and middle fingers of his left hand in a V. For victory. The sweetest victory for Georgia Tech and Bobby Dodd.

The Yellow Jackets then annihilated Georgia 37-6, with Lothridge scoring three times. Their first visit to the Bluebonnet Bowl ended with a

14-10 loss to Missouri. Still, Georgia Tech had finished the 1962 season 7-3-1. And, after four successive failures, Bobby Dodd had finally beaten Bear Bryant again.

In 1963, Tech again won seven games, losing three. The Yellow Jackets lost by a point at LSU, by eight points to the Auburn combination of quarterback Jimmy Sidle and running back Tucker Frederickson, and at Alabama 27-11. Georgia was beaten for the third straight year, 14-3. Lothridge was the runnerup in the Heisman Trophy balloting to Navy's Roger Staubach, and both Lothridge and Billy Martin made all-American.

Come 1964, Billy Lothridge was gone. But then, Georgia Tech was gone, too. Gone from the Southeastern Conference, for good.

"The hardest thing that I had to do as a coach," said Bobby Dodd, "was to get my coaches to have the same philosophy that I had about football players. Whitey Urban and some of the tougher ones that I had, well, when a boy came in here that we'd recruited and he didn't come up to what we thought he was gonna be—knew he wasn't a football player, knew he was gonna be B team or third or fourth string all the time—they wanted to get rid of him. They wanted to treat him bad, scrimmage him."

Dodd always came back with the argument, "All right, how would you feel if you were a high school star? Every one of these boys were stars in high school, and we recruited them and thought they were good football players. And if we made a mistake, it wasn't that boy's fault. So long as he's giving us effort, we're gonna keep him here and we're gonna graduate him.

"I felt sorry for those boys who had always been stars but were now playing third string. I was for the underdog, for that person who was not as fortunate as I was. And that came from my mother.

"I know that because she cared so much about people. She loved people, they loved her. I got my sensitivity from her. So, anyway, I treated my third-stringers like they were first-stringers. I fed 'em well, I treated 'em good with tickets. I cared about 'em, and I wanted to keep 'em happy."

His care, concern, and commitment to his players were Bobby Dodd's greatest attributes. Yet it also prompted one of his most agonizingly painful decisions: to withdraw from the Southeastern Conference. It was Dodd's most controversial decision and brought heavy criticism from throughout the conference, as well as from many Tech people.

"We never got a fair shake on the story, the publicity about why we got out of the SEC," Dodd said. The only reason, Dodd insists, was the 140

SEC rule. Not any desire on Tech's behalf to keep all bowl and TV revenue for itself. The 140 rule.

Conference rules permitted a combined total of 140 players to be on scholarship in football and basketball. Since there were usually no more than 10 to 12 basketball players on scholarship, there were only about 130 scholarships left for the football team.

"In other words," said Dodd, "if you signed 45 players each year (the SEC limit at that time), you'd end up with 180, so you had to run off about 40 of 'em. You couldn't be over the limit. Alabama and Ole Miss and Tennessee and these people were all doing that. They'd bring in 45 players, look at 'em for three months—September, October, November—and then they'd get rid of all of 'em but about 30. When they checked 'em at the end of the year, they weren't over the limit.

"It was nothing but a legal tryout. That's what it was, a legal tryout."

Dodd, on the other hand, only recruited 32 to 35 players annually and still had trouble staying under the limit because his five-year players were counting against him. "We wouldn't run off anybody and hardly anybody flunked out," he said. "We didn't lose but one or two boys a year. Vanderbilt and Tulane were the only other schools in the conference running a program like ours, and they weren't beating anybody."

Dodd had already implored the conference a couple of times to recognize the inequities in the rule and change it. In SEC Commissioner Bernie Moore, Dodd found a sympathetic, but powerless, ear. Dodd implored, "Why don't you put the premium on keeping boys instead of putting the premium on running 'em off?

"We said we'd live with 10 boys a year, 20, 30, 40, 50, we don't give a damn how many boys you let us take," Dodd said. "But don't tell us we gotta run 'em off. And I can't compete with these schools that are taking 45 and me taking 32. They're gonna get better boys than I get. I got so damn mad for two or three years there."

Dodd finally convinced five other SEC schools of the wisdom of his ways and the folly of the 140 rule. Thus, the conference divided evenly, six for altering the rule, six for maintaining it. Dodd needed a seventh, and majority, vote to change the rule: either to eliminate the 140 maximum, or restrict the number of recruits you could sign annually.

The controversy finally came to a head in 1964 at the annual off-season SEC meetings in Atlanta. Georgia Tech President Edwin Harrison had already polled the Tech athletic board, which agreed unanimously that if the 140 rule wasn't changed, Tech would withdraw from the conference. "We couldn't live with it," Dodd said. "We're gonna be on probation [for being over the limit], and we're the good guy."

The SEC athletic directors met on Thursday, January 23, 1964. During that meeting, Dodd said, "I got Bear to agree to vote with us. He said,

'We'll vote with y'all.' So we're not gonna have to get out of the conference."

On Friday, when the 12 SEC presidents were to meet and cast votes for their schools, Dodd was supremely confident. "Bear, he had Dr. Rose in the palm of his hand," Dodd said. "Whatever he wanted, Dr. Rose did."

Custom called for each athletic director to sit beside his president. Bobby Dodd sat beside Edwin Harrison. "And I'll be damned if we don't come up Friday morning and Bear is not there," Dodd said. "And there's Dr. Rose sitting over there by himself."

The voting began, in alphabetical order. The first vote: Alabama. Dr. Rose. "He voted against us," Dodd said. "I couldn't believe it." Edwin Harrison rose, walked down the aisle to the front of the room, and announced that Georgia Tech, regretfully, must resign from the Southeastern Conference. In the wake of Tech's withdrawal, the committee voted 11-0 to retain the 140 rule.

"Bear felt like a damn dog about it," Dodd said. "He never did tell me whether he told Dr. Rose, or didn't tell him, or where he was that morning. I never found out what happened.

"But he tried to get us back in the conference. He tried to get the conference to ask us to come back. But the Mississippis hated us, because I wouldn't play 'em. And I had dropped LSU, too, 'cause playing in Baton Rouge is a loser. So I had enough enemies in the conference to where Bear, even with his influence, could not get 'em to invite us back."

Tech's enemies included two perennial rivals. Ray Graves recalls that in the mid-1960s, Bryant called him and wanted to get Georgia Tech readmitted to the Southeastern Conference. "He said, 'I don't want to die with Bobby and me feeling about each other the way we do.' Bear worked his butt off and so did I. It came down to two teams, Auburn and Georgia. They kept Tech out. We needed Atlanta and the exposure, but those two said, 'If you let Georgia Tech back in, we'll get out.' "

Georgia Tech remained on the outside looking independently at the SEC. "We did not want to get out of the Southeastern Conference," Dodd still maintains, "even though it's a terrible conference for Georgia Tech to be in. You see, people don't seem to realize—and I never have heard anybody have enough sense to realize—how handicapped a school is against a state university.

"The state universities have all the big advantages. Hell, they can get any boy in the state in their school. The mothers went there, the sisters went there, the girls went there. You try to recruit at Vanderbilt against the University of Tennessee. Hell, they can't get two boys in the state that Tennessee really wants. Tulane against LSU. Mississippi State against Ole Miss. Tech against Georgia. Only reason I got 'em is because we just sold 'em on coming to play for me."

At that time, seven state universities belonged to the Southeastern

Conference. The other schools were Vanderbilt, Tulane, Georgia Tech, Mississippi State, and Auburn. And the only ones winning that weren't state universities were Georgia Tech and Auburn.

Immediately after Georgia Tech withdrew from the SEC, Dodd said, the Atlantic Coast Conference approached him about joining the ACC. Dodd declined, for two reasons. He thought Tech couldn't compete in basketball in the ACC. "That's a miracle—what Bobby Cremins has done in basketball at Tech," Dodd said.

Secondly, Dodd knew that many ACC football schools would not draw large crowds to Grant Field, a chronic problem Georgia Tech still faces after joining the ACC in 1979. Yet in some ways, Dodd would have dearly loved to join the ACC in 1964.

"There are three state universities in there [Maryland, Virginia, and North Carolina]," Dodd said. "Everybody else is just like Georgia Tech: Wake Forest, N.C. State, Clemson, Duke. None of 'em state universities. All of 'em just like we are."

In 1964, though, Bobby Dodd did not switch allegiances to the Atlantic Coast Conference. He chose to go it alone. Georgia Tech, a member of the old Southern Conference from 1902 to 1932 and a charter member of the Southeastern Conference in 1933, became an independent.

"Everybody said, 'Georgia Tech can get along fine as an independent,' " Dodd said. "Hell, Notre Dame's an independent, Penn State's an independent, Miami too. If you have a good football team, it don't make any difference whether you're in a conference or not. If you got a weak football team, a lot of people think you oughta be in a conference 'cause you get to split their bowl and TV money. But if you're in a conference, it's more obvious when you put the standings up there that you're down near the bottom.

"If we had stayed in the conference, hell, all the SEC teams would've been beating us, except Vanderbilt and Tulane," Dodd said. "So, it wasn't getting out of the SEC that hurt us. It was the quality of football."

The quality of Georgia Tech football did not diminish while Dodd was still coaching. In 1964, its first season as an independent but still playing a predominantly SEC schedule, Tech won its first seven games. But then came the season-ending crucible of Tennessee, Alabama, and Georgia. The Yellow Jackets lost all three games, including a 7-0 defeat in Athens, to again finish 7-3.

That 7-0 loss to Georgia was Dodd's first meeting with the Bulldogs' new coach. Vince Dooley had left the womb in Auburn and taken on the job of rebuilding Georgia after three unsuccessful seasons under Johnny Griffith. He had also taken on Bobby Dodd.

"I guess I was just so young and foolish," Dooley said. "I felt like I'd have to try to outwork him, and I had youth on my side. I was gonna be everywhere I could possibly be. I just jumped into it, and I was young enough to be oblivious to all the things around me, which was probably an asset."

In 1965, Tech won seven games for the fifth straight season. After starting out 0-1-1, the Jackets finished the regular season at 6-3-1. Kim King, a sophomore, started at quarterback. The young left-hander obliterated the school single-season total offense mark with 1,676 yards. That was one of 13 Tech records King set that season, including a 319-yard passing performance against Virginia.

Yet King feels his performance against Auburn that year was his best ever. Auburn was favored that day. Before the game, King was warming up, throwing in the south end zone in Grant Field. Bobby Dodd sidled up near the goal post and told his quarterback, "Auburn's a better football team than we are."

"I didn't need to hear that," King said. "I was a sophomore. I was already tight as a tick."

"But I'll tell you what," Dodd told King. "You're gonna have a great day today and we're gonna beat 'em."

Duly inspired, King helped Tech upset Auburn 23-14.

Georgia Tech concluded the 1965 season in the Gator Bowl, against Donnie Anderson and Texas Tech. It was Lenny Snow, though, not Anderson, who ran with abandon. The sophomore set Tech and Gator Bowl records for carries with 33, and rushing yardage with 139; he also scored a touchdown and won the most valuable player trophy in a 31-21 Georgia Tech victory. Collectively, the Yellow Jackets gained 364 yards rushing. They ran the ball 79 times and rushed for 23 first downs, both Gator Bowl records.

After three post-season losses, the 1965 team gave Bobby Dodd his first bowl victory since the 1956 Gator Bowl. It was also the ninth bowl victory of Dodd's coaching career. And it would be his last.

With Lenny Snow and Kim King in 1966.

Chapter 16
Sixty-six, the Last Team

THOUGH FREE OF THE SCHOLARSHIP limits of the Southeastern Conference, in 1966 Bobby Dodd still tried to compete while coping with the more stringent academic entrance requirements and curriculum at Georgia Tech. He was having even more difficulty getting players, particularly Georgians, into Tech.

For three years, Dodd had been seeking some academic relief, some concessions, from the Tech administration. Specifically, Dodd asked for changes in three required courses for management majors, including the dreaded calculus. One of the opposition's finest recruiting tools against Tech.

"Worst one thing that's ever happened to a school—put in calculus," Dodd said.

Instead, Dodd proposed substituting business math, communications, and public speaking, courses more compatible with recruiting more football players and keeping more of them eligible. "Just give me those three courses and that same degree," Dodd said, "and I can live with it."

But Tech was unwilling to have the curriculum changed as Dodd proposed. His only concession, which Dodd thought was inadequate, was to offer a humanities course.

Tech has never changed the calculus requirement.

"My coaches were doing a good job recruiting. But we just couldn't sell boys on Georgia Tech. They didn't think they could pass.

"So when I had the good year in 1966—and I didn't have any idea we'd have good a year, I thought we'd have about a 6-5—but when we won nine, I said, 'This is my time to quit. This is when I oughta get out. I'm frustrated, I'm getting bitter.' I was getting bitter at the administration up here on the hill. I was getting mad about the fact that Georgia and Auburn could take these boys I couldn't take. So I said, 'It's time for me to get out!'"

After telling his beloved Mimi, Dodd confided in Furman Bisher but asked the *Journal* sports editor not to make public his decision. "And

Furman kept it a secret," Dodd said. "I knew I was going to coach in a bowl game, and I thought announcing my retirement would hurt us in recruiting and hurt us in the bowl game. So I waited till after the Orange Bowl."

About the middle of the season, Dodd knew he was going to quit. "I just could not compete with those damn state universities," he said. "And Auburn is just as easily a state university. They could take these same boys that we couldn't take, who wanted to come and play for me. And it just broke me down.

"I couldn't beat 'em. You can just outcoach 'em some of the time, even when they have better players. But you can't outcoach 'em all the time, brother. Better football players will beat you."

The impending racial integration of southern universities and southern football also figured into his decision. Initially, that would only further hamper the football program at Tech. Many of the black players who would become available to previously segregated southern football schools had had separate, but hardly equal, educations. Thus, many of them would not be prepared academically for Tech, either for admittance or for doing the schoolwork. So Tech would be at a further recruiting disadvantage.

Another factor: Georgia Tech was no longer the only game in town. In 1966, the Atlanta Falcons joined the National Football League. That same year, major-league baseball came to the southeast when the Braves, the team that made Milwaukee famous, moved to Atlanta.

"I felt like if our football team fell off in quality, the pros were gonna hurt us crowd-wise in the stands, and publicity-wise in the papers," Dodd said. "And not just football. Baseball, too."

In the fall of 1966, though, nothing could hurt Georgia Tech and Bobby Dodd, at least not through the first nine glorious weeks.

On Friday evening, October 24, 1986, the 1966 Georgia Tech football team—Bobby Dodd's last football team—held its 20th reunion party at the Hyatt Regency Hotel in Atlanta. Players from all over the country had returned to Atlanta to reminisce, to rejoice in the past and the present, and to honor the old coach again.

As always, Bobby Dodd told his story, the stories of Galax, of Kingsport, of Knoxville and the University of Tennessee. As always, the people roared, even those who had heard the stories dozens of times. Then Dodd grew serious.

"Min, I don't think there's ever been a football team at Georgia Tech that played up to its abilities as you min did," Dodd said. "You don't know how proud of y'all I was as the season went on. I was pretty sure I was gonna drop out of Georgia Tech after that season, and I never thought I'd go out with a team as good as you.

"Min, I'm so proud of you, and I love each of you so much. If I could, I'd go around and hug all of you. My memories are always with y'all, 'cause you're the last team I coached. And I love you more than any other football team."

The memories of that 1966 season are misty, wistful memories. Trailing 3-0 at halftime of the opener, Georgia Tech erupted for 28 fourth-quarter points and a 38-3 rout of Texas A & M. After a 42-0 win over Vanderbilt, the Yellow Jackets edged Clemson 13-12 and Tennessee 6-3 on two Bunky Henry field goals. Then an elusive, quicksilver specialist named Jimmy Brown returned a punt through the rain and mud of Legion Field to help beat Auburn 17-3.

Following decisive victories over Tulane and Duke, Tech barely survived Virginia 14-13 to run its record to 8-0. The Grant Field crowd—already anticipating a bowl game—was chanting, "We want 'Bama, we want 'Bama!" as Tech left the field.

"Well, you might want 'em," Dodd said that day, "but I don't."

The next week, Penn State came to Atlanta with its young head coach, Joe Paterno. Anticipating a thunderstorm and muddy turf, Dodd wore duck-hunting boots that day. It was Paterno and Penn State, though, who had to duck. The rain never fell, but Tech thundered down on Penn State 21-0. Afterward, Paterno called Georgia Tech the quickest team he'd ever faced.

"I expect," said Dodd, "that's one of the few times Joe Paterno has ever been thrashed."

Georgia Tech was now 9-0 and ranked fourth in the country. Georgia, though, was also undefeated. "The stage was set," Vince Dooley said, "and we played very well."

Although Tech took an early 7-6 lead on King's seven-yard run and Henry's point after, Georgia was clearly the superior team that day in Athens. The Bulldogs won 23-14. It was Dooley's third win in three meetings with Dodd. And it could have been worse.

"We had them in a position," Dooley said, "where we really could've beaten them bad."

Bobby Dodd realized that. The next day, Dooley arrived at the WSB studios in Atlanta to do his Sunday TV show. Dodd had just completed his show. When the two coaches met, they shook hands and Dodd told Dooley, "You were mighty kind to me yesterday."

"That meant a lot to me," Dooley said. "Those were the kind of things he'd try to do. I had kept some down-the-liners in longer at the end of the game."

Georgia Tech returned to the Orange Bowl for the first time since the 1952 season. This would be the first appearance for Tech in an Orange Bowl played at night. Ironically, Bobby Dodd would conclude his coaching career against Florida and his one-time, long-time assistant, Ray Graves. Graves, too, had heard the rumors, rumors of Dodd's possible retirement. But publicly at least, they were just that. Rumors.

On January 2 in Miami, Tech took an early 6-0 lead. At halftime, Florida led 7-6. But in the third quarter the Yellow Jackets were driving, threatening until King's pass was intercepted near the goal line. Larry Smith then bolted 94 yards for the touchdown that stunned Tech and effectively decided the game.

Lenny Snow ran for 110 yards and caught a 52-yard pass from King, but could not prevent the 27-12 Florida victory. For Georgia Tech, the season was still an unexpectedly smashing 9-2 success, despite the last two losses. On January 3, the Yellow Jackets returned home. The next month, Dodd would leave coaching forever.

On Monday morning, February 6, 1967, 58-year-old Bobby Dodd walked into the office of Tech President Edwin Harrison and submitted his resignation as head coach. "Bringing to a sudden and somewhat stunning end," Furman Bisher wrote in the lead story on the front page of the *Journal*, "an athletic era that glittered with glory and grandeur at the only place he ever coached."

As Bisher wrote, "The news broke with seeming suddenness, because the rumors that he would resign had subsided, but the decision was one that had undergone months of deliberation."

Reluctantly, Dr. Harrison accepted Dodd's resignation, citing "our great admiration for him as one of the finest men and one of the great teachers ever to grace our campus."

Although Bisher had known of Dodd's intention to retire, there had been recent indications that he might reconsider. Just the previous week, Dodd had told the *Atlanta Constitution* and UPI that, health permitting, he would coach another four or five years. But by Friday, February 3, Dodd had definitely decided to quit. He even told a few confidants at Georgia Tech. At a hastily called press conference Monday morning following his resignation, Dodd made this formal statement:

"After numerous talks with my doctor and months of deliberation, I have regretfully asked to be relieved of my position as head football coach at Georgia Tech.

"In resigning, I would like to say that no coach has had more cooperation from the president, the athletic board, the faculty and the students than I have had. I am grateful to all of them.

"All of us here at Georgia Tech have been blessed by having the finest of men represent us in football that a school could have, and although I have had many wonderful players and teams, this past year's team was probably closer to my heart than any of them."

Dodd began the press conference by peering through the window at a steady rain falling outside. When he started to speak, he struggled to control his emotions. "The weather is pretty gloomy out there," Dodd said, "and it has been gloomy for me since Friday when I decided I would have to ask the athletic department to relieve me of my duties as head coach. It has been a difficult year for me physically. Not only this year, but since the last half of last season. Whenever you men asked me if I planned to retire this year, I had not made a final decision. But I did feel it might have to be my last year."

In addition to Dodd's growing dissatisfaction with Tech academic policies that inhibited his recruiting—he admitted Georgia Tech had just suffered poor recruiting years in both 1964 and '65—Dodd had health problems. A kidney and prostate condition had plagued him as far back as the previous season.

There were other health considerations, as well. Besides the headaches, chronic upset stomach, and fever—sometimes as high as 104 degrees—which often accompanied his kidney-prostate condition, Dodd's personality and sleeping habits had changed. In recent months, Dodd had seldom slept a full night, usually waking two or three times during the night. That, Dodd said, was as psychological as it was physical. That, he said, was the pressure the football coach feels. Any football coach. Even Bobby Dodd.

"I know people have always said I looked calm, but football eats at every man," Dodd said. "On some, it shows and on others, it doesn't.

"I've often wished I could have gone in the locker room and kicked a headgear and bawled out the officials or somebody, but it just wasn't my nature. I kept it all inside, but it bothered me just like it does every coach."

Those pressures, Dodd said, were both internal and external. "Georgia Tech supporters want to have a good football team and win so badly that it creates terrific pressure," Dodd said. "I've always felt the same way, of course. But the pressure is a lot easier to live with when you're young.

"In recent months, I feel like I've been irritable and moody and neither one of those is my nature. I don't want to disappoint our players and fans, and in the final analysis, I think that really was what worried me most."

After consulting with his immediate family and closest friends, Dodd made this decision just as he'd made almost every big decision in every big game. Alone. "Once I'd made up my mind," he said, "it was like a great weight lifted from my shoulders."

The reaction to Dodd's retirement was widespread, swift, and sorrowful. Even considering Dodd's age and health, the most common response to his announcement was shock.

"You mean he actually retired?" said Bitsy Grant, a close friend of Dodd's and the tiny tennis champion who ran the Bitsy Grant Tennis Center until his death in 1986. "It comes as a shock to me. I mean, he's been so active playing tennis. He was out here playing tennis yesterday. I thought he could coach for at least another five years. The coaching world has lost a great guy."

"Just heard the news, and to tell the truth, it surprised me," said Clemson's Frank Howard. "But if my health were bad, I'd retire too. . . . All my dealings with him have been above board. With all those little geniuses around, I hate to see a regular ol' fellow like Dodd retire."

Bear Bryant issued a surprisingly short statement. "Coach Dodd's retirement will be a great loss to the profession," he said. "No doubt he is one of the great coaches of our time."

"Certainly the game is losing one of the great coaches," said Florida's Ray Graves, who described himself as "a longtime friend, one who owes much of his career to Coach Dodd." Said Graves, "He probably contributed as much to the modern game of football as any coach in the country, both offensively and defensively."

"I knew his health was not as good as it has been, and with all the pressures of coaching, I'm happy he is getting out," said Wally Butts. "But personally, I will miss him very much, and so will football."

"When you think of Georgia Tech football, you think of Coach Dodd," said Larry Morris, an all-American linebacker under Dodd and Tech captain in 1954. "Anyone who has played for him has the utmost respect for him, not only as a coach but as a fine gentleman. He built an image no other institution in the United States has. Personally, I respect no man more."

"He was more considerate and more concerned for the individual boy than any person I've ever known or been associated with in sports," said Bill Curry, then a center for the Baltimore Colts.

Dodd's active players were especially shocked and emotionally upset, but no more so than their coach. As personally involved as he was with his players, as much as he cared about them as people and not just performers, Bobby Dodd simply could not bring himself to tell them in person that he was quitting coaching. Dodd knew he would become too emotional, and he did not want his players to see such a display of emotion in a man who was always so unflappable.

So Dodd dispatched an assistant coach, Bill Fulcher, to read a message Dodd had written to the players explaining his resignation. "I'm afraid I couldn't have delivered it very well myself," Dodd said. "I'll see most of them individually, of course, but facing them as a group would have been tough. This team and I were close."

"It's a total shock and a surprise," quarterback Kim King said softly, slumped in assistant coach Jess Berry's office. "I had no idea this was going to happen. Coach Dodd is the kind of guy everyone looks to as a second father. He treated us like that. To him, we were men, not animals. He put us above him."

"I knew his health wasn't up to par, but this greatly surprises me," said Tech tailback Lenny Snow. "Athletes come not only to play football at Tech, but to play for Bobby Dodd. I want to play my senior year under a man just like Coach Dodd."

The Atlanta newspapers lavished praise on Dodd. And not just the sports sections. Editorial cartoons lauding Dodd appeared in both the *Journal* and *Constitution.* "Dodd: Remarkable Coach" was the headline on the editorial page of the *Constitution.* "Bobby Dodd," the editorial began, "has been one of those Georgia institutions, like Bobby Jones or Peachtree Street. He could kick on third down, unschedule Alabama, or even lose to Georgia, and the Georgia Tech crowd would still wisely nod and say, 'Well, Dodd knew what he was doing.'

" . . . there was something in him that transcended the victory-at-any-price syndrome that sends many muscle-headed coaches to grudged notoriety and swift obscurity. . . .

"His retirement is a tug; the lank Gray Fox will be missed, for it has been a part of other autumns to see him standing tall on the sideline, mildly directing the Tornado. But his record is a proud one, his withdrawal comes with usual grace, and his place is an assured one in the annals of the White and Gold."

In its editorial, the *Journal* recounted Dodd's 22-year record: 165 victories, 64 defeats, and 8 ties. In 13 bowl games, Dodd was 9-4, including eight straight wins before losing.

"The record alone is enough to establish Bobby Dodd's reputation," the *Journal* declared. "But there was and is much more to Coach Dodd than the won and lost record.

"For years he has given Georgia Tech and Atlanta (since they are inseparable) the reflected glow of his own personality."

"A Great Career" was the headline on *Constitution* sports editor Jesse Outlar's column. "Bobby Dodd never forgot that he was coaching teenage college football players," Outlar wrote. "He won with a system very few coaches, if any, could have used and remained a national power."

"Bobby Dodd has been everything to Georgia Tech that he was hired to be when he came there in 1931," wrote *Journal* sports editor Furman Bisher.

"He has always been the affable one," Bisher wrote. "He has always made himself accessible. He has a mind carefully adjusted to thinking in terms of headlines and human interest. Writers of all drafts have walked away from him after a session in the glow of his charm saying, 'What a pleasure it must be to live in his society.'

"Another plank in Georgia Tech's platform of national integrity and affluence is this: In all the years Dodd has been head coach, the school has never been on NCAA probation or even investigated."

Furman Bisher, who loves his children even more than his beloved left-handed golf clubs, saved his highest praise for last. "I have no other means of judging a football coach than this: Would I want my sons to play for him?

"Bobby Dodd—I would want my sons to play for."

Vince Dooley's reaction to Dodd's retirement was dramatic, and telling. Dooley and his wife, Barbara, were vacationing in Jamaica when the phone rang in their hotel room. Dooley answered. It was a reporter asking Dooley about Dodd's retirement.

"Has he really?" Dooley said over the phone. "That's really too bad."

Barbara Dooley was in the hotel room, listening and watching worriedly while her husband spoke on the phone. When he hung up, she asked, "Who's dying?"

"I told her, 'Coach Dodd retired,' " Vince Dooley recalled. "She was relieved that no one was dead.

"It was like, 'No, I can't believe it,' " Dooley said. "It was kind of like he was coaching forever. I was in shock when I heard about it. It was like it *was* a death."

And something was dead, or at least dying: Georgia Tech football, as it had come to be known under Bobby Dodd.

Discussing strategy with Bobby Jr.
in the family box at Grant Field, 1985.

Chapter 17
Legend Emeritus

FOLLOWING THE 1966 SEASON, the Football Writers Association of America voted Bobby Dodd its national coach of the year, as the *New York Daily News* had done after Tech's glorious 1952 season. The 1966 award was no sentimental farewell gift to an aging coach. Dodd had earned the honor, with as fine a coaching job as he and any of his staffs had ever done.

Friday, May 6, 1967, was proclaimed Bobby Dodd Day in the state of Georgia. The following day, May 7, was named Bobby Dodd Day in the city of Atlanta. That night, one thousand people—including players representing each of Dodd's 22 Tech teams—gathered at the new Hyatt Regency Hotel to honor Dodd.

Frank Broyles was the featured speaker that evening. He was so nervous, he wrote out his speech, then typed it, the first time Broyles had ever done so. Broyles stressed three of Dodd's finest characteristics: "His fine perspective on things, his ability to inspire confidence, and his originality. During his career these traits have worked in beautiful harmony to help bring about Bobby's uncommon success."

Broyles stressed Dodd's "ability to take the eagle's-eye view—to get up above things so he could see them in their true relations. And I wonder today if that wasn't the reason he spent so much time up on the tower." There was Dodd's philosophy of "Football for fun," which, Broyles said, "doesn't in any sense mean playing soft football."

There was Dodd's inspirational air, his knack for inspiring players to believe in him, and in themselves. Said Broyles, "We felt that he had our personal welfare always at heart." But the practical football side also had to be considered. "The proof of the pudding lay in the eating," Broyles said. "We saw his methods get results on Saturday afternoon."

There was Dodd's Luck, and also Dodd's mystical ability to perform extraordinary feats: that onside kick in practice; the punt that hit his chair in the tower; calling the Chappel Rhino running pass play in the 1952 Georgia game. And, of course, there was Dodd's original football thinking and innovations: the chairman of the board concept, short practices, no spring practice for many upperclassmen, no scrimmaging once the season began, volleyball, and all these swift, shifty little specialists Dodd deployed so masterfully.

"General Neyland once observed that Bobby Dodd had the greatest backs of any football team in America," Broyles said that night. "I think they averaged around 170 pounds. Someone asked Neyland how many of these boys could make his team, and his reply was, 'Not a darned one of them.' Bobby knew that football was not a game of muscle, but a game of quickness. He realized that ability can come in any size package."

And, of course, there was Dodd's notion that football players should actually be students, too. "I believe that Bobby Dodd's innovations have helped save the game of football," Broyles said. "Academic demands have grown more rigorous and demanding as the years have passed. Players have had to invest more and more time in the classroom, the laboratory, and the library. Bobby's innovations in football have made more time available for academic uses. I seriously doubt that the game of football could have survived under the older system of practice with its grueling hours and hours of practice. As academic demands grew heavier, interest in football would have waned. And we would have lost support."

Broyles concluded by referring to "the great Georgia Tech football tradition," which he called "an unrivaled football tradition in which the weak were made strong and the strong were made stronger." Finally, there was Dodd's greatest contribution and achievement, "the achievement of developing human beings. He molded youngsters into men—men who believed in themselves, men with direction and purpose and high moral character."

Dodd spoke humbly to the audience that evening.

"I'm a little like Tom Sawyer. He didn't like to go to school and neither did I. But we both had some teachers who took an interest in us and a principal who believed that there was more to learning than can be written on a report card, and somehow we got through because of these people.

"I never felt more like Tom Sawyer than I do tonight. You remember when Tom snuck into the house and hid under the table and listened to his own funeral services and heard all those folks praising him when they thought he was dead. Well, I keep feeling like you all are going to realize that I'm still around and come up here and take back all those nice words and all those gifts that mean so much to Alice and me.

"The good Lord had to burn a lot of midnight oil staying up nights to let my life come out as it has. For at times, I have done a lot of things to hinder Him."

In 1967, Bobby Dodd was still the Georgia Tech athletic director, but the new coach of the Ramblin' Wreck was Dodd's defensive coordinator from the previous season, Bud Carson, only the fourth official head coach in Tech history.

Carson's first season had begun promisingly. Tech won its first three games in 1967. But then Kim King was injured and missed much of the remainder of the season. When the Yellow Jackets lost the final three games, Georgia Tech had its first losing season since 1950.

With the exception of a fine 1970 season, when Carson's Jackets went nine and three, football on the Flats, in performance and in the won-lost column, was not up to the standards Bobby Dodd had set.

Carson, like Bowden Wyatt at Tennessee and Ray Perkins at Alabama, found that following a beloved hero is a thankless job. In 1971, after compiling a five-year record of 27-27, Bud Carson was dismissed.

At Bobby Dodd's urging, Georgia Tech hired Bill Fulcher to replace Carson. Fulcher was a 180-pound guard and linebacker in the mid-1950s at Tech. Fulcher represented, Dodd hoped, a homecoming of sorts, a return of the old days at Tech. "Bill was what looked like a very fine Georgia Tech football coach," Dodd said. "A young person, very enthusiastic, what I thought would be a real good man for Georgia Tech for many years, and when I offered him the head coaching job, he said, 'That's what I've always wanted. I'll be there for the next 20 years.' "

He was there for two.

Fulcher's first year was a success, as Tech recorded a 7-4-1 mark in 1972, including a breathtaking 31-30 victory over Johnny Majors's Iowa State team in the Liberty Bowl.

"Bill had a good year," Dodd said. "I was real pleased with him." Dodd was shocked, however, when, following spring practice in 1973, Fulcher abruptly came to him and said, "Coach, I've just got to quit coaching."

"I know it must have had to do some with some personal things, family things," Dodd said.

Dodd, though, would not accept Fulcher's resignation. "I told him he couldn't do it now," Dodd said, "that it was too late in the year, and I couldn't get anybody. I couldn't take a head coach away from anybody else, and I didn't believe there was anybody there who could take over."

Instead, Dodd offered a compromise: Fulcher would coach another season. After the season finale against Georgia, should Fulcher still want to resign, Dodd would accept his resignation. "He still wanted to," Dodd said, "and he did resign. And I did accept his resignation. His heart just wasn't in it."

After a disappointing 5-6 season in 1973, Fulcher resigned to enter private business. His two-year record was 12-10-1. Thus, Georgia Tech, once a bedrock of stability, was about to hire its third coach in eight years.

"That's when we went after Pepper," Dodd said. Pepper Rodgers, Dodd's quarterback and kicker in the early 1950s, later Bobby Dodd, Jr.'s quarterback coach at Florida, then a highly successful head coach at Kansas and, when Tech approached him, at UCLA. "I went after him," Dodd said, "because my former players had recommended him."

But not before an influential group of former Tech players had made one final, futile attempt to lure Frank Broyles back to Georgia Tech. George Mathews, who had become extremely wealthy and influential in the Tech community and in Atlanta, was part of that group pursuing Broyles, Mathews's old Tech teammate.

According to Mathews, the financial package that Broyles was offered went far beyond the salary and traditional perquisites afforded most football coaches. Total value of the package, including real estate opportunities: two million dollars.

Even as athletic director, Dodd was unaware of the offer. "Maybe they didn't want me to know," Dodd reasoned, "because I had never made much money coaching at Tech."

Once again, Broyles could not be persuaded to leave Arkansas, where his own dynasty and legacy were assured, where he was also the athletic director and where his wife, Barbara, had vowed that their children would grow up. Thus, George Mathews recalled, the search for a new Tech coach turned toward Pepper Rodgers. At Frank Broyles's suggestion.

"Frank said Pepper had grown up, that he'd matured," Mathews said.

"Pepper was ready to come, and I was ready to hire him," Dodd said. "I thought he would be good for Georgia Tech. He's enthusiastic, he's colorful, he's a good PR man with the newspaper people. And we needed all that, because the pros had come to town."

In 1975, in Rodgers's second season back at the Flats, Bobby Dodd turned 67, the mandatory retirement age for state employees, and had to step down as athletic director. In March 1976, Tech named Dodd's successor, Doug Weaver, an old friend of Pepper Rodgers. "I recommended John McKenna [Dodd's assistant athletic director], but Pepper wanted Doug," Dodd said. "The football coach always swings a lot of weight, and he got the athletic board to give Doug the job. I liked Doug Weaver. I thought he was very personable, but John McKenna had worked for me and knew the ropes at Tech, and I thought he would have been a good athletic director. I still think he would have been."

On October 17, 1975, hundreds of Dodd's friends, former players, and colleagues gathered at yet another testimonial dinner, this time in honor of his impending retirement as athletic director. It was a joyous and poignant occasion, made even more memorable by the fact that Bobby Dodd was lucky to even be there. Lucky to even be alive.

After retiring as head coach in 1967, Dodd was continually treated and monitored for his prostate troubles. By 1974, his doctors discovered a malignancy: prostate cancer. A good friend and frequent tennis companion, a urologist named Dr. Charles Scott, made the diagnosis.

"I had it bad," Dodd admitted. "I could have died. We were all upset. Before Charlie even operated on me, he told me 'You're in bad shape now.' After the surgery he came in and said, 'Coach, it was just touch and go. I don't know whether I got it all or not. I hope I did.'

"Of course, we didn't know whether it was gonna recur. If it does recur, I'm gone. When that malignancy gets out of that sack, it goes into your bones. That's the way Bitsy died [Bitsy Grant, in 1986], exactly. He had cancer of the prostate and they didn't get it quite quick enough. They thought they might have it but it came back all over him and he died in six months."

Publicly, the Dodds maintained an air of optimism and confidence. Privately, though, family and close friends knew how fragile Dodd's health was and how frightened his wife was. George Mathews still remembers the call he received from Alice Dodd, when she broke down over the phone, so distraught over her husband's condition.

Fortunately, Charlie Scott's operation was as thorough as it was timely. Within a month, Bobby Dodd, then 65, again roamed the baseline at Bitsy Grant Tennis Center, playing doubles. For that, Dodd may have been as responsible as the doctor. Unlike his father, Bobby Dodd did not succumb to the looming horror of prostate cancer.

"He didn't let it disturb him," Dr. Scott said. "He went ahead with his everyday activities. The main thing was his attitude. He didn't get down in the dumps. He went right back onto the tennis courts as soon as I let him go."

So by October 17, 1975, Bobby Dodd was still alive and kicking the baseline over a missed return of service. That evening, he reveled in the affection and appreciation of those who honored him. Many of those who could not attend also extended their love and gratitude in writing. Those expressions are remarkable for their diversity as well as their sincerity. And not from just the big names.

Raymond Holt, class of 1962, recalled the two knee injuries he suffered his senior year and how he sat down with Dodd, and together they decided it was best for Holt not to play. "I appreciate the fact that you were interested in my well-being," Holt wrote.

Tom Winingder, captain of the 1962 team, remembered what Bobby

Dodd had said while recruiting him: "We make football fun at Georgia Tech and treat you like a man." And that Dodd had delivered on that promise.

Leon Hardeman, perhaps Dodd's greatest back, remembered his freshman year, when he was summoned to the head coach's office so Dodd could "explain the facts of life about athletics and education."

Paul Duke, Dodd's first all-American and captain, was grateful to Dodd "for believing in me early when I perhaps lacked confidence to believe in myself," and for "guiding me . . . when I didn't have a father at home."

Sam Lyle, Dodd's assistant in the early 1950s, who came to Georgia Tech after coaching at LSU under Bernie Moore and Gaynell Tinsley, at Florida under Bob Woodruff, and at Oklahoma under Bud Wilkinson. On observing Dodd's coaching style, Lyle's first thought: "This will never work."

Dave Davis, Dodd's outstanding punter in the early 1950s, wrote, "Everyone knew that all they had to do was to act like human beings and keep their noses clean, and they would receive outstanding treatment."

That meant everyone, even if they didn't always keep their noses clean. Phillip Baum, who eventually became Maxie Baughan's backup center in 1958, recalled that as a sophomore, he'd married on December 23, 1955, and went on his honeymoon while the Tech traveling squad went to New Orleans for the Sugar Bowl. Baum returned to Atlanta on the thirty-first, settled into an on-campus apartment for married students, went out to celebrate on New Year's Eve, and promptly celebrated to excess. The following day, New Year's Day, he was kicked out of his apartment. Naturally, he went to Bobby Dodd. "You asked me when I was going to grow up now that I was a married man, among a few other choice comments. You then proceeded to pick up the phone, call the Atlanta Biltmore, and tell them you wanted the best accommodations in town for one of your new honeymooners. Coach Dodd, at that time, I was just a third-string left guard who didn't know which end was up. The impression that you made on me that day will be something that I will cherish for the rest of my life."

George Humphreys, a fullback from 1952 to 1954, and the most valuable player in the 1955 Cotton Bowl, was associate director of the Domestic Council at the White House in 1975 when he wrote, "you had the magic ability to see beyond the frivolous in us, and discover the essential. You brought out the very best in your men. For most, you allowed it to happen. For some of us, you demanded it. But all of us knew we were being guided by you as individuals."

Mackey Mulherin was a seldom-used substitute who lettered in 1949. He reiterated in 1975 what he said while playing: "I would rather sit on the bench at Georgia Tech for Coach Dodd than play for any other team."

For Ken Owen, Tech's fine fullback in 1955 and '56, the most vivid memory of Bobby Dodd was "that personality which held all us punks in absolute awe . . . as if a spirit came over the field."

Dick Bestwick, who became head coach at Virginia, later director of the Peach Bowl, and then an assistant athletic director at Georgia, had wanted his son to play for Bobby Dodd. For good reason. "You set a standard for treating players with dignity that no one has ever been able to match," Bestwick wrote.

Frank Broyles allowed that "I would have hated trying to coach without knowing the things that you taught me." Regarding Dodd's role as chairman of the board, Broyles described it as "a concept that has lengthened the working lives of coaches, opened up a multitude of jobs, and brought exceptional organization into our game." Frank Broyles had only one regret: "For the sake of our profession, it is a shame that you coached mostly engineers! If you had served at a large university with a general curriculum where most of the players are P.E. majors, I believe that Dodd students would blanket the coaching field."

For years, Margie Bennett had served as Bobby Dodd's secretary and right-hand woman at Georgia Tech. "She was indispensable to me," Dodd said. And so ferociously loyal to Tech that she joked of being so nervous before the nationally televised 1955 opener against Miami, that she even considered leaving a Coca-Cola bottle right outside Miami's locker room door. Something for someone to slip on.

Margie Bennett could have been speaking for thousands of people when she declared, "Those were the halcyon days, the golden days, the days of wine and roses. It was a stay in Camelot, and it has taken me some years to become adjusted to the 'other world.' It was rather like losing my right arm when I left Georgia Tech."

And the late Don Stephenson, Dodd's all-American center in 1956 and '57, described life with Bobby Dodd this way: "Most of all, we had fun."

Upon Dodd's official retirement in 1976, Furman Bisher wrote that the coach "led Georgia Tech into a football game like a scoutmaster taking a troop on a picnic." Professionally speaking, Bisher was also very grateful for Bobby Dodd.

"Dodd never tensed when they [writers] walked into his practices," Bisher wrote. "He never tried to hide anything from them. Sometimes he did everything but write the headline for a kid he could see needed help."

By 1979, football at Georgia Tech had lost all of its lustre. The golden years were distant memories, attendance was down, and recruiting was increasingly difficult. There was growing friction within the ranks of the faithful. As always, the attention focused on the head coach.

The same bold cockiness that attracted Dodd's confidence in Pepper Rodgers, the player, was not as appealing a trait for Pepper Rodgers, the head coach. At least not to many of the older, more sedate and traditional Tech alumni and boosters, who opposed Rodgers's way of doing things. This, after all, was the man who led his first UCLA team on the field by doing cartwheels.

Regardless of Rodgers's modern appearance and free-spirited attitude, he just didn't win enough to satisfy the conservative following in the west stands. A 16-3 loss to Georgia was the sixth defeat in 1979 and marked the finish of Rodgers's coaching career at Tech. His six years at the Flats ended with a record of 34 victories, 31 defeats, and 2 ties.

"I still believe if Pepper had gotten equal material to the people he was playing against, the big schools, I believe he would've whipped 'em with his wishbone," Dodd said. "He was doing a terrific job of coaching the wishbone. He just didn't get enough football players, just like Bud didn't and Fulcher didn't and I didn't there at the end.

"But Pepper won some big games with what I thought was inferior material. He beat Notre Dame. He beat Georgia with inferior football material."

Following the 1979 season, Bobby Dodd and everyone else who cared to look could see that Georgia Tech football needed help. Badly. Although he was officially retired by then, Dodd still maintained an office in the Tech Alumni House, as he does now in 1987. He serves as a paid consultant to the alumni association, primarily to speak at Georgia Tech functions around Atlanta, the state, occasionally the southeast, and sometimes even the nation. Generally, though, Dodd's status became, and remains, legend emeritus. He remains the last link to a glorious age at Georgia Tech. In 1979, Dodd sought to add another link to the past: Bill Curry.

"When they let Pepper go," Dodd said, "we needed somebody very badly who could bring the Georgia Tech people back together. They got splintered off during the years after I had quit. They had just gotten kinda disenchanted with what we were doing. Pepper's style was not appealing to a lot of them. I had nothing to do with letting Pepper go because I was out of the athletic department by then. But as soon as the job was open, I immediately started telling everybody that would listen to get Bill Curry. I don't know how much influence I had, if any, in getting him. But I told everybody, 'He is the man to get.' "

This despite the fact that Curry had never been a head coach and had scant coaching experience: one season as an assistant to Rodgers in 1976, then three years as an assistant with the Green Bay Packers, the first of four professional teams Curry had played on after serving as Dodd's captain in 1964.

"He hadn't had much [coaching] experience," Dodd said. "But he had played football—high school, college, and pro—and been around football enough. But he had what I thought we needed: a dominating Georgia Tech man with a lot of personality who could bring the Tech people back with his charisma. And he had it, he had it. If you ever saw a guy who was endowed with all the talents that one man oughta have, Bill Curry did."

Dodd often introduced Curry at Tech functions in the following years and always took great pleasure in pointing out Curry's lone shortcoming. "I'd say he was a fine high school player, a great college player, and an all-pro center," Dodd recalls fondly. "He's handsome, he's a leader, he's got character, and he's the best speaker in college football today. But call offensive plays? He's terrible. You can understand it, though, 'cause as a center, he's spent most of his life looking at the world upside down between his legs. I tease Bill and say that's the only bad thing about him.

"But thank goodness for Bill Curry."

Bill Curry still looked, acted, and dressed the part of the Tech man, that most privileged of collegiate football heroes in the 1950s and early '60s, when the Yellow Jackets were the palace guards and tackles, quarterbacks, and kickers of southern football.

"To be a Tech man was to be among the elite," Curry said. "The other programs surrounding us were not what we were, with the exception of Alabama. Auburn was awfully good, but they were on probation. Tech was the place to be. We were so successful, it was so perfect and 90 something percent of us graduated. We were hated for that, and still are. And when hard times fell on us, the piranha came out and enjoyed that."

Hard times fell immediately, and for the piranha, it became a weekly buffet of buffoonery. Despite all of his assets, Bill Curry knew little about being a head coach when he returned to Tech. That inexperience, coupled with a dearth of talent and a savage schedule, led to a 1-9-1 debut for Curry in 1980. After shocking Alabama 24-21, to open the 1981 season, the Yellow Jackets proceeded to lose their last 10 games.

For Bill Curry, the pain of those two seasons was searing. He could only imagine what it was like for Bobby Dodd, sitting up in his private box in Grant Field, watching the horror below. Said Curry, "Here's something you give your whole life to and build it into a national power, and he watched it deteriorate into a laughingstock."

"It was very tough for me to swallow," Dodd admitted. "I had been a winner all my life. I hated to see us go through some bad years and some bad decisions. But I can lose as long as I've got class. Curry's got class. I always think of Tech as a school with class."

Dodd supported Curry in two crucial ways. After the disastrous seasons of 1980 and '81, Dodd began meeting on Monday mornings in Curry's office during the season. He carried with him a yellow legal pad, on which he had jotted down notes during the game concerning decisions Curry had, or hadn't, made. Then Dodd would critique the Jackets and their coach. Once, Dodd's legal pad bulged with 44 items for discussion. The two men discussed, and parried, each one.

"Bill is the only coach that followed me who's wanted any of my advice," said Dodd, who was only too happy to give it. Particularly since Dodd, the master strategist, was a quarterback and Curry a center, with a narrow, inverted view of the football world.

Dodd's greatest assistance to Curry, though, may have been the numerous public votes of confidence the old coach gave the new coach while he struggled. Dodd, who remembered those tough years Alexander had suffered and knew firsthand the recruiting problems Georgia Tech presented, publicly defended Curry, whom he said would transform Georgia Tech back into a winning program, and would do so without cheating.

Dodd defended not just Tech but Curry, whom Dodd calls "like a son to me." And in 1984, Curry rewarded Dodd's faith in him with a 6-4-1 victory and a 35-18 thrashing of Georgia. The 1985 season was even more satisfying. Tech finished 9-2-1, the best record since Dodd's last team went 9-2 in 1966. The Jackets again beat Georgia, 20-16, and were ranked 18th nationally after upsetting Michigan State 17-14 in the All-American Bowl in Birmingham. That game was particularly satisfying to Dodd and Curry, who had to suspend four Tech players—including starting quarterback John Dewberry and starting wide receivers Gary Lee and Toby Pearson—for missing curfew three nights before the game.

On an even grander scale, it was the kind of decision Bobby Dodd had made with Billy Teas. Curry placed principle ahead of expediency and victory—and then, with backup quarterback Todd Rampley giving a superb performance, went out and won the bowl game anyway.

"That year, I thought Bill and his coaching staff—and I told them this—did the finest coaching job that anybody at Georgia Tech's ever done," said Dodd. "When you consider the material and the games they won, well, I said before the season started that if they won six games, it'd be good. Seven would be great. Eight, I'd change the name of Grant Field to Curry's Field. I didn't even mention nine."

In 1986, Georgia Tech appeared destined to compete in its second straight bowl game, but Wake Forest upset the Jackets and spoiled their holiday plans. When Georgia survived 31-24 Tech finished a disappointing 5-5-1.

And then something remarkable happened. Alabama ushered in the New Year by ushering in a new era, a new philosophy toward football and intercollegiate athletics. With Ray Perkins having left his alma mater to return to the NFL, this time with the Tampa Bay Buccaneers, Alabama hired Bill Curry, the quintessential Tech man, as its head football coach. And this despite the fact that Curry was the only losing coach in Georgia Tech history, with a seven-year record of 31-43-2.

Alabama president Dr. Joab Thomas was more impressed by Curry's commitment to academics and running a program of integrity. Thomas interviewed Curry at the urging of Perkins, Curry's old teammate on the Baltimore Colts. Before talking to Thomas, and before accepting the job, Curry sought the counsel of Bobby Dodd.

"He called me and asked me what I thought," Dodd said. "I said, 'Well, you know I'd hate to see you leave Georgia Tech. But I'm certainly not gonna try to hold you back.'

"I didn't think they'd offer him the job, for only one reason. I didn't think Alabama people could stand to hire a coach with his record. I knew that a lot of Alabama people were not particularly fond of Georgia Tech because of our falling outs, about Graning-Holt, and Bisher and the sportswriters kinda fussing at each other. I didn't think they would offer him the job. But I said, 'If they offer you the job, I don't blame you if you take it.' "

Alabama did offer Bill Curry one of the premier coaching jobs in the country in spite of his won-loss record. Curry took the chance Dodd didn't take with Texas. Although Dodd can only wonder what might have been, Bill Curry will find out.

"I didn't ask him why he took the job and I never have asked him, because I know why he took it," Dodd said. "It's a challenge. It's a chance to be a big-time major football coach, which he could never be at Georgia Tech. I doubt if he could have won an ACC championship to say nothing of being at the top nationally, the top ten or the top five. Which he can do over at Alabama, if he makes it over there. I don't know whether he'll make it or not. I just pray he will. I love Bill."

Indeed, Bobby Dodd's favorite tie clasp is a gold one featuring a football, with two names to the left and one to the right. It reads: HEIS ALEX DODD. Heisman, Alexander, and Dodd, the three greatest coaching names in Georgia Tech history. Bobby Dodd has tried to get a jeweler to enlarge the tie clasp, to add a fourth name beside his own: CURRY. The jeweler said it couldn't be done.

"His record at Georgia Tech was real, real bad. But he did what we needed most. He brought all the Georgia Tech people back into the fold, and they're still here. We needed that more than anything. Tech people started giving more money to the school and still are.

"So now, when Curry left, we hit the jackpot again. Homer has that knack of coming up with great people."

This time, Tech athletic director Homer Rice came up with Bobby Ross, the enormously successful coach at Maryland who had resigned after the 1986 season. "I approve of Bobby Ross very much," Dodd said. "I've been impressed with him. I already knew a little bit about his coaching. I watched his Maryland team play a number of times. They were well coached. I checked his background. I liked the idea he'd gone to VMI, one of the schools near my section. He played under John McKenna. That's a plus. I found out about his two boys, one went to Annapolis, one went to the Air Force Academy. That's good, that's good.

"When we got Bobby Ross, I went and had a long talk with him about football. And I approve of him. I approve of him very much."

But, of course. As a young high school football coach, one of the first books on coaching that Bobby Ross studied was, *Bobby Dodd on Football*.

"I think that he will be a fine football coach at Georgia Tech," Dodd said, "and will be very successful *if* he can get equal football material, or near equal to the people that he's playing against. He won't get out-coached, but he may get out-materialed.

"So, that's where we are today."

In retirement, there is nothing retiring about Bobby Dodd. In retirement, he continues to do what he has always done best: live life to its fullest. His life's work is being Bobby Dodd.

Each weekday at mid-morning, Dodd hops into his Tech yellow Chevrolet station wagon—presented to him upon his 50th anniversary on the Flats—and drives to his office at the Alumni House. He reads his mail and answers phone calls. For the Tech Alumni Association, Dodd's role is essentially one of goodwill ambassador and great public speaker, primarily at alumni club gatherings.

"Whenever we start a new club, he's the motivator, the guy who can get people out," said John Carter, Tech's alumni executive director. "If I call down to south Georgia and say, 'I'm John Carter, and I'd like to come down and start a club,' not many people may come out. But if I say, 'I'm John Carter, you don't know me, but Bobby Dodd is coming down and his wife, too,' everybody in a one-hundred-mile radius will show up."

At alumni functions, Dodd will invariably begin by saying, "In this room are the greatest people in the world. 'Georgy' Tech people." And he will have the audience, as if he already didn't. He will tell the tale of his life story yet again: Of his high school days in Kingsport. His obsession with graduating players. Bear Bryant's recruiting tricks (once disguising an assistant coach as a priest, complete with collar, to dissuade a prospect from attending Notre Dame). A $125-a-plate roast and fete for Curry after the 1984 season. ("After he won *six* games. I won six major bowl games in consecutive years, and you know what they did? They had a little luncheon over at the student center.")

The time Bear, faced with a limited number of scholarships at Alabama, gave 20 football players swimming scholarships. ("Twenty of the biggest swimmers you ever saw. They damn near drowned when they put 'em in the pool, but they could play football.") The diplomatic and political purpose Bear might have served had he lived longer and accompanied Ronald Reagan to the Reykjavik summit with Mikhail Gorbachev. ("If they'd let Bear go up to Iceland and negotiate with those damn Russians, we'd own Moscow and have all their vodka—except what Bear drank up.") How Bear, who had an awful time for the longest time trying to win a bowl game, once decided, out of desperation, to use Dodd's easy-going approach to bowl preparation. ("Bear said, 'I Dodderized my boys, and it still didn't work'.")

And the first time Dodd's grandpappy saw him play football at Tennessee. ("Girls in short dresses yelling for volunteers. Men in striped shirts like convicts. People with orange gourds and blue gourds on their heads. And then the littlest one went out and smelled the biggest one, and the damnedest dog fight you ever saw broke out!")

Dodd will often wear his camel's hair sport coat and a Georgia Tech yellow power tie fastened with his HEIS ALEX DODD tie clasp. His silver hair flows long and wispy and curls up over the collar of his blue button-down Oxford shirt. And his big hands will gesture vividly, animating the stories he has told so often and so well.

Dodd's office walls are adorned with plaques, photographs, and awards he has accumulated over the last half-century. Ironically, many were on display in "Bear," the movie made of Bryant's life story starring Gary Busey. Bryant's family would not cooperate with the moviemakers, so much of the film was shot in Georgia. Agnes Scott College in Decatur served as the Alabama campus, and Dodd's football memorabilia were hung in the office Busey used.

Two of the most treasured trophies in Dodd's office are mounted and displayed behind his desk: a pair of 13-pound, large-mouth bass. Dodd remains an avid fisherman, casting for bass with his beloved silver doctor lure, but not nearly as often as he once did. Now, Dodd and his wife and son usually fish on friends' private lakes up in Paulding County or down in Thomasville.

In earlier times, it was difficult to determine which kind of tackle—football or fishing—Dodd preferred.

In 1949, on the morning of the Florida game, Dodd and Ray Graves snuck out of a Gainesville hotel and went bass fishing before dawn. The day before the 1952 Orange Bowl, Dodd was out on the hotel pier, casually fishing in Biscayne Bay. Later that summer, before coaching the college all-stars against the Los Angeles Rams, Dodd flew to Canada for a week of fishing. The following winter, he was introduced at a banquet as "the man who finds time to coach football at Georgia Tech between fishing trips."

Bobby Dodd still fishes regularly, and he plays tennis doubles daily at Bitsy Grant. He plays for the health of it, for the camaraderie, for the competition. When he isn't hitting out on one of the three main courts, Dodd watches from the veranda, or plays checkers or gin rummy in the clubhouse. Whatever game he's involved in, he has a small wager placed on the outcome.

Dodd plays tennis much like he coached football. He plays the odds, he plays the angles. He plays defensively, keeping the ball in play, rallying, not trying to hit winners but rather waiting for the other guy to make the mistake. He does things his way, schedules opponents craftily. And usually, he wins.

Dodd hobbles around on an arthritic left knee, a nagging reminder of arthroscopic surgery in 1980. He bends only, and rarely, from the waist. He plays with an enormous Weed racket that makes opponents' Prince rackets look like paupers. He has no strokes, marshmallow-soft serves, switches the Weed from right hand to left when he can't reach a backhand, and taps little wrist dinks. And there is his trademark: the Scoop, the two-handed, underhanded shot that simply keeps the ball in play. In football, you quick-kick on third down, maybe even second, and make your opponent drive 70 yards without making a mistake in order to score. In tennis, you hit the Scoop.

For a while, Dodd shuffled about the clay courts in tennis shoes that were slit open at the toes. "I have a simple philosophy: Don't ever let a shoe give you blisters when there's a knife handy," said Dodd, who bought the shoes only to find they were too snug for sweatsocks. So he sliced them.

He peers out across the net from beneath a white tennis cap and from behind black sunglasses. Dodd would wear the shades even if he hadn't had two cataract operations. Even with the shades, he always makes sure the sun shines in his opponents' eyes.

"I had three great tennis wins," Dodd said. "I'm very proud of 'em. The first one, no one will ever equal. In the city tournament, I entered four different events. I entered the men's unlimited. I must have been in my sixties then. I got the best partner in the tournament, Crawford Henry, who had played at Tulane and was a real fine college player. I'm gonna play doubles with him. All of these were doubles. I couldn't play singles, I was a doubles specialist.

"Then I entered the seniors, and they only had one seniors then, anything above 45 years old. I got Bitsy Grant, who was the best senior player in the South, for my partner. Then I entered the father-and-son, with Bobby Jr. Strangely enough, I never liked to play mixed doubles, with girls, but I some way decided I'm gonna play, and I get the best woman player in the tournament, Sally Seebeck.

"Believe it or not, we won all four events. I won 'em all. Nobody has ever done that and now they'll never do it, 'cause they won't let you enter but two events now.

"The second great tennis win I had, they say, was the biggest upset since David slew Goliath."

At the 1961 Atlanta Invitational tennis tournament, one more team was needed to fill out the doubles field. Dodd was chosen and paired with another senior player, Larry Shippey. Their opponents were the number one seeded team: Whitney Reed and Gene Scott, who also happened to be the number one ranked doubles team in the United States. In singles, Reed was the top-ranked amateur nationally, while Scott was ranked eighth. Later that year, they would represent the U.S. in the Davis Cup against Canada.

"The first set, Whitney Reed kinda played around," Dodd said. "He didn't mind, he was kinda laughing, trying to hit the ball through me. Gene Scott didn't like it much, though."

Particularly after Dodd and Shippey took the first set, 6-4. "In the second set," Dodd said, "they went to work. But we beat 'em in the second set, too, when they were trying."

Beat 'em 6-3. "So we put 'em out of the tournament," Dodd said. "Just before the final point, I told Shippey, 'Larry, we oughta default. We're ruining the tournament. They're the special guests.' He said, 'Hell, no, we'll beat 'em if we can!' And we beat 'em."

(Bobby Dodd, Jr., has seen that side of his father, who is still competitive but also compassionate. On occasion, when father and son are about to win a wager from an opponent they've already taken a set from—and perhaps an opponent who shouldn't be losing as much tennis money as he is—Dodd will suggest to his son that they purposely, but inconspicuously, drop that set.

Linda Thompson understands. "I think Daddy's very empathetic," she said. "He's very sensitive. He also gets depressed easily. That's why he always stays around young, talkative people. That's why he's always got the lights and TV on.")

"The third thing was when I was 67," Dodd said, "and took Joe Becknell, who was 37, and entered the state men's championship. Just above men's unlimited. They had good players then, good college players. And we won that tournament, even though we lost the first set to everybody we played. I was very proud of that. Nobody else thought we had any chance of winning the tournament.

"So anyway, we won those three things. The 35 doubles, the four divisions I won, and beat Whitney Reed and Gene Scott. When you realize my age, well, I was up in age in all of those. But I got a big kick out of it. Since then, I've won some minor tournaments. Bitsy and I won some tournaments playing together, but these are the big things."

Although Bobby Dodd seldom misses a chance to play tennis, or to fish, he seldom misses coaching football. Usually, he misses it only one day a week, about three months a year.

"Only when they blow the whistle on Saturday afternoon to start the game," Dodd said. "I would be running the game. I could run a football game as well as anybody. Bear would tell you that. Anybody who's been around me will tell you that. How could I not run it? I played six years in high school, four years in college. I coached for 36 years. Why wouldn't I know how to run a game?

"I was a quarterback all those years, and a quarterback knows more than anybody else on the field. He has to know assignments, he has to know everything going on. I knew everything that was going on. And I was a good coach during the game."

Indeed, Bear Bryant always readily acknowledged Dodd's greatness. "The best ever on the sidelines," Bill Curry said of Dodd. "Coach Bryant told me, 'You know he was the best on Saturday.' " (In Bryant's autobiography, *Bear*, he stated, "Bobby was one of the best at-the-game strategists who ever lived, a coach who came up with the right decision at the time when a decision was needed. So-called Dodd's Luck and Grant Field Luck was really Dodd Smart.")

During the week, of course, was another matter. Dodd's lighthearted, no-scrimmage approach to football baffled veteran coaches like Bryant and Jess Neely. "No one else in the country can coach like Dodd and win," Bear said. "I want to find the guy that coaches like Dodd and play him," Neely said. "Not Dodd, but someone else that coaches like him."

"I don't feel I was a better coach than anybody else during the week," Dodd said. "Except that I knew what would win football games. Penalties, turnovers, kicking game, things like that. I stressed those things. But the best thing I did was pick assistants."

Others insist picking plays was Dodd's forte. Even Dodd admits there may have been only one coach better at play selection and running a game. "Paul Brown, to me, is the greatest football coach that's ever been," Dodd said. "He's one of my few heroes. He was successful in high school, Ohio State, the Cleveland Browns, the Cincinnati Bengals. Whatever team he touched, he just changed that team.

"He knew the things that win football games. First, his teams were disciplined. They didn't make mistakes, didn't jump offsides, didn't get holding penalties. One of the greatest talents he had was he called the right play at the right time. He was the greatest play caller. I thought I was a great one and I may be second to him.

"He was just the best of our era, and I knew some great football coaches. I have about five great coaches I rate, and I rate Paul Brown the best."

The best of the rest: Wallace Wade. Bob Neyland. Bear Bryant. Bud Wilkinson.

"They're all about a notch above the rest," Dodd said.

"All the great coaches of my era knew that defense was the name of the game. That's changed some now, with the modern passers and catchers and wide-open offense. But back in our days, particularly in college, defense was the name of the game. If you had a good defensive team, and you played the kicking game, and kicked that ball and made that other team start on their 30, they couldn't score many points on you. You see, you didn't have field goals back then. Nobody hardly kicked any field goals.

"Neyland and Wade were great defensive coaches, and I would put Bear in there, too. Those three stressed defense better than any of the rest of them. If you look at my record, look at Neyland's record, there's not many points scored. We'd go through a season and have 50 points scored on us—during a *season*. Nowadays, they score more than that in one game many times. Neyland went through the 1939 season with no points scored on him. Bear, tough to score points on. Wade, tough to score points on. Most of those people, you had to score points on a long run from a kickoff, maybe, or a punt return, or a lucky pass.

"Bud was an offensive coach. He was gonna outscore you, and he did, with the split-T. Bud would score 50 points on a pretty good football team, but he'd get 20 points scored on him.

"Paul Brown was more, to me, an overall coach. Great offense, great defense. A great signal caller. Bear was a weak signal caller until he started having his backfield coach call plays for him. I used to tell him, 'You can't call plays. You played end!' "

Among current college coaches, Bobby Dodd has a clear preference. "Paterno." Joe Paterno of Penn State. "He runs a program just like I hoped I ran," Dodd said. "He graduates his players. He treats 'em good. He runs a good sideline. You watch him on the sideline. He runs a good program. He has a good football team every year, and he's a class guy. He also stands for something in football that I stood for: honesty. He'd never buy a football player in a million years.

"So Paterno, I'd have to put way ahead of anybody. When Frank [Broyles] coached, he ran a great program out at Arkansas. And I thought Darrell Royal ran a good program at Texas."

A program Bobby Dodd could have run. "I might have made a mistake in not going to Texas," Dodd said. "I might have gone down as one of the real great coaches if I could have gone out there and won a couple of national championships. But I don't really regret that.

"I always wanted to be happy in what I was doing. It wasn't the fame as much as it was being happy. I wanted to have a good family and be happy here in Atlanta rather than go to Texas and not enjoy living out there but win the national championship. I'd rather have been happy."

He would not be happy coaching today, however, not even at Georgia Tech, the engineering school where Bobby Dodd offered the finest brand of engineering. Human engineering.

"I wouldn't want to be coaching college football today at all," Dodd said. "There's some cheating, too much cheating, because there's too much pressure involved. And that's because there's too much money involved. There's just too many problems nowadays. I know the recruiting would just drive me up a wall.

"I guess the most basic reason I would not want to be coaching now is the practice sessions. You would have to go through all those practice sessions in the spring. They'd bore me. They'd *bore* me. Spring practice. I wasn't enthusiastic about it in the years I was coaching, and I was young then. That's probably why I made it so easy on the players. I didn't enjoy spring practice. It's dull."

Had he not become a college football coach, Bobby Dodd might have been a minor-league baseball manager. He thinks he would have been a good one, too. "I'd a ended up running a baseball team somewhere for somebody," Dodd said. "I knew baseball, like I knew football, and I knew how to play the odds, play the percentages. I think I would've done that."

Instead, he came to Georgia Tech, transformed the game of football, and transformed countless lives.

"When I look back after all is said and done," Dodd said, "about all of my football career, I felt like we probably enjoyed football as much, played it the way it ought to be played, and won our share of the football games under the best conditions that football could be played in college. I didn't realize at the time when I was doing it, but that's the way football ought to be played and ought to be coached."

"I think the award in his honor pretty well sums it up," said Vince Dooley, the first recipient of the Bobby Dodd Coach of the Year Award in 1977. Sponsored by Delta Air Lines, the Coca-Cola Company, and the *Atlanta Journal*, the national award is given annually to a coach who has had a successful season while epitomizing the principles for which Bobby Dodd stands.

"Bobby Dodd was a special individual in a tough, very competitive business," Vince Dooley said. "He always tried to keep the higher things, the higher aspects of it all, uppermost. And in perspective."

In recent years, Dodd's friends, many of them former players, have presented him with special gifts in appreciation of his devotion to them as individuals and his loyalty to Georgia Tech.

In March 1987, he was overwhelmed with gratitude when a small group of people gathered at the Capital City Club to toast their friend. Each person had contributed five thousand dollars for the old coach. A seventy thousand dollar thank-you.

A few months earlier, on the evening of October 24, 1986, at the 20th reunion of Bobby Dodd's last football team, the old coach was honored with a more modest, but equally touching gift.

After dinner that night, members of the 1966 team presented Dodd a check for four thousand dollars and a plaque whose inscription described Dodd as, among other things, "the gentleman coach of college football." Even for a man who has been honored so often in his lifetime, Bobby Dodd was genuinely touched.

"That's the nicest thing ever written about me," Dodd said upon receiving the plaque. "I would've read it myself, but I was afraid I'd get choked up. And you boys aren't used to seeing me choked up.

"I love you so much," Dodd said that evening. "I love you more than any other football team."

Then he turned to his wife and said, "When I die, Alice, I want you to put this on my tombstone: He loved his family and his football players more than any other person."

He is Robert Lee "Bobby" Dodd of Georgia Tech—the gentleman coach of college football, and a ramblin', gamblin', *hell* of an engineer.

The Bobby Dodd Scrapbook

Top left. Playing baseball with brother John in Galax, about 1920. *Top right.* Suited up for the Kingsport basketball team, about 1926. *Bottom left.* Typically casual on campus at Tennessee, about 1927. *Opposite page.* In the news.

Top. Great Tennessee backfield 11 years later. Left to right, Bobby Dodd, Quinn Decker, Buddy Hackman, and Gene McEver. *Bottom left.* With freshman sensation Clint Castleberry, in 1942. *Bottom right.* General Robert Neyland.

 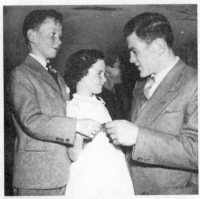

Top left. With Coach William Alexander and officers from the Navy V-12 program at Tech, about 1943. *Top right.* Paul Duke, Bobby Dodd's first captain and first all-American, was presented the Joe Rhodes award as Tech's most valuable player in 1945 by Jimmy Robinson III and Frances Robinson. *Bottom.* With key men from 1946 squad. Kneeling from left to right, Walter Kilzer, George Mathews, Pat McHugh, Frank Broyles, and Bob Davis, and Bill Healey, standing.

Top. At the blackboard with Ray Graves, Ray Ellis, and Dwight Keith, about 1947. *Bottom left.* With quarterback Darrell Crawford in 1951. *Bottom right.* On the tower watching spring practice with Woody Hayes of Ohio State in 1952.

Top. The ol' coach with all-Americans George Morris and Hal Miller in 1952. *Middle.* The 1955 coaching staff. Left to right: standing, Jim Luck, Joe Pittard, Bob Bossons, Byron Gilbreath, John Robert Bell, Bob Miller, and Trainer Buck Andel. Kneeling, Lewis Woodruff, Jack Griffin, Ray Graves, Bobby Dodd, Tonto Coleman, Frank Broyles, and Whitey Urban. *Bottom.* At press conference before Tech vs. Kentucky and Georgia vs. Ole Miss doubleheader at Grant Field in 1955.

Top. With Frank Howard of Clemson.
Bottom. Quarterback Wade Mitchell and
offensive coordinator Frank Broyles, 1956.

Top. With the tri-captains from the 1961 team, Billy Williamson, Chick Graning, and Willie McGauhey. Bottom. The Dodds at home. From left to right, Linda, Bobby Dodd, Bobby Jr., and Alice.

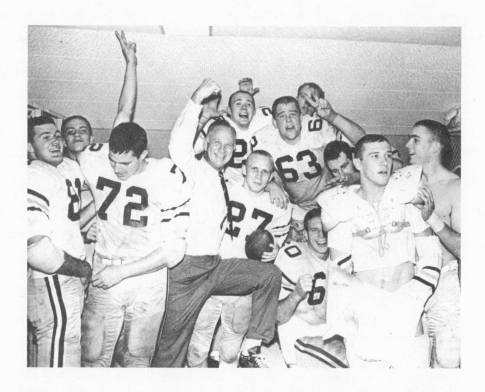

Top. Celebrating the 1962 victory over top-ranked Alabama. Billy Lothridge and Rufus Guthrie hold up V's for victory while Coach Dodd hugs Don Toner. Game hero Mike McNames stands in front on the far right. *Bottom left.* At the Bluebonnet Bowl in 1962. *Bottom right.* On the court with Bitsy Grant, 1962.

Top left. Meeting with Penn State coach Joe Paterno after the 1966 game at Grant Field. *Top right.* With L.W. "Chip" Robert in 1964. *Bottom.* Alice Dodd in the family room.

Top. Surrounded by former players and assistant coaches at the 1967 retirement dinner. From left to right: John Robert Bell, Pepper Rodgers, Charlie Tate, Bobby Dodd, Frank Broyles, Whitey Urban, Bo Hagan, and A.M. "Tonto" Coleman. *Bottom left.* Being honored at the state capitol in 1966. Lieutenant Governor Zell Miller greets Coach Dodd as Mrs. Dodd and Speaker Tom Murphy look on. *Bottom right.* With Dave Garrett of Delta Airlines, Bo Schembechler of the University of Michigan, and Vince Dooley of the University of Georgia at the 1978 Bobby Dodd Coach-of-the-Year banquet.

Top left. With new head coach Bill Curry in 1980. *Top right.* At Grant Field ceremony honoring longtime Tech radio announcer Al Ciraldo. *Bottom.* Relaxing in his office at the Alumni House.